REFORMATION & RESILIENCE

Lutheran Higher Education for Planetary Citizenship

Ernest Simmons and
Erin Hemme Froslie, Editors

Lutheran University Press
Minneapolis, Minnesota

Reformation & Resilience

Lutheran Higher Education for Planetary Citizenship

Ernest Simmons and Erin Hemme Froslie, Editors

ISBN 978-1-942304-30-2

Lutheran University Press, PO Box 390759, Minneapolis, MN 55439
www.lutheranupress.org
Manufactured in the United States of America

TABLE OF CONTENTS

V. Whole College

INTRODUCTION

Five hundred years ago the Protestant Reformation became a major turning point in Western history. Born in a university setting, the dialectical interaction of the life of the mind and the life of faith has been a hallmark of Lutheran higher education from the beginning. Luther insisted on the Christian life being lived right in the midst of the world so that the resources of faith must be brought to play on daily life and work. This means that a sharp distinction between the sacred and the secular cannot be drawn for the Lutheran tradition. All of the finite world can in some way be revelatory of God and must therefore be kept in constant relationship with faith. One of the central tasks of a liberal arts college of the church is to maintain this dialectical interaction between faith and learning, and so it is highly appropriate at this time to undertake reflection upon the beginning of the Lutheran tradition, the Protestant Reformation, and its continued relevance.

As Concordia College observes this anniversary, it is important to ask what is in need of reform today and what resilience remains within the tradition to help effect such reform? At its core, Lutheran liberal arts education emphasized preparation for vocation in service to neighbor. Today, the understanding of "neighbor" must be expanded to include all faith traditions and the natural world. *The thesis of this book is that Lutheran liberal arts education must move beyond an anthropocentric to an ecocentric understanding of vocation in order to foster planetary citizenship and sustainability leadership.* Our contemporary society encourages a person to be preoccupied with the self and the satisfaction of one's selfish desires. To be liberated from such a condition is one of the main objectives of a liberal arts education. Only with a changed vision can we begin to talk about a viable foundation for a sustainable future. *It is in light of what might be that one can become empowered to challenge and change what is.* The essays in this volume attempt to do just that. Following the structure of the college's strategic plan, this text addresses questions of reform in the areas of Whole Self, Whole Life, Whole World, and Whole College, and encourages the interaction of faith with contemporary life and thought.

The first section does not directly correspond to the sections of the strategic plan but is intended to provide the foundation for the remainder of the book. "Establishing the Context" seeks to explore four major areas to be of use for later reflection: Luther's understanding of creation and his maturing conscience, the nature of sustainability, and the reform of liberal arts education. Since we are observing the 500th anniversary of the Reformation, it is appropriate to begin by spending a bit of time reflecting upon the life and thought of Martin Luther. This is undertaken not only to provide some historical perspective but also retrieval; in effect, to employ Luther to critique the tradition that bears his name. What in Luther's life and thought is of use to us today in our quite dramatically different context? The first essay will point out that while later Lutheranism became rather anthropocentric, focusing almost exclusively on human salvation, Luther himself had a broader view including the love of nature and the importance of the creation as bearing witness to God's presence. This can be drawn upon to enlarge the understanding of neighbor and expand the concept of vocation to move towards equipping for planetary citizenship and sustainability. The second essay does a winsome job of elaborating on the maturing of Luther's conscience and how he came to draw strength from Scripture and reason to stand up to the most powerful forces of church and state in his time. In the case of indulgences, Luther struggled with the niggling question, "Is this true?" The third essay dives into the difficult waters not only of defining sustainability but of addressing how this commitment can inform college curriculum. This essay then turns to specifically address the curriculum and sustainability practices of Concordia College and seeks to have sustainability become "part of the DNA" of Concordia. The section closes by introducing the reader to the broad discussion of the reform of liberal arts education taking place on the national scene and the return to character formation and moral reflection that was once the heart of such education. If we are to find ways out of our current thicket of crises everyone must work to restore the common good for the global commons. May we all hope that we are not too late.

The remainder of this introduction will be devoted to brief overviews of each section of the text. Since each begins with its own introduction, there is no need to repeat what is to be found there about each individual paper, rather a brief look into what each section addresses as part of the strategic plan and the wider need of reform in today's world will be undertaken.

- "*Whole Self: In a time of constant distraction and clashing ideals, we will lead our students into a life-long habit of reflection on their identity, purpose, and leadership in a deeply interconnected world.*" Forming the focus for the second section, the first strategic goal helps unpack the challenges and opportunities we have with an increasingly diverse student body seeking alternatives to the values and commitments of a consumerist society. Discussions of the importance of retaining the Lutheran heritage of the college, redefining the self away from consumerism, and employing moral judgement to inform vocation in a business context open up ways to critiques consumer culture. Finally, the argument is made that we need to come to see our students as "whole-broken" and become a more compassionate and inclusive campus.
- "*Whole Life: In a time of rapidly shifting work environments, we will guide our students to complete a baccalaureate composed not of an atomized collection of credits but of a coherent and increasingly challenging experience to build competence, creativity, and character.*" The third section expands out of the subjective self to the nature of life itself. By addressing the need for better science education, the role of power relation-

ships in and out of the classroom, communicating in a digital world with accelerated decision making and critique of Luther's treatment of the Jews and Muslims, this section opens the reader up to the diverse challenges we face today and provides insightful reflections on how they can be addressed.

- "*Whole World: In a time of heightened national and international distrust, we will open the world to our students so that they understand and embrace the call to national and global citizenship.*" How to achieve wholeness in such a world as described above is the focus of the fourth section. A diverse number of topics present in today's dynamic world of change are addressed. Beginning with two articles that draw upon faculty experience in south Asia and its resources for addressing environmental and economic change, this section then turns to the challenge of adjunct faculty, the need for racial and cultural inclusion, and the politics of energy conversion away from fossil fuels. A vision of sustainability must be for all and not just for the privileged few who can afford it.
- The fifth section, "Whole College" is not a specific category of the strategic plan but is implied throughout the plan as the wholeness of the college is addressed. This section focuses upon a number of different student activities that in the life of the student come to compose a "Whole College" experience. A recurring theme of this section is that for students to have a more holistic college experience the divisions between curricular and co-curricular as well as academic and professional programs must be bridged. Drawing upon the understanding of integrative learning and PEAK experiences, these essays argue for the transformation of everything from residential life into a "laboratory for planetary citizenship" to professional and music programs equipping students for "compassionate citizenship." "Whole Col-

lege" thus seeks to develop all dimensions of a student's life, from curricular to cocurricular, so that it can be seen as an inclusive and integrated whole contributing to a unified college experience.

- The book ends with a section on case studies to provide some concrete examples of best practices and applications for developing planetary citizenship and sustainability leadership. It involves doing education in sometimes non-traditional ways and in non-traditional places. The case studies range from using Community-Based Research (CBR) for classes to address social issues in the community or food waste on campus, to the development of a more integrated model for academic affairs and student affairs that enables students to allow their ideas to emerge and then learn how to lead them to be enacted. In another case study the classic approach of "teach the controversy" is challenged in deference to "explain the controversy," which moves beyond posturing on controversial issues toward more agreement when listening to the evidence. The final case study addresses how chemistry lab, having to deal with hazardous waste, can be taught in a way that is integrative, making students more environmentally and sustainability conscious. These case studies provide rich and varied examples that will hopefully be springboards for readers to consider how they might do old things in new ways.

Reformation and resilience, two words that are not often used together. Reform implies change and doing away with present structures that perhaps were not resilient. Resilience, on the other hand, often connotes endurance and the absence of change. This book, in good Lutheran paradoxical fashion, asks the reader to keep both in mind at the same time. True reform, to have lasting power and be truly effective, must have some element of resilience within it. True resilience, if it too is to remain effective, must also have an element of reform built in it as well to adapt to the continuing changes of life.

The truth is, we need both. We need change because many times the old ways do not work in a new environment. Learning tells us that. However, without some sense of continuity how can we know who we are, much less what to value and where we would like to go? Faith tells us that. So faith and learning today, as in the past, need to be dynamically related to provide morally informed decisions that take into account the details of our changed context. Graduates who seek to be planetary citizens and sustainability leaders will need both. They will need to be both reforming and resilient.

—Dr. Ernest Simmons, Professor of Religion and
Co-director of the Dovre Learning Center
for Faith and Learning

ESTABLISHING THE CONTEXT

INTRODUCTION

Identity is a process, not a position. It is always undergoing dynamic change because of historical conditions in space and time. Traditions and institutions are no exception. Since change is inevitable, it is not something to be mourned or simply obstructed but rather to be embraced so that a trajectory may be channeled and developed in consonance with tradition. This challenge and opportunity has also to be found in Lutheran higher education. This section intends to provide background in several areas that form the foundation of the later sections of this book, by looking first at Lutheran liberal arts education and a widening of the understanding of vocation (Ernest Simmons), then moving to the development of Luther's ethical conscience (Roy Hammerling), continuing with a deeper understanding of the complexity of sustainability (Kenneth Foster), and closing with an evaluation of the new paradigm for liberal arts education as proposed by the American Association of Colleges and Universities (Per Anderson).

Human existence is so intricately woven into the ecological fabric of earth that to denigrate nature is to denigrate the human. Human anthropocentrism, over the centuries, has argued for separation from and superiority over nature. Such arrogant anthropocentrism must no longer persist if humanity itself is to survive. The overall argument of this section and of the book is that Lutheran liberal arts education must move beyond an anthropocentric to an ecocentric understanding of vocation in order to foster planetary citizenship and sustainability leadership.

Simmons begins his essay by arguing that the classic liberal arts of the *Trivium* (grammar, rhetoric, and logic) are still essential for navigating and critiquing the information of our contemporary world. This then prepares the foundation for drawing upon Luther's understanding of creation to enlarge the concept of vocation by widening the arena of "neighbor" to include not only persons of other faith traditions but especially the natural world as well. In effect he is using Luther to critique the anthropocentricism of the Lutheran tradition. By preparing students to be citizens not just of the city or nation but rather of the planet, we are preparing them to understand principles of sustainability more deeply across disciplines and equipping them to be effective leaders of sustainability in the future.

Through a thoughtful and winsome historical summary of Luther's life, Hammerling explores the interesting development of Luther's moral conscience as he moves from a general acceptance of the church's teachings to significant challenges of certain teachings and practices, such as that of indulgences. It is because of the niggling question "Is this true?" that Luther grows in moral conscience and conviction to challenge all the powers of church and state in his time. In 1510, after reaching the top of the *Scala Santa*, (the stairs that Christ ostensibly walked up to reach Pilate's trial room) in Rome, which were to bestow enough indulgence to release someone from Purgatory, Luther was brought to ask, "Would God allow himself to be pinned down this way?" This question persisted as he contemplated whether God could be bought off so easily and whether this is really the way to reconciliation. This then led to further study and the growing conviction that the answer was no. We are forgiven by grace not by works. Luther eventually became so concerned that he thought a scholarly debate was necessary to settle the question and the rest is history. What started out as a niggling question led to the posting of theses on the Castle Church door and a turning point in Western history.

Foster dives deeply into the understanding of sustainability developing its central principles and then applying them to inform the nature of liberal arts education across the curriculum. After demonstrating the need for addressing sustainability, "Our Unsustainable Trajectory," he then goes on to address some of the challenges and confusions about the concept, such as its perceived "negativity" and the established forces arrayed against change including human self-interest. He then moves to the most important sections of the essay where he addresses sustainability education in general and its particular application on the Concordia campus. Foster affirms the progress Concordia has made in creating a more sustainable and carbon neutral campus as well as the significance of the college's "Vision for Sustainability." While acknowledging the vision's "expansiveness," he also acknowledges that a lot of work lies ahead, particularly in transforming the curriculum to be more sustainability oriented. In his final section, "Towards a Future of Human Thriving on a Vibrant Earth: Putting Sustainability at the Center of the Educational Enterprise," drawing upon the work of David Orr and Frank Rhodes, he lays out some concrete steps and concludes, "Closer to home, we need to make sustainability part of the DNA of Concordia College and an anchor of the curriculum—not as an add-on, but as a frame that helps animate the curriculum and makes the college an engine of exploration into complex issues, for the good of students and the world." A good part of the remainder of this book works to develop that challenge.

Anderson has done significant research and reflection on the trends in liberal arts education at the national level. Drawing upon the imagery of Dietrich Bonhoeffer of a "World Come of Age," Anderson sees higher education in the years ahead having to deal with a series of "unscripted problems." Beginning with a clear and distinct summary of Lutheran ethics in the first section on "Lutheran Christian Morality in Outline," he then moves to employ the thought of the philosophical ethicist Hans Jonas to critique the impact of technology on society and how that is producing the diverse crises that we are experiencing today from information overload to climate change. What can liberal arts education contribute to preparing future generations to deal with such a situation? Here Anderson draws upon the thoughtful work of the Association of American Colleges and Universities (AAC&U) in their groundbreaking study of the transformation of liberal arts education, *Greater Expectations: A New Vision for Learning as a Nation Goes to College*, to embody, "global citizenship education," that for Anderson, ". . . marks a shift in the purpose and aim of public education to include moral formation toward international cooperation and societal change." This would signal a sea change in higher education to return to the formation of character and moral education as had once been the case before the turn to emphasize "value neutral" objectivity and scientific thought. In the 2012 national taskforce study on higher education entitled *Crucible Moment: College Learning and America's Future,* the role of education for civic responsibility was emphasized which does give Anderson a sense of hope. In creating an "Anticipatory Academy for Unscripted Problems" Anderson hopes to see a change in education to address the moral, civic, technological, and political issues of our time. In such a case we would perhaps have, "A Turn to Responsibility, Perhaps in Time." May we all hope that he is right.

—Dr. Ernest Simmons, Professor of Religion and
Co-Director of the Dovre Center
for Faith and Leaning

LUTHERAN LIBERAL ARTS EDUCATION

Nurturing Vocation for Planetary Citizenship

DR. ERNEST SIMMONS
Professor of Religion
Co-Director, the Dovre Center for Faith and Learning

> A city's best and greatest welfare, safety, and strength consist rather in its having many able, learned, wise, honorable, and well-educated citizens.
>
> —Martin Luther, *To the Councilmen of All Cities in Germany That They Establish and Maintain Christian Schools*

> A constituency able and willing to fight for the long-term human prospect must be educated into existence.
>
> —David Orr, *Earth in Mind*

"The human imprint on the global environment has now become so large and active that it rivals some of the great forces of Nature in its impact on the functioning of the Earth system."[1] So begins an article co-authored by several of the world's leading geologists and climatologist as they begin to assess the appropriateness of naming our current geological epoch the "Anthropocene" to signify such human impact. Such impact raises the question of the sustainability of life on this planet as well as of human civilization. What could be the role of Lutheran higher education in such a changed global and interfaith context and what resources in the Lutheran tradition can contribute to preparing our students to be more effective sustainability leaders? These are the two questions this chapter will focus on.

Today we are called to formulate a new sense of what constitutes Lutheran higher education. At its core this education has emphasized *vocation in service to the neighbor*. Today, "neighbor" must be expanded not only beyond the Christian to other faith traditions but also beyond the human to include the natural world. Human existence is so intricately woven into the ecological fabric of earth that to denigrate nature is to denigrate the human. Human anthropocentrism, over the centuries, has argued for separation from and superiority over nature. Such arrogant anthropocentrism must no longer persist if humanity itself is to survive. The thesis of this chapter (and the book) is that Lutheran liberal arts education must move beyond an anthropocentric to an ecocentric understanding of vocation in order to foster planetary citizenship and sustainability leadership. There are roots in Luther, particularly his understanding of creation, to make such a change, in effect, using Luther to reform Lutheran liberal arts education. For Luther, the purpose of education was the preserving of the Gospel and the equipping of the priesthood of all believers for their vocation of serving others within the world. Today this understanding of vocation must be enlarged to also include the natural environment and skills for sustainability leadership.

Identity is a process not a possession, so it is always undergoing dynamic change.[2] Traditions and institutions are no exception. Luther and his Wittenberg colleague Philip Melanchthon understood this well as they attempted to effect change in many areas of church and society in the sixteenth century. Change, as re-forming for the common good, is something to be embraced so that a trajectory may be developed in consonance with tradition. Here we will briefly explore the roots of Lutheran higher education in Luther and the later tradition before moving to Luther's understanding of creation to inform an enlarged, interfaith conception of vocation for sustainability.

I. Sustainability and the Liberal Arts

What does sustainability mean and what is its significance for higher education? Leslie Paul Theile observes, "The word 'sustainability' derives from the Latin *sustinere*, which literally means to *hold up*. Something is sustainable if it endures, persists or holds up over time."[3] In this context, to call Lutheran liberal arts education for sustainability it *must* become education for the long term to hold up society and creation for mutual benefit. As we may recall, in the Greek city-state the purpose of what became known as liberal arts education was to prepare a person for thoughtful and responsible citizenship in the *polis* (the Greek city-state). Today the challenge is to prepare our students to be citizens of the planet, that is, to prepare them for planetary citizenship.

Historically, this education meant having knowledge of the fundamental "liberating" arts of grammar, logic, and rhetoric, referred to by Plato in Book VII of the *Republic* and elaborated in the *Phaedrus.*[4] During the middle ages they became known as the *Trivium,* literally "where the three roads meet," and were considered the foundation for all other arts. The classical descriptions are that,

> Grammar teaches the mechanics of language to the student....Logic or dialectic is the 'mechanics' of thought and analysis the process of identifying fallacious arguments and statements,...Finally Rhetoric is the application of language in order to instruct and to persuade the listener and the reader. It is the knowledge (grammar) now understood (logic) being transmitted outwards, as wisdom (rhetoric).[5]

While this is later supplemented by the *Quadrivium* of arithmetic, geometry, music, and astronomy, for our purposes these three basic "liberating arts" are the most important. One need only look at the recent dissembling discussions of climate change to see the importance of these three arts.

Noami Oreskes and Erik Conway in their book *Merchants of Doubt: How a Handful of Scientists Obscured the Truth About Issues from Tobacco Smoke to Global Warming,*[6] indicate that by supporting fringe scientific research, the energy industry has engaged in the same tactics of sowing doubt or uncertainty about climate change that the cigarette industry did for decades concerning the carcinogenic character of cigarette smoking and nicotine addiction. As horrible as that loss of life is, this is still a personal decision. Climate change, however, is not, and whole cultures and nations are at stake as well as the viability of human civilization. We no longer have time for such distracting and fallacious arguments. We must prepare our students to think clearly and critically about the matters at hand as well as creatively to formulate viable responses and then communicate them clearly, effectively and persuasively to their social context. To be able to name something clearly and to ferret out the illogical and fallacious arguments that have been made are today survival skills for society. Students must become able to critique and dismantle such obstructionist thinking and call out the powers that have a vested interest in promoting such arguments. To move in this direction, however, we must first reflect upon where we have come from and what resources are available within the Lutheran tradition to help foster such a constructive change.

II. Luther and Learning

Justification by grace through faith is the heart of the Reformation for Luther and the article by which "the church stands or falls."[7] It forms the basis for the priesthood of all believers where everyone is equal before God. It is necessary, then, that this priesthood be adequately prepared for the task of expressing faith in life (vocation) which leads not only to an informed clergy but to a civil and informed society as well. The reality of late Medieval Saxony, however, was something less than this ideal. Luther faced strong opposition to sending children to school from the people who had struggled and been disenfranchised for so long. The pressure was on to go to work and earn money in the world of trade and craftsmanship. Unless they planned for one of the three major professions; law, medicine, or theology, those who went to school were considered "daft" (*Gelehrte sind verkehrte*, "the learned are daft").[8] Education was an unnecessary luxury and a waste of time for the average person who could not afford it, so the general population believed. It was much better for a child to learn a useful trade and thus insure their livelihood.

In this late medieval climate, Luther advocates generalized public education for both boys and girls for the first time in western history. His major treatises on education, *To the Councilmen of All Cities in Germany that They Establish and Maintain Christian Schools*

(1524),[9] and his famous sermon, *On Keeping Children in School* (1530) [10] are intended not only to establish an educated leadership for the church and government but also an informed laity to serve both the church and society. The situation was quite serious for not only had there been limited educational opportunities before the Reformation, the reform movement led to decreasing support and dismantling of church related schools, such as the cathedral and monastic schools. The monastic schools were in a state of disrepair and even abandonment as the monasteries closed and their properties and endowments were confiscated by the local authorities. A new form of educational system was desperately needed. Some radical reformers (e.g. Andreas Carlstadt and Thomas Muntzer) even spoke against education, saying that one only needed the Holy Spirit to be fully informed.[11]

At first Luther thought that parents would see to the education of their children but he soon realized they had neither the training nor the willingness to do so. This drove him to encourage government officials to establish schools and libraries in their communities.[12] This appeal was successful with numerous schools being supported and several new ones, including universities, being started (e.g. at Marburg, Jena and Konigsburg). Luther's colleague Philip Melanchthon oversaw major educational reforms throughout Protestant Germany and in so doing established the secondary school (*Gymnasium*) between the Latin (elementary) school and the university, developing the pattern for German university education which has persisted until today. That is why Melanchthon is known as the *Praeceptor Germaniea*, the "schoolmaster of Germany."[13]

These reformers were practical leaders who foresaw the need for education and especially the value of the liberal arts in training for Christian ministry and the life of faith. For Luther, and especially Melanchthon, from the beginning there was a strong connection between the emerging liberal arts humanism of the Renaissance and the claims to justifying grace of the Reformation.[14] If the Bible is the "cradle of Christ" as Luther referred to it, then surely liberal arts education, especially language study, can be one of the hands that rocks the biblical cradle. In his treatise of 1524, *To the Councilmen of All*

Cities in Germany That They Establish and Maintain Christian Schools, Luther states this in a very practical manner,

> Now the welfare of a city does not consist solely in accumulating vast treasures, building mighty walls and magnificent buildings, and producing a goodly supply of guns and armor. Indeed, where such things are plentiful, and reckless fools get control of them, it is so much the worse and the city suffers even greater loss. A city's best and greatest welfare, safety, and strength consist rather in its having many able, learned, wise, honorable, and well-educated citizens. They can then readily gather, protect, and properly use treasure and all manner of property.[15]

Luther's commitment to education emerged rather naturally from his own experience. Scholarly investigation, or inquiry, provided the tools by which Luther unlocked "the Book" and discovered the gift of faith. For Luther that book, the Bible, was fundamental and so, he believed, it should be accessible to all. Accordingly, education became an imperative and led Luther and his colleagues to develop the common schools where education would be made available to all.

Luther's commitment to education also was shaped by his doctrine of the two realms or kingdoms. The earthly realm, God's "left hand," is a place of service, of vocation where God rules through designated authorities. The affairs of the earthly realm, where one is called to serve the common good (without self-interest), are to be ruled by reason, hence education is essential to fulfill one's vocation.[16] The heavenly realm is God's "right hand" where God rules directly through grace which is embraced in faith by the believer. Through God's grace manifest in faith, the Christian lives in both realms and is called to relate to God through faith and make that faith active in loving service to one's neighbor. Christian vocation becomes the everyday expression of this faith. This is most succinctly explained in Luther's classic work, *The Freedom of a Christia*n where Luther talks about being simultaneously related to both God and neighbor.[17]

Closely related to Luther's commitment to academic inquiry was his commitment to academic freedom. Luther was given the freedom to pursue the truth by his colleagues at Wittenberg and by the princes of the realm. That freedom led him to faith in God's creation of this world and the redemption of humans within it. Indeed, if the world is God's creation then there is surely no inhibition to the pursuit of inquiry for any truth discovered is yet another truth about what God has done. In this sense, open inquiry is both privilege and mandate. Accordingly, within the Lutheran tradition academic freedom is understood as an application of the two realms to academia. The integrity of creation requires nothing less than the integrity and freedom of disciplines devoted to its study. In the world of today, for persons of faith, reason dominates as the means to study the order God has placed in creation thus granting each discipline its own integrity and freedom. Luther himself asserts,

> No science should stand in the way of another science, but each should continue to have its own mode of procedure in its own terms. Every science should make use of its own terminology, and one should not for this reason condemn the other or ridicule it; but one should rather be of use to the other, and they should put their achievements at one another's disposal.[18]

While "science" for Luther does not mean the same thing that it does for us today in a post-Enlightenment perspective, still in Luther's view, reason reigns in the earthly kingdom and Christ's revelation has no exclusive claim on earthly truth.

Human reason, however, has its limits and can make mistakes. He believed that human reason is subject to error. More importantly, Luther said that while reason is essential and helpful in dealing with things below or in the human realm, with matters of faith, i.e. the heavenly kingdom, it is not definitive. Human reason cannot provide definitive answers to things that are above the human, such essential questions of faith as: Who is God? What is it to be human? What does it mean to be saved? Revelation plays an essential role in matters of faith, or the heavenly realm, and when reason begins to legislate for the heavenly realm, when it confuses human justice and the righteousness of God, when it rationalizes divine revelation, then it is misused.[19] This is to say that reason is being abused in trying to prove or control matters that are above the human. It is turned into a work. It was such a use of reason that Luther had objected to when it was used to justify the sale of indulgences, for example. Learning alone cannot transform the self or the world in a spiritual sense. It cannot grant forgiveness of sins—only God can do that. Perhaps this view is best capsulized in Luther's explanation to the third article of the Apostles' Creed in *The Small Catechism*:

> I believe that by my own understanding or strength I cannot believe in Jesus Christ my Lord or come to him, but instead the Holy Spirit has called me through the gospel, enlightened me with his gifts, made me holy and kept me in the true faith, just as he calls, gathers, enlightens and makes holy the whole Christian church on earth and keeps it with Jesus Christ in the one common, true faith.[20]

For Luther, reason and education are for the earthly realm where they can guide and enlighten human action for the common good and must be free to do so. In matters beyond human comprehension (such as salvation), one must rely on the grace and love of God embraced in faith. Reason and faith thus exist in a complementary, dialectical relationship where each contributes to the other for the benefit of both the individual and society.

III. Lutheran Education After Luther

Later Lutheran reformers were also committed to education and continued to affirm the value of a specific form of education, namely the liberal arts. Understanding "the Word" required knowledge of language, literature, philosophy, science, history and music, which Luther had a particular interest in.[21] The great church historian Sydney Ahlstrom described the flow of the Lutheran tradition as it moved into the post-Reformation era in terms of three currents: the scholastic, the pietistic, and the critical.[22] The scholastic emerged in the context of the fierce debates and religious wars of the late sixteenth and early seventeenth centuries as Lutherans struggled to define themselves against the Roman Catholic counter-reformation on the one hand and the reformed and radical Protestants on the other. Focusing especially on doctrinal formulation as a way of preserving the Reformation heritage, the scholastic movement argued that Lutheran doctrine could be expressed in formalized statements such as the Formula of Concord of 1580. Richard Solberg observes that Lutheran scholasticism became rigid and ". . . resulted in finely drawn expositions of Lutheran theology that tended to become intellectual exercises rather than professions of faith."[23]

In reaction to this rigid intellectualism, the movement of Pietism emerged in the late seventeenth and early eighteenth centuries. Centered at the University of Halle, Pietism emphasized the inner spiritual life, engagement in mission work and deeds of mercy. Less concerned about intellectual formulations, Pietism stressed the commitment of the individual believer in living out an active life of faith which gave a strong impetus to lay involvement in the church.

Finally, the critical current emerged in the late eighteenth and nineteenth century in response to the rise of natural science and Enlightenment Rationalism. Housed primarily in the universities, the critical tradition was marked by a sense of intellectual freedom and a desire to ask deep questions and challenge accepted assumptions. This tradition includes such scholars as Kant and Hegel.[24] It is important to remember that this critical spirit that significantly influenced nineteenth century scholarship in many disciplines is an academic expression of one of the currents of the Lutheran tradition in education, indeed of the "Freedom of a Christian."

As we turn to Lutheran immigration to the United States, however, not all these currents would find expression in America. Richard Solberg observes,

> In the migration of Lutherans from Europe to America, however, the "critical tradition" was largely left behind. Most German immigrants in the eighteenth century were peasants and came to a country still in the frontier stage. The few university-trained clergy who came to care for their spiritual needs had been trained in centers of German Pietism. As the supply of European clergy dwindled, the earliest Lutheran ventures in higher education were primarily directed to the preparation of more pastors. Colleges were founded to provide the basic classical lan-

guages necessary for theological study. Thus, a tradition that had been broadly involved in the intellectual milieu of European thought was narrowed to a concern for preparing frontier pastors in an institutional climate strongly flavored by American evangelical revivalism.[25]

Taken together, however, these Lutheran roots suggest a vigorous, open and for the most part free approach to education in which "the Word" has full sway in dynamic relation to academic freedom and integrity. There were (and to some extent still are) some expressions of the tradition that are in tension with academic life and do restrict academic freedom but today they are by far the minority voice in Lutheran higher education. Richard Solberg concludes, "This conviction, that a thorough intellectual preparation of professional leadership for church and community is fundamental to the broad intentions of the Reformation, has provided the driving impulse for higher education within the Lutheran tradition."[26] This connection between faith and education was so firmly planted in the followers of the Reformation that it has lasted for centuries and was carried to other parts of Europe, particularly Scandinavia, and by immigrants to the New Zion of America. Faith, especially in its Pietist expression, did influence and direct the academic enterprise, especially through its immigrant theological heritage. It was the persistent pastoral need as well as the need to educate and socialize immigrant populations forming their faith in the context of life in a new land (through "normal" schools as well as later colleges) that were to become the driving forces for the establishment of Lutheran colleges and universities. Lutheran education in America began as immigrant education.[27]

IV. From Anthropocentrism to Ecocentrism: Luther, Creation, and Sustainability

In his explanation of the first article of the Apostle's Creed (on creation) in his *Small Catechism*, Martin Luther says, "I believe that God has created me together with all that exists."[28] At first reading, this sounds very arrogant. He seems to place himself before all of creation. However, as one reflects upon this more thoroughly, one can come to see that this is far from the truth; indeed, the truth was quite the opposite. In his explanation of the first article of the Apostle's Creed, what he was getting at is that our own existence, our own creation, body, mind, and spirit, is the most intimate experience of creation that we will ever have. It is through our own experience of being created that we have a window into the rest of creation and to the creator God to be found "in, with, and under" it.

There are profound environmental implications in this theological affirmation of the goodness of material existence. Matter is not to be opposed to spirit but rather can be the embodiment of spirit. The Creative Spirit (*Spiritus Creator*) of God which voiced forth the creation has become one with it and continues to animate it in a continuing creation (*creatio continuua*). The material creation is not void of God but rather animated by the ongoing presence of God. God is "entangled" with the very creation that God has brought about.[29] All of creation, and not just the human, must be viewed as embodying the ongoing dynamic spirit of God, helping to challenge the anthropocentrism that has justified wanton abuse and destruction of the creation for human purposes alone. Luther's understanding of creation is key to moving education to an ecocentric perspective.

Luther on Creation

Human beings are part of God's creation and intimately connected with it. Our bodies are our little corner of the cosmos, from which we are enabled to perceive the rest of the universe and all that it contains. The heavy elements in our bodies, like copper and zinc, were forged in the thermonuclear fusion reactions of stars that later exploded as supernovae spewing out their material into the vastness of space. We are quite literally made from stardust.[30] It is from within this intimate experience of wonder at our own creation that we can begin to consider the nature of creation itself. To understand Luther on creation, we must begin with a brief description of creation mysticism, mysticism of the everyday.

Luther was deeply influenced by German creation mysticism, particularly as expressed in the *Theologia Germanica*.[31] The experiencing of God in all things runs throughout this short treatise and forms its mystical groundwork.[32] Heiko Oberman clarifies, however, that it is not "absorption mysticism."[33] It is not a mysticism of being merged or united into one being with God-in-nature, but actually rejects such an understanding. Bengt Hoffman explains that the *Theologia Germanica* knows nothing of abnormal or unusual experiences, of absorption or merging. On the contrary, it involves the apprehension of the divine in the everyday, the wisdom of experience, which influences Luther's understanding of the presence of divine grace. Hoffman writes: "The theological term for experience of divine presence is *sapientia experimentalis* [experiential wisdom]. Martin Luther used this term as part of what 'justification' is."[34] Philip Watson puts it this way, "For Luther, God is not to be sought behind His [*sic*] creation by inference from it, but is rather to be apprehended in and through it."[35] This position builds upon the classical understanding of the two books, that of nature and of Scripture, both of which God authored and therefore do not conflict.[36] Niels Henrik Gregersen further explicates that "Creation is a mystery, not because it is esoteric, not because it forces us to believe in a variety of supernatural truths, but because the mystery of creation takes place in the midst of everyday existence."[37] God is in all things, even though God is also more than the creation as well. Steven Churchill writes,

> Martin Luther is a *normal* creation mystic. This modified claim is good news for us: nature-mystical experiences—ordinary, daily, available-to-all, wonder-filled sightings of God in all creatures, neither more nor less—is open to you, me, all people. Truly Luther is trying to wake us up to the amazing spiritual truth that we are all creation mystics, through Christ's redemptive act.[38]

There is a normalcy in Luther's nature mysticism that has him affirm the wonder, beauty, and grace of God in the everyday. Luther calls us to go and do the same.

The Incarnation for Luther is the most intimate presence of God within the world and demonstrates that God is truly capable of entering into the reality of the finite. Gregersen further explains, "From this premise Luther proceeds to the logical conclusion that also the world of creation must be able to host the infinite God: *finitum capax infinitum*" (the finite bears the infinite).[39] Truly the finite can contain the infinite in the Incarnation. Just as God in Christ is incarnate within the finite natural world, so too is Christ transcendent and everywhere present by being at the right hand of God. For Luther, there is an intrinsic connection between creation and salvation because the same God is present in both. In some ways one could say that Luther reads the creation Christologically, which provides the basis for Luther's sacramental theology.[40] Christ's presence in the Eucharist is a particular example, for the forgiveness of sins, of the general presence of God in all creation. This intimate Divine connection with all of creation, humanity included, provides the theological basis for a creative and constructive relationship between theology and science as well as the potential for a faith-based commitment for the care of the creation.

From a theological point of view, God's *creatio continuua* (continual, sustaining grace of creation) runs "in, with and under" (to borrow from sacramental imagery) the processes of nature such that science and theology need not be in conflict but rather in dialogue or even consonance. Science and theology both begin in wonder at the natural world with its complexity and its beauty. But by intention they try to answer two different types of questions: how and why? By design, scientific methods in general restrict themselves to instrumental, "how" types of questions: what can be observed, measured, quantified, repeated and, ideally, expressed in a mathematical formalism. Newtonian physics is the paradigmatic example of such an approach. Science is concerned with what philosophically is called secondary causation. It assumes something already exists. Theology (and philosophy) on the other hand, ask the intrinsic, "why" questions. Why does something exist, where did it come from and what is its purpose? This is known as primary, originating or foundational causation. When observing the appropriate boundaries of analysis, science and theology can together contribute to deeper understanding of the creation and be complementary.[41] This is critical if we are to formulate a meaningful joint response for sustainability.

Sustainability

As Genesis 2 points out, humans are made from the "dust of the earth" of creation and are intimately connected with the rest of the natural world. But in Biblical understanding humans are also created with "the breath of God" and so in the image of God and called to be caretakers of the creation as creatures within it. Environmental science has increasingly pointed to our intimate connection to everything on this planet. But as St. Paul and the nightly news remind us, "We know that the whole creation has been groaning in labor pains until now." (Romans 8:22) All is not well with the creation. Creation is groaning, suffering, and much of that suffering today is due to the human impact upon the planet. Humanity has even succeeded in lighting up the planet at night.[42] But human planetary impact goes much deeper, even if invisible, in such areas as species extinction or chemical genetic mutation. Here, in the intersection of humanity and the environment, science and faith must join forces. Creation theology provides a theological justification for environmental science and sustainability. The ELCA's social statement, "Caring for Creation: Vision, Hope and Justice" (1993)," affirms this theological foundation for creation and sustainability and formulates four major ethical principles for its member churches as "communities of deliberation" to utilize, namely, justice through: participation, solidarity, sufficiency and sustainability. [43] The reconnection of fact and value can empower all of us to not only reach out to other human beings but to seek sustainability for the systems of Earth that make our lives possible.

To seek to sustain the environment is to seek to sustain the human species.[44] The Preamble to the Earth Charter released in June, 2000, clearly states;

> We stand at a critical moment in Earth's history, a time when humanity must choose its future. As the world becomes increasingly interdependent and fragile, the future at once holds great peril and great promise. To move forward we must recognize that in the midst of a magnificent diversity of cultures and life forms we are one human family and one Earth community with a common destiny. We must join together to bring forth a sustainable global society founded on respect for nature, universal

> human rights, economic justice, and a culture of peace. Towards this end, it is imperative that we, the peoples of Earth, declare our responsibility to one another, to the greater community of life, and to future generations.[45]

This interconnection is clearly articulated in the guiding principles of the Earth Charter:

1. Respect Earth and life in all its diversity.
2. Care for the community of life with understanding, compassion, and love.
3. Build democratic societies that are just, participatory, sustainable, and peaceful.
4. Secure Earth's bounty and beauty for present and future generations.[46]

The Earth Charter's ethical vision affirms that environmental protection, human rights, equitable human development, and peace are interdependent and indivisible.[47] These principles are key to formulating a sustainable society and world and may also guide the expression of education for vocation and sustainability.

David Orr, who has thought about sustainability and education for decades, offers six suggestions for such a sustainability education:

1. All education is environmental education.
2. The goal of education is not mastery of subject matter, but of one's person.
3. Knowledge carries with it the responsibility to see that it is well used in the world.
4. We cannot say that we know something until we understand the effects of this knowledge on real people and their communities.
5. Education has to stress the importance of "minute particulars" and the power of example over words.
6. The way learning occurs is as important as the content of particular courses.[48]

To incorporate such educational principles into liberal arts education could empower students not only to see the wider picture but also begin to understand the multivalent and interdependent character of sustainability. It could restore (or improve) wonder at nature back into the curriculum, to see it as more sacred, and to help move our thinking from anthropocentrism to ecocentrism. As Lisa Sideris argues, "Loss of direct contact with nature and immersion in overly specialized and balkanized disciplines creates a narrowness of vision that is the antithesis of wonder. Thus, depending on how education is designed, wonder can be cultivated or deadened through learning."[49] It is truly the case, as the David Orr quote at the beginning of this essay states, "A constituency able and willing to fight for the long-term human prospect must be educated into existence."[50] This sense of wonder can also open up the possibility of interfaith dialogue as education works for cooperation between faith traditions to enable vocation for sustainability.

V. Vocation and Interfaith Dialogue

Interfaith dialogue leading to interfaith cooperation is perhaps one of the greatest needs of our time if we are to address the profound global issues that face us today. It is because of (not in spite of) the Lutheran theological heritage that colleges and universities in the Lutheran tradition are open to interfaith dialogue. Lutheran colleges were created and are partially sustained by the church. By being church related, colleges are expected to provide regular occasions for worship and proclamation of the gospel. In such a grace filled context, the college also practices hospitality to all present on campus regardless of belief. It is a way of understanding the relationship between God and the world characterized by justifying grace embraced through faith. This is the principle contribution of Lutheranism to ecumenical dialogue and affects the way faith and learning are exemplified in our institutions of higher learning. It also grounds what Darrell Jodock calls the "third path" a position between rigorous defense of a theological tradition on the one hand and no affiliation on the other, a middle way between extremes. This position also affirms that Lutheran higher education can be both "rooted and inclusive" paving the way for creative interfaith dialog.[51]

Concordia College's Interfaith Cooperation Statement reads, "Concordia College practices interfaith cooperation because of its Lutheran dedication to prepare thoughtful and informed global citizens who foster wholeness and hope, build peace through understanding, and serve the world together."[52] In such a dialogue, one enters the relationship with mutual respect and affirmation of the integrity of the other. The goal is not conversion but dialogue leading to deeper understanding and cooperation, indeed, to "mutual transformation."[53] This is at the core of the "theology of accompaniment" which is the main model for mission work in the ELCA today.[54] In *Global Mission in the Twenty-First Century*, the model of accompaniment is affirmed:

> Recognizing that the nature of the Triune God and the nature of God's mission is fundamentally relational, the ELCA's Division for Global Mission seeks to express its mission activities in relationship and in cooperation with companion churches, agencies, and institutions. Mission is also lived out in respectful and listening relationships with those with whom we would proclaim the gospel and share the life of God: people of all living faiths and those who claim no faith.... Religious pluralism is a reality of the global environment for mission for both the ELCA's membership and companion churches. The ELCA is committed to include interfaith witness and conversation in its programs in order that there might be mutual understanding and respect between the ELCA and people of diverse faiths.[55]

Confessional theology, then, coupled with open ecumenical and interfaith commitment, allows one to enter dialogue with both a witness to bear as well as a witness to hear.

Diana Eck, founder of "The Pluralism Project" at Harvard University over twenty-five years ago, in her fine book, *Encountering God: A Spiritual Journey from Bozeman to Banaras*, states,

> Today the language of dialogue has come to express the kind of two-way discourse that is essential to relationship, not domination. One might call it mutual witness: Chris-

> tians have not only a witness to bear, but also a witness to hear. In the process of mutual testimony and mutual questioning, we not only come to understand one another, we come to understand ourselves more deeply. It leads to what John Cobb calls "mutual transformation."[56]

Cynthia Moe-Lobeda, concerning global climate change, observes that,

> The world's great faith traditions are called to plumb their depth for wisdom to contribute to the great moral challenge of our day: to forge ways of being human that allow earth to flourish and all people to have the necessities for life with dignity. I believe that all religious traditions have particular gifts to bring to the table, and are called to put these in dialogue with each other and with other bodies of knowledge including the natural and social sciences.[57]

After clarifying that pluralism is different from relativism, Eck goes on to elaborate why dialogue is important. She states,

> The language of dialogue is the two-way language of real encounter and it is for this reason that dialogue is the very basis for pluralism. There must be constant communication—meeting, exchange, traffic, criticism, reflection, reparation, renewal. Without dialogue, the diversity of religious traditions, of cultures and ethnic groups, becomes an array of isolated encampments, each with a different flag, meeting only occasionally for formalities or for battle.[58]

Eck goes on to affirm that the three aims of dialogue include mutual understanding and mutual transformation leading to cooperative transformation of our global and local cultures.[59] These aims of dialogue are at the core for addressing religious pluralism and for developing leaders today who can work with others to address common global problems.

The Interfaith Youth Core, founded by Eboo Patel, is one of the most effective organizations for bringing awareness of the need for interfaith dialogue to college campuses as well as providing respectful guidelines and principles for interfaith dialogue to help educate interfaith leaders for the future. The IFYC Core Values are:

1. We are serious about our mission. We lead with religious pluralism.
2. We are all interfaith leaders.
3. We cultivate interfaith leadership as a craft.
4. We engage diversity in pursuit of pluralism.
5. We achieve as a team.
6. We steward relationships and resources with conviction.
7. Our staff is our most powerful and valuable asset.
8. We pursue excellence with grit, grace, and energy . . . and we have fun doing it.[60]

These principles are also in consonance with the goals of a theology of accompaniment and of the Lutheran understanding of education conducted in an open, respectful, and dialogical manner.

The character of Lutheran identity began, and must be sustained through, public debate and dialogue in the arena of contemporary intellectual and religious opinions. At their best, scholars at ELCA institutions of higher education eagerly bring their tradition and confessions to the ecumenical and interfaith table in the spirit of openness and commitment to the discernment of new truths about God and God's world. Taken together, these theological resources provide both content and context for the engagement of faith and learning, a dialogue which is explicit in Concordia College's mission.[61] The tradition provides us with both the freedom and the responsibility to confront culture. We are not saved by our intellectual or ideological constructions, so we are free to pursue analysis of the world and search for truth wherever it may lead. That is the character of an educational vision which affirms diversity within the overarching unity of God's creation. Born in the liberal arts setting for reflection on faith and life, Lutheran liberal arts education can remain a vital force for sustaining such an interfaith dialogue.

Conclusion: Vocation for Planetary Citizenship

The Lutheran tradition's emphasis upon vocation is one way to give theological grounding to Lutheran higher education. Why are any of us here? The answer is vocation. Vocation addresses the practical from the context of the existential. It seeks to connect purposes and practices, ends and means and does not allow them to fall apart into separate realms. *Vocation occurs at the intersection of these two dimensions of the why question.* It is through work in the world that faith is incarnated and by so doing helps to sustain the creation. Vocation rejects the separation of the material from the spiritual, of nature from grace, insisting that they be kept together. In this context, education and scholarship have their own religious integrity.

Luther sought to reform the church by clarifying the nature of the Gospel through debate in the public arenas of the university and society. In this regard the character of Lutheran identity began and, to remain vital, must continue to be sustained as a matter of public debate and dialogue, particularly at colleges and universities. This is to say that "Lutheran liberal arts" is not an oxymoron but rather an essential statement of one of the ways in which the character of Lutheran identity is formulated and sustained in the ongoing dynamic between faith and life.

The Lutheran model of such an education is particularly helpful because of its dialectical openness to alternative viewpoints and their dynamic interaction. It allows for mutual critique between contemporary society and the realm of faith. Such a model avoids what Tom Christensen has termed the "fallacy of exclusive disjunction."[62] There are middle positions between doctrinal imposition and cultural accommodation in higher education and the Lutheran dialectical model is one. Such a theological perspective can and should confront any claim to absoluteness or finality, including in its secular expressions.

Our students come to us formed by mass media merchandizing, disposable, material consumption, and social media patterning for human relationships. Our contemporary society encourages a person to be preoccupied with the self and the satisfaction of one's selfish desires. To be liberated from such a condition is one of the main objectives of a liberal arts education and the faculty who facilitate such an education. Only with a changed vision can we begin to talk about a viable foundation for a sustainable future. *It is in light of what might be that one can become empowered to challenge and change what is.* We need a grace from beyond the self to reform the self and provide both forgiveness and hope. Judgment is easy and there is more than enough of that to go around. Cynicism breeds self-defeat. What is needed is reconciliation that motivates beyond the despair and hopelessness that inevitably result when one finally comes to terms with one's own responsibility for destructive actions.

We are becoming aware of our collective environmental responsibility and now forgiving, motivational grace is needed to transcend self-interest for constructive change. The Christian tradition, among other religious traditions, can provide grace-filled change if education will only step up to the challenge. Such a grace-filled hope can sustain one in the face of enormous challenges. As Viktor Frankl observed in his classic work *Man's Search for Meaning,* "Everything can be taken from a man [sic.] but one thing: the last of human freedoms—to choose one's attitude in any given set of circumstances, to choose one's own way."[63] Lutheran higher education must foster a realistic but open and hopeful attitude towards the future and the systemic changes that we are all facing. It must provide an education for vocational service which connects both the practical and the existential in relation to sustainability for both the natural as well as the human world. Accordingly, environmental education for sustainability must be supplemented with religious and ethical education which provides hope in the face of impending cultural and climatological change. Fostering hope and feasible practical responses will provide a foundation for our graduates to become sustainability leaders in their future communities. To engage the challenges of the twenty-first century, the epoch of the Anthropocene, would indeed be to conduct education for planetary citizenship.

Endnotes

1 Will Steffen, Jacques Grinevald, Paul Crutzen and John McNeill, "The Anthropocene: Conceptual and Historical Perspectives," *Philosophical Transactions of the Royal Society*, A 2011 369, 842-867, doi: 10.1098/rsta.2010.0327. For a more complete summary of the Anthropocene, please see, Christian Schwagerl, *The Anthropocene: The Human Era and How It Shapes Out Planet* (Santa Fe: Synergetic Press, 2014). For a more personal account, see Gaia Vince, *Adventures in the Athropocene: A Journey to the Heart of the Planet We Made* (Minneapolis: Milkweed Editions, 2014).

2 Some of the material in this chapter was published as "Lutheran Education in the Anthropocene," in *Dialogue: A Journal of Theology*, 55 (2016): 2-5, "Semper Reformanda: Lutheran Higher Education in the Anthropocene," *Intersections*, 43 (2016): 33-38, "Liberal Arts for Sustainability: Lutheran Higher Education in the Anthropocene," in *Eco-Reformation: Grace and Hope for a Planet in Peril*, ed. Jim Martin-Schramm and Lisa Dahill (Eugene: Wipf and Stock, fall, 2016) and "A Lutheran Dialectical Model for Higher Education," *Intersections*, 37 (2013):27-31. This chapter also draws heavily on my book *Lutheran Higher Education: An Introduction* (Minneapolis: Augsburg Fortress, 1998) esp. Chaps. 2-3.

3 Leslie Paul Thiele, *Sustainability* (Cambridge, UK: Polity, 2013), 7. See also, "The Earth Charter," *Earth Charter Commission*, 2000, www.EarthCharter.org.

4 *Plato, the Republic, and Phaedrus, in The Collected Dialogues of Plato, Including the Letters*, eds. Edith Hamilton and Huntington Cairns, Bollingen Series LXXI (New York: Random House, 1966) Republic Bk. VII, 747, Phaedrus, 475. See also Edward Goodwin Ballard, "The Liberal Arts and Plato's Relation to Them," in *Philosophy and the Liberal Arts, Contributions to Phenomenology*, vol. 2 (Springer, Netherlands, 1989): 93-112.

5 "Trivium" in Wikipedia.

6 Naomi Oreskes and Erik Conway, *Merchants of Doubt: How a Handful of Scientists Obscured the Truth About Issues from Tobacco Smoke to Global Warming* (New York: Bloomsbury Press, 2010).

7 See Carl Braaten, *Principles of Lutheran Theology*, 2nd edition (Minneapolis: Augsburg Fortress, 2006): Chapter 5, "The Christocentric Principle."

8 Walther Brandt, "Introduction" to *Luther's To the Councilmen of All Cities of Germany That They Establish and Maintain Schools*, LW 45: 342 (Philadelphia: Muhlenberg Press, 1962).

9 LW 45: 347-378.

10 LW46: 207-258.

11 Richard Solberg, *Lutheran Higher Education in North America* (Minneapolis, Augsburg, 1985), 14.

12 See *To the Councilmen of All Cities in Germany that They Establish and Maintain Schools*, LW 45.

13 Richard Solberg, "What Can the Lutheran Tradition Contribute to Christian Higher Education?" in *Models for Christian Higher Education*, eds. Richard Hughes and William Adrian (Grand Rapids: Eerdmans, 1997): 72. See also Bernard Ramm, "Phillip Melanchthon: Christian Humanism" in *The Christian College in the Twentieth Century* (Grand Rapids, Eerdmans, 1963), 31-51.

14 See Philip Melanchthon, *The Loci Communes of Philip Melanchthon: with a Critical Introduction by the Translator* (Eugene: Wipf & Stock, 2007).

15 Luther, LW 45:355.

16 See William Lazareth, *Christians in Society Luther, the Bible and Social Ethics* (Minneapolis: Augsburg Fortress, 2001).

17 Luther, "The Freedom of a Christian," *Luther's Works* (Philadelphia: Fortress, 1961), 31:327-77.

18 LW 1:47-48.

19 David Lotz, "Education for Citizenship in the Two Kingdom: Reflections on the Theological Foundations of Lutheran Higher Education," *Institutional Mission and Identity in Lutheran Higher Education*, LECNA (1979), 15.

20 "The Creed," from the Small Catechism of Martin Luther, *Evangelical Lutheran Worship* (Minneapolis: Augsburg Fortress, 2006), 1162.

21 Mark Noll, "The Lutheran Difference," *First Things* (1992): 37.

22 Sydney E. Ahlstrom, "What's Lutheran about Higher Education?—A Critique," *Papers and Proceedings of the 60th Annual Convention* (Washington, D.C.: Lutheran Educational Conference of North America, 1974): 8-16.

23 Solberg, 1985, 20.

24 Solberg, 1997, 72.

25 Ibid., 73.

26 Solberg, 1985, 15.

27 For more detail on the origin and development of specific Lutheran Colleges and Universities in America, please see my *Lutheran Higher Education: An Introduction*, pp. 11-20 and for great detail, Richard Solberg, *Lutheran Higher Education in North America*.

28 Martin Luther, "The Creed" from The Small Catechism in *Evangelical Lutheran Worship* (Minneapolis: Augsburg Fortress, 2006), 1162.

29 For more elaboration on divine entanglement see Ernest L. Simmons, *The Entangled Trinity: Quantum Physics and Theology* (Minneapolis: Fortress, 2014).

30 There are many texts that affirm this. See Ian Barbour's *Religion in an Age of Science* (San Francisco: Harper San Francisco, 1990) Chapter 5, Arthur Peacocke, *Theology for a Scientific Age* (Minneapolis: Fortress, 1993) Part III and, more recently, Paul Wallace, *Stars Beneath Us* (Minneapolis: Fortress, 2015).

31 Bengt Hoffman, *The Theologia Germanica of Martin Luther*, Classics of Western Spirituality (Mahwah, NJ: Paulist, 1980).

32 Ibid., 6. See also Bengt Hoffman, *Luther and the Mystics: A Re-examination of Luther's Spiritual Experience and his Relationship to the Mystics* (Minneapolis: Augsburg, 1976).

33 Heiko Oberman, "Simul gemitus et raptus: Luther and Mysticism," in *The Reformation in Medieval Perspective*, ed. Steven E. Ozment (Chicago: Quandrangle Books, 1971): 225, 232.

34 Hoffman, *Theologia Germanica*, 6.

35 Philip Watson, *Let God Be God: An Interpretation of the Theology of Martin Luther* (Eugene: Wipf & Stock, 2000, 1947), 78.

36 See both Augustine and Thomas Aquinas.

37 Niels Gregersen, "Grace in Nature and History: Luther's Doctrine of Creation Revisited," *Dialogue: A Journal of Theology* 44 (2005): 23.

38 Steven Church, "'The Lovely Music of Nature:' Grounding an Ecological Ethics in Martin Luther's Creation Mysticism," *Currents in Theology and Mission* 26 (1999): 192.

39 Gregersen, 24.

40 Larry Rasmussen, "Luther and a Gospel of Earth," *Union Seminary Quarterly* Review (1997): 2.

41 See Simmons, *The Entangled Trinity*, esp. chap.7, "Theology, Science and Quantum Theory," for more development on the relationship of theology and science.

42 See NASA website, "Earth at Night," at https://www.nasa.gov/topics/earth/earthday/gall_earth_night.html.

43 The statement can be found at: https://www.elca.org/en/Faith/Faith-and-Society/Social-Statements/Caring-for-Creation or download at: https://www.elca.org/en/Faith/Faith-and-Society/Social-Statements/Caring-for-Creation

44 See *Eco-Reformation: Grace and Hope for a Planet in Peril*, Jim Marti-Schramm and Lisa Dahill eds. (Eugene: Wipf & Stock, 2016). See also, Larry Rasmussen, *Earth Community, Earth Ethics and Earth-Honoring Faith*, Willis Jenkins, *Ecologies of Grace: Environmental Ethics and Christian Theology*, James Martin-Schramm, *Climate Justice* as well as his co-edited work, *Earth Ethics*. For an earlier text please see, James Nash's *Loving Nature: Ecological Integrity and Christian Responsibility*,

45 *The Earth Charter*, Preamble, www.earthcharter.org, 1.

46 *The Earth Charter*, www.earthcharter.org, 2.

47 *Earth Charter*, Wikipedia.

48 David Orr, "What is Education For?"10-16. See also Orr, *Earth in Mind* (Washington: Island Press, 1994, 2004): 7-15.

49 Lisa Sideris, "Environmental Literacy and the Lifelong Cultivation of Wonder," in *Teaching Environmental Literacy: Across Campus and Across the Curriculum* (Bloomington: Indiana University Press, 2010): 91.

50 Orr, op.cit., 126.

51 Darrell Jodock, "The Third Path, Religious Diversity, and Civil Discourse," *The Vocation of Lutheran Higher Education*, ed. Jason Mahn (Minneapolis: Lutheran University Press, 2016), 82-99. See also, Jodock, "Religious Diversity and the Vocation of a Lutheran College," *Intersections* (2016): 24-35.

52 "Interfaith Cooperation Statement," accessed at Concordia College website at https://www.concordiacollege.edu/studentlife/spiritual-life/.

53 John B. Cobb, Jr., *Beyond Dialogue: Toward a Mutual Transformation of Christianity and Buddhism* (Eugene: Wipf & Stock, 1998) and Diana Eck, *Encountering God: A Spiritual Journey from Bozeman to Banaras* (Boston: Beacon, 2003):19.

54 See "Global Mission in the Twenty-First Century" at www.elca.org > global_mission_21 for the full statement and to download the PDF.

55 *Global Mission in the Twenty-First Century*, PDF, "The Accompaniment Model" 12 and "Interfaith Witness and Dialogue," 30. Access at www.elca.org > global_mission_21.

56 Dianna Eck, *Encountering God: A Spiritual Journey from Bozeman to Banaras* (Boston: Beacon, 2003): 19.

57 Cynthia Moe-Lobeda, "Cross, Resurrection and the Indwelling God," in *God, Creation and Climate Change*, ed. Karen L. Bloomquist, LWF Studies (Minneapolis: Lutheran University Press, 2009):145-146. See also her more recent work, "A Haunting Contradiction, Hope and Moral-Spiritual Power," Chap. 3 in *Eco-Reformation* as well as her major theological work, *Resisting Structural Evil: Love as Ecological-Economic Vocation* (Minneapolis: Fortress, 2013).

58 Eck, *Encountering God*, 197-198.

59 Eck, *Encountering God*, 199.

60 See the Interfaith Youth Corps website at www.ifyc.org.

61 "The mission of Concordia College is to influence the affairs of the world by sending into society thoughtful and informed men and women dedicated to the Christian life, accessed at Concordia College, Moorhead, MN, website at https://www.concordiacollege.edu/about/our-mission/.

62 Tom Christenson, *The Gift and Task of Lutheran Higher Education* (Minneapolis: Augsburg Fortress, 2004), 12.

63 Viktor Frankl, *Man's Search for Meaning*, 92.

THE WITTENBERG DOOR

Reconsidering Martin Luther's Reforming Conscience

DR. ROY HAMMERLING
Professor of Religion

Introduction: A Distraction from Reality—Martin Luther's View of Indulgences

In 1518, an ambassador from Venice wrote a letter explaining how upset he was when he heard that the proceedings at an Imperial Diet in Augsburg had bogged down over what he considered to be a trivial theological debate concerning a question over indulgences. Apparently, an upstart Augustinian friar by the name of Martin Luther from a small, recently founded university in Wittenberg, Germany, offered a challenge to the Catholic Church; at a debate with Johannes Eck, another young professor, Luther raised questions about the pope's theological right to issue indulgences. As Heiko Oberman puts it, the ambassador thought it "ridiculous, to let indulgences distract one from reality!"[1]

For the Venetian diplomat, "reality" meant promoting a tariff called a "crusade penny" to raise funds for a "Holy War" that Venice was engaged in against the Ottoman Turks. About a half a century earlier, Constantinople, the capital of the Byzantine Empire, had fallen to the Ottomans and the ambassador at last wanted to win the prize city back for the "glory of Christendom," and his own economic advantage. He also intended to tie up his papal ally, and sometimes rival, in a war so that the Papal States would be unable to expand further into his territory. He hoped that together they would suppress the "Muslim threat" and gain land, security, and financial fortune in the process. The Holy Roman Emperor, Maximillian I, at the Diet of Augsburg on August 28, 1518, agreed to come to the aid of Venice by signing a treaty that allowed the Venetians to go on a crusade to fight the Sultan. However, Maximillian, nearly bankrupt, also needed other tax hikes besides the "Turkish Penny" to keep his own empire afloat.[2]

At the diet, however, when the issue of the crusade tax came up, various representatives from the empire, especially the German contingent, voiced deep grievances against Rome's demands to increase taxes and especially levy a tax on German churches. In other words, the German princes, led by Duke Frederick the Wise, Martin Luther's lord and protector, wanted less of a tax burden, not more, upon their territories.[3]

Luther's criticism of the papal indulgence policies, which many saw as just one more way to support papal programs with hard-earned German coin, began in earnest when he posted the 95 Theses in 1517. Luther's concerns were theological, but the attack resonated with the German nobility and their concern about their pocketbooks. Even if the theological implications of this debate were lost upon most people, the idea of indulgences and the crusader penny together rubbed many the wrong way. Perhaps some things never change. At the Diet of Augsburg in 1518, Luther was hardly little more than a minor irritation for the papacy and emperor, even though Luther had issued the 95 Theses a year earlier on October 31, 1517. After all, such criticism had come and gone before, and no doubt they thought as the Venetian ambassador did, that this was simply a distraction from more important realities concerning the spiritual and secular realms of the day.[4]

After the Diet of Augsburg was over, superiors told Cardinal Cajetan to find a solution to the "Luther problem." The cardinal summoned his scholarly Augustinian friar to an audience and questioned him from October 12-15, 1518. The young Luther proved more frustrating for the cardinal than his eminence had expected; Luther stubbornly refused to recant unless he was shown by "scripture and pure reason" the error of his ways. Cajetan wrote to Luther's direct sovereign, Frederick the Duke of Saxony, "I exhort Your Highness to consider Your honor and Your conscience and either to have the monk Martin sent to Rome or to chase him from Your lands. Your Highness should not let one little friar (*unum fraterculum*) bring such ignominy over You and Your house."[5] Frederick politely refused. Although he never met Luther personally in life, he would support him as a loyal subject of his land until the duke died in 1525. Frederick believed that Luther, as a campus pastor and professor at Frederick's recently founded young Wittenberg University (est. in 1502), had a right from God to preach the Word as his conscience demanded and the academic freedom of a professor to speak his mind. Luther used his liberty not only to challenge the church and papacy directly, but he also even attacked his protector, Frederick, who had his own admirably large collection of relics, which the duke used to draw pilgrims to his lands to spend money and promote local businesses. Therefore, the decision by Frederick to protect Luther, even when attacked by him on occasion, proved fateful and earned the duke a moniker, "The Wise."[6]

If we ask how Luther got to be a "problem," a pattern emerges that is useful to consider in more detail: in other words, we may determine by means of an examination of the development of Luther's conscience, how others may in turn develop their own consciences and means of producing change in their worlds. Indeed, how did Europe get to the point where an insignificant friar from an obscure university became a remarkable agent of change and catalyst for a "reformation" that would transform the whole Holy Roman Empire? To explore this question, let us examine how Luther became a distraction from reality for the emperor and pope. The story hinges upon various aspects and stages of Luther's life. They are: 1. Luther's upbringing as a normal child. 2. A life-changing event that caused Luther to change his focus of academic study. 3. Luther's awakening of conscience and the discovery of his passion and vocation. 4. The persistence of a niggling question, "Is this true?" 5. Luther's studies that led him to take the risk of going public and bring truth as he saw it to light. 6. Luther's clinging to his conscience in the face of opposition. 7. And despite the threat of death, Luther remaining true to his convictions and his highest authorities that had captivated his conscience, namely the Word and reason. This paper is a shorter version of a much longer text. Here the focus will be upon points 1-4 above in order to introduce the reader to the early development of Luther's conscience.

I. The Extraordinary Quality of Being Just a Normal Kid

Luther in most ways was just a normal German kid, who happened to be born in Eisleben about midnight of St. Martin of Tours day, November 10, 1483. Luther proudly declared, "I am a peasant's son. My father, my grandfather, and my great grandfather were all true peasants."[7] Modern archeological research, which in recent years excavated the boyhood home of Luther in Mansfeld, suggests that for Luther the word "true" applied to his ancestors, but was not accurate when applied to his father. Luther would have been more accurate had he said he was born of hard-working parents, who made the most of difficult life situations, so that they became successful and even wealthy. His father, Hans, a successful copper miner supported his four sons and four daughters with a certain amount of luxury as the excavations of the "Luder" Mansfeld home shows. Hans could afford to send his talented son, Martin, off for a good education, when such an education was beyond the grasp of a clear majority of folk. Margarethe, Luther's mother, as far as scholars can tell, came out of a middle-class Frankish background, but speaking about her Luther noted that she often "carried all the wood on her back . . . enduring hardships the world today would no longer put up with."[8] What Luther appears to have learned from his parents and from a rather normal advantaged upbringing was a hard-working dedication to succeed and a clever ability to take advantage of whatever life set before him.[9]

Luther's overall education in the church, at home, and in schools was typically medieval; "strict." Martin appreciated his parent's faithful dedication to the church and their religious convictions, even if his father was not overly religious and usually quite cynical about a greedy, money-seeking church. In this, Hans was like other Germans of his age.[10] Luther became religious himself in this atmosphere. In his later youth, while on a trip, he accidentally cut his femoral artery in his thigh with his sword and he nearly bled to death. Thanks to a good doctor and his pleas to the Virgin Mary, Luther declared, he was spared.[11] This last story indicates how Luther respected both scientific knowledge, such as it was in his day, and faith together as essential to life.

Luther when talking about education and discipline in his home emphasized its oppressive nature. On one occasion, he reacted to such harshness by arguing, "One shouldn't whip their children too hard,"[12] because it can break their spirits; it had, in fact, done so at times when he was young. Luther notes that his parents were so tough on him that he became timid, something that is hard to imagine given his later fiery disposition. In his later years, he was also able to see that their severity did have a positive side, namely that through it they cared for him. Luther declared, "The best thing I received of all my father's possessions was that he educated me."[13] The schools of his day believed that the rod was the best motivator of performance; however, Luther loathed such techniques and referred to his school experiences as his "prison" and "hell and purgatory."[14] He later on encouraged instead that children be taught through joyful play.[15]

Despite the torture of education, Luther proved a good student. Recognizing his son's considerable academic talent, Hans eagerly prepared his son for a noble profession and eventually sent Martin off to law school in Erfurt. There is nothing in all this that suggests Luther had exceptional qualities that destined him to be a reformer, even if he was a gifted student. He was a typically talented youth who did alright by himself; he, like other timid youth, worked hard to make his parents proud. He was on his way to a better life than his so-called peasant ancestors, because his father had the means to allow Luther to better himself through education. Like his parents, hard-work and talent paid off for the copper miner's son. Then not unlike other college students of any age, Luther had a change of heart about the direction of his life. The normal youth, however, was about to find his conscience through crisis.

II. Conscience and Passion Through Crisis

The story of Luther's change of heart has taken on mythic proportions over the ages. Luther's admirers have eagerly perpetuated and exaggerated the almost legendary tale of Luther getting caught in a life-threatening thunderstorm on July 2, 1505 as he returned from a break to Erfurt to continue his studies in law. A bolt of lightning knocked him to the ground and fearing death he cried out to the patron saint of his father, and miners in general, and of people in trouble in storms; none other than the mother of the Blessed Virgin Mary herself, St. Anne. His plea was simple, as he tells it, "St. Anne, St. Anne save me and I'll become a monk!" As has already been hinted at, Luther's religious convictions were strong, and he was in the habit of turning to saints in times of trouble. One should not be surprised that he did so now in a time of fear.[16]

What is impossible to know is whether Luther might have made this turn in his career anyway without his near-death experience. Certainly, later at a less thunderstruck moment, Luther no doubt had to wonder about the circumstances of his private, and rather rash, vow. He might simply have ignored his vow, who would know besides God, and moved on with his law degree, but he chose not to. Why? Luther later described the experience to his friend Melanchthon, "I am uncertain with what kind of an attitude I took my vow. I was more overpowered than drawn. God wanted it this way. I am afraid that I, too, may have taken my vow in an impious and sacrilegious way."[17] By this he meant that he proceeded to the monastery in an involuntary state of mind rather than joyously, or even willingly. But for Luther, a vow is a vow, his conscience would not allow him to go back on his word, and so after two weeks, and after numerous attempts by friends and family to dissuade him, Luther entered the Augustinian Mendicant Monastery of Hermits in Erfurt, which was dedicated to St. Anne, on July 17, 1505. The way he saw it, he had no choice in the matter, he had to do what God pushed him to do, and he would interpret this and other storms as being the clear voice of God. What clearer sign could there be than a lightning bolt from heaven? Once at home among the Augustinians he did not look back; Hans expressed grave concern at his leaving the noble profession of law for what he considered to be a more ignoble religious life.[18]

College students throughout the ages have disappointed parents and others with their choices of careers, especially if the change was from what was considered to be a stable profession to one that does not provide the same economic advantage, and Luther in this can be said to be typical. Sometimes the choices people make cannot be helped, conscience compels, and the road of life opens in a way that is unexpected.

Even so, it is also normal to doubt one's conscience, to go against what one knows is right for whatever reason; still Luther could not be dissuaded from his path, no matter how serious his friends', families', or his own doubts were. Diarmaid MacCulloch notes, "Martin Luther was typical of the recruits to the monastic and clerical life on whom the smooth running and reputation of the church depended, a bright boy from a hard-working middle-rank family with a shrewd respect for education."[19]

Once Luther entered his advanced religious studies, however, life on the surface for Luther appeared to proceed slowly. Two years after the thunderstorm he was ordained a priest on April 4, 1507, and then after another five years, in October of 1512, he received his doctoral degree and became a professor of biblical theology at Wittenberg University. Then for the next five years he taught and worked with students to make them into good mendicant friars, priests, and people of God. Somewhere along the 12-year journey, his studies began to change him in a way that he could not have imagined earlier.[20] What changed in him was his passion. The study of theology, unlike his studies in law, sparked a deep enthusiasm for study henceforth unknown in young man Luther. His passion for biblical studies developed with a vigor that few, especially Luther, anticipated upon his entrance into the monastery. Indeed, on the surface, one would anticipate that Luther was doomed to hate the monastic and academic life, especially if he had entered it under duress, as the thunderstorm story suggests.

Indeed, Luther talks a good deal about becoming depressed and overcome by a sense of despair after entering the monastery. The spiritual despair of Luther is known as an *Anfechtung* (or plural *Anfechtungen*). The term is not easily translated into English so scholars leave it as is, but it means a deep spiritual anguish, which in Luther's case manifested itself in a feeling of being abandoned by God and resulting in a sense of hopelessness. Luther does not appear to have had any *Anfechtungen* early on as a novice after entering the Augustinian Order in 1505, but when he conducted his first mass as a priest in 1507, he was overcome with a depth of trembling emotion.[21] Oberman notes that Luther "nearly ran away in the midst of the service" not as a part of "stage fright but of an overpowering awe at the majesty of God."[22] Something was happening. Luther hints at a part of the issue when he writes, "I was a good monk, and kept the rule of my order so strictly that I may say that if ever a monk got to heaven by monkery, I would have gotten there as well. All my brothers in the monastery who knew me will bear me out. If I had kept on any longer, I would have killed myself with vigils, prayers, readings and other works."[23] The never-ending drive to please God and force the divine to save him overwhelmed the friar. He began to wonder, why is God like this? Luther concluded that this type of God could not be a loving God, but only a vengeful and vindictive Deity who created people to condemn them. At the heart of his *Anfechtungen* lay the overwhelming sense that his Just God, had it out for him and all of humanity.

Luther desperately needed help with his spiritual struggles and fortunately for him at this time he developed a relationship with his most important mentor, Johannes von Staupitz, whom he fondly called his most beloved father in Christ ("*in Christo suavissimo Patri*").[24] Staupitz, a notable leader among a strict reform movement of the Augustinian Hermits, the Observants, was a genuinely spiritual man and a noted academic in his own right. When Staupitz later was called away from the monastery at a formative time in Luther's life, Luther anguished over his spiritual father's absence. Staupitz's death in 1524 left a tremendous emptiness in Luther's life. As Heiko Oberman points out, Luther would not be able to speak about Staupitz until his own father, Hans, died in 1530, or five years later. Luther mentioned the influence of both of these men in the well-known table talks and in his sermons regularly. Staupitz, in the end, was the one who helped Luther come to grips with his *Anfechtungen*.[25]

Staupitz decided that Luther's *Anfectungen* required a multi-leveled solution. First, Staupitz offered the young anguishing Augustinian friar the comfort of a confessor, guide, superior, and close spiritual friend. Then, when Staupitz learned of Luther's abilities and interest in scripture, he had him removed from doing menial labor and promoted him as a candidate for the priesthood and for a Ph.D. program in the study of the Bible and theology. Staupitz hoped that the young friar's spiritual malaise would be overcome by a budding young mind being put to its best use.[26] Luther was reluctant and unsure that this was right for him, but he had taken a vow of obedience and said that he would die trying, if Staupitz insisted. He did. Staupitz told his spiritual son that God needed the counsel of good doctors in heaven, so off Luther went.[27] For all intents and purposes Staupitz's plan worked, even if Luther's *Anfechtungen* would remain with him at varying levels for the rest of his life. They would never again overcome him in the same way they did early on. The young Luther threw himself into his studies not only to be obedient to his superiors or simply to gain a prestigious career, but to find insight and comfort for his anguish, and ultimately to enlighten his students by remaining true to God's initial call in the thunderstorm.

Let us take an aside at this moment briefly to discuss the type of education that Luther received, and how Staupitz hoped that it would help Luther. The program Staupitz urged was both a rigorously academic and a focused spiritual-formation exercise. His education was rooted in the Augustinian Order, which was noted for its passion for the liberal arts, as well as critical spiritual self-examination. Indeed, there is evidence that Luther chose the Augustinian Order in Erfurt because of the Augustinian educational emphasis, and because the local Augustinians were a fraternity of St. Anne, the same saint he had taken his vow to in the thunderstorm, who was known as the great teacher of her daughter, the Virgin Mary.[28]

As an Augustinian hermit and later as a professor, Luther began to study and develop his ideas and lifestyle about the meaning of his own life, as well as what a good society should look like. The ancient writings, especially those of St. Augustine, and excellent teachers, like Staupitz, helped him come to grips with his emotional and religious anguish and to find a way forward. Luther himself noted that "Staupitz laid all the foundations" for his future life and Luther thus was loath to give up his monastic heritage, even after it was clear that the Protestant reforms would move forward outside of Roman Catholic influence. He would wear his religious habit, for example, nearly up to the time he was married, or seven years after the posting of the 95 Theses. Historians often overlook the reality that Luther's religious formation that opened Luther up to reform developed out of a mendicant religious order or what is sometimes more broadly called a monastic setting, as well as an academic context.[29] Why does this matter? Luther's life, once again, was not something out of the ordinary. He followed the normal path of the career of others like him in religious orders of his day. There was nothing that made him stand out, especially early on, as a reformer who would change Europe.[30] He developed scholarly, mendicant, pastoral, and passionate sensitivities, and no one could possibly have suspected the remarkable trajectory of his life.

The road to reformation, as Oberman calls it, at this point in the story was invisible and extremely unlikely.[31] As a priest, Luther led mass and preached. As a professor, he taught and engaged his students with passion and vigor. Life had a comfortable rhythm to it. What happened? It appears that after Luther immersed himself in study and teaching, a series of seemingly insignificant events took on unexpected significance in a way that can only be understood through retrospective analysis as a road to reformation.

III. A Niggling Question: "Is This True?"

Luther went to Rome in 1510 at the behest of the Augustinian Order on official business. Alongside the duties Luther was to perform, he was given the freedom to be a pilgrim. Pilgrimage was an important spiritual exercise of late medieval Europe whereby people traveled to holy sites to do penance and get right with God. People are perhaps most familiar with the practice because they've read Chaucer's *Canterbury Tales*. Luther's official task was for the Augustinian Order, but his personal goal was to deepen his faith by visiting holy shrines. In any case, what transpired next was unexpected.

While in Rome, Luther found a city full of pilgrims anxiously scurrying about, venerating relics in order to do penance and earn, or buy, indulgences, so that their relatives might be freed from time in purgatory. Luther too felt the longing to see the great churches of Rome and their treasures. So great was the appeal to make, or pay, for a penance for his ancestors that Luther even noted that he was sorry his parents were still alive because, as he put it, "I would have loved to deliver them from purgatory with my masses and other special works of prayer."[32] He lamented not being able to do masses at St. John Lateran's Church, the pope's cathedral, because he was not able to wait out the long lines. However, what he could do was walk across the street to buy an indulgence for his grandfather who had passed away; all Luther needed to do was climb the famous *Scala Santa*, or steps that Christ had climbed before his death, which had been transported from Jerusalem and reassembled in Rome. The penance was twofold; first he bought an indulgence and then Luther went on his knees, saying a Lord's Prayer on every step as he climbed to the top. As Luther started shuffling up, he notes that at first he had a strong sense that he was freeing his grandfather from purgatory. Somewhere along his climb Luther tells us that his mind began to wonder, in the words of Heiko Oberman, "Would God allow himself to be pinned down this way?"[33] What would be the point? Why would God allow money and a few Our Father's to be such a powerful means of reconciliation? After all Augustine in his explanation of the fifth petition of the Lord's Prayer, "Forgive us our debts as we forgive our debtors," had acknowledged that forgiveness cannot be bought with money. If forgiveness could be bought, then the rich would have a very distinct advantage over the poor and that did not make sense. Rather Augustine argued that the fifth petition reveals that everyone has access to forgiveness not through money but through repentance. For Augustine, God simply did not and would not act this way.[34] Luther knew Augustine's work and so it stands to reason that something of it, or a similar analysis at least, now sparked a logic in Luther's mind that created a seed of doubt that had been planted as he climbed the *Scala Santa*. It was no great sudden revelation of skepticism, notes Oberman, but a germination of an idea that would niggle at Luther. A simple niggling thought, an apparent inconsequential idea, a question that would prick his conscience, and once pricked, his conscience would not rest easily afterward. Perhaps all reformations start with the simple niggling question, "Is this really true?"[35]

Likewise, the ideal of Rome, as the holy city, now had been tarnished for Luther. He saw much and heard even more about the lure of pleasure, greed, power, and fame, which together with the concerns about indulgences, now pressed even harder upon his conscience. His passion was for the gospel and the church, but now he could not reconcile the two. He would conclude, "The closer to Rome, the worse the Christians."[36] His worldview altered and with it his concept of reality and truth. When he returned to Germany from Rome in 1511, the trip, done largely on foot, and which had taken him some six months walking over the Alps, gave him plenty of time to ponder and consider. The pilgrimage had worked. He was changed, but not in the way originally expected. Still the day of October 31, 1517, and the posting of the 95 Theses was still six years away.

IV. Study and Small Risks

Luther returned from Rome, finished his doctoral studies and began to teach. By the fateful year of 1517, he had lectured upon the Psalms, Romans, Galatians, Hebrews, and also written works on *The Seven Penitential Psalms with a German Exposition*, *The German Exposition of the Lord's Prayer for the Laity* (which heavily relies on Augustine), The Ten Commandments, as well as prepared a public debate called, "The Disputation of Scholastic Theology." Luther had settled into his passion of study, teaching, and preaching. Walther von Loewenich suggests that "the years of 1513-17 were, in a certain sense, the greatest period of Luther's life . . . He gave himself completely to his work as a professor—someone responsible for his students—and to those issues that moved him most deeply."[37] Staupitz's nudging insistence now bore fruit and Luther came into his passion and along with his passion, his conscience began to awaken in a new way. The niggling questions just wouldn't go away. And a calling to a greater purpose was born within Luther.

What Luther awakened to is what scholars have called "Luther's breakthrough:" that he and all are saved by grace and that works and indulgences are of no avail.[38] When the breakthrough happened is a hotly debated scholarly topic. Luther says little about it until late in his life, in 1545, when he wrote in his preface to his Latin writings, "I had indeed been captivated with an extraordinary ardor for understanding Paul in the Epistle of the Romans [1:16-17,]..., 'He who through faith is righteous shall live' . . . Paul was for me truly the gate to paradise. Later I read Augustine . . . he, too, interpreted righteousness in a similar way."[39] What Luther came to was a confidence in what he called a "theology of the cross" or a theology of grace, that he found both in the Bible and the church fathers. Now armed with certainty that the ultimate authority of scripture revealed that the Roman Catholic Church over-emphasized works (buying indulgences, pilgrimages, venerating relics, doing acts of charity, all without regard to the state of the heart and repentance) for salvation, he decided to take a small risk. His studies had moved him to continually ask the question that first appeared upon *Scala Santa* about indulgences, "Is this true?" However, now he raised the question out in the open for all to hear. He no doubt worried that few would care, nevertheless, he would put forth his questions in a most ordinary way for a scholar of his day, that is by producing theses for academic debate. This common practice of discussing issues in an academic setting Luther thought was the right place for him to explore whether he was right or wrong. And he had a lot of ideas that he wanted to discuss; 95 to be exact. To give his ideas greater impact, he not only took on the idea of indulgences, but he focused his theses upon a person, Johannes Tetzel, the indulgence seller in Germany, known for his ruthless methods and outspoken manner, and his defense of the validity of indulgences. For the young Luther, his passionate research told him Tetzel was wrong in thought and deed, and Luther's conscience said that it was time to ask publicly, "Is this true?" and "Can we trust a church in which Tetzel operates with such blatant disregard for scripture, God, and the faithful everywhere?"

Conclusions

Later on Luther's studies led him to take the risk of going public to bring the truth as he saw it to light by posting the 95 Theses. Luther relied upon and clung to his conscience in the face of remarkable opposition and despite death threats, Luther remained true to his convictions and his highest authorities that had captivated his conscience, namely the Word and reason.

The above examination of Luther's life and his journey from an ordinary child to a reformer, who many argue changed the western world, points to a pattern that may be useful. First, who among us does not start out longing with ordinary hopes and dreams to make something of ourselves and make the world a better place, whether we come from disadvantaged or advantaged circumstances. Opportunities present themselves and whether one has wealth or not, choices about how we can serve the neighbor and greater society should and must be made. In Luther's case, he chose to follow the road his father set before him. Luther's goals in life were rather ordinary, namely to get a law degree and succeed in a way that would make his life better financially, first of all, and also in the long run better for others. Hans Luther's dream was to give his children an even better life than he had, which was tied to physical comforts and the same standards we cling to today, namely a belief that happiness is tied to the security of affluence.

Then came a fateful day when a thunderstorm changed everything. Not all are so fortunate to get a physical thunderbolt to show them the way, but generally some crisis happens when events of a day make people question what is important in life. Luther already had deep religious inclinations but now they replaced his path toward an ordinary life of an up-and-coming lawyer with another ordinary path toward a religious life. Luther's family was not happy, and probably others had thought he had lost his mind. He went anyway. Rash vow or not, it was still a vow. Or was it an excuse? Why our lives turn upon seemingly insignificant events is hard to say, but it does seem that often there comes a moment, when a choice needs to be made, namely to continue following the well-laid plan, or to take a risk in order to follow a meaningful calling. The call may be as dramatic as a major change like Luther's from law to theology, or perhaps it is less dramatic, within a life plan only altering the path slightly by reimagining why one is doing what one is doing. Motives matter; motives change everything. But in the end, the choice gives meaning and purpose to life, even if others, and perhaps because others do not understand the choice. People think the reason makes no sense because it is often a choice away from financial security to a purpose that aids humanity in some greater way. In the end, it costs people something, but that is of little or no concern given a grander sense of purpose.

The choice often feels as if it cannot be helped. Certainly, Luther did not think he had a choice in the matter. And once he had become an Augustinian, a priest, and a doctor of theology, it seemed like things were going smoothly, until another fateful day in Rome, when climbing the *Scala Santa*, a niggling question presented itself, "Is this true?" It would never go away. So, Luther immersed himself in his studies and a sense of wonder as he read the scriptures that moved him to a deep dedication to its lessons. The gospel understood through clear reason, moved him to wonder about the authority of the pope and councils, and God's justice and love for humanity, and how indulgences made sense. The niggling question burst forth as a call to debate in the Ninety-five Theses; to nail those theses to a door, and then see what would happen. It was a small risk, an ordinary act and early on few of the intended audience cared or even knew about the challenge; Luther nevertheless kept pursuing his quest for clarity and truth. Along the way, others, outside of the intended audience, however, took notice. They copied the theses, printed them, and took up Luther's cause in a way that he never could have imagined. One small act, like a match, caught on, and those in authority feared its light. Many rallied to Luther's ideas, and the depth of his convictions. A movement began; resistance was inevitable.

Luther's conscience had been pricked, his convictions solidified, and slowly his confidence grew. Conscience is a great motivator, but more importantly it offers a sense of clarity, if not always certainty, amid the doubt and assault of those who would rather not raise such questions. Luther not only wanted to raise the hard questions but could not have done otherwise. For him, to do otherwise would have meant to place his own soul in peril. So he forged ahead and wrote, debated, and longed for a broader audience.

Finally, the opportunity to present his ideas in a public forum, the Diet of Worms, presented itself. Luther baulked at first, but then found courage rooted in the gospel and pure reason, and here he found the strength to refuse emperor and pope; he would not recant unless convinced otherwise, his conscience was captive to the Word of God. He knew he was taking his life in his hands, but the only other choices would have been to place his own soul in peril, allow tyranny free reign, or to refuse the world the truth that is always offensive to the powers that seek their own advantage.

Oberman notes that at the end of his life Luther was about 100 kilometers from Wittenberg in Eisleben, the town of his birth, to work with local officials to solve the problems of the day. While preaching, he became ill and was taken to a nearby inn, where he would die. On his deathbed, he was asked, "'Reverend father, will you die steadfast in Christ, and the doctrines you have preached?' 'Yes,' replied the clear voice for the last time." Oberman points out that ". . . Luther was not spared a final public test, and not granted privacy even in this last, most personal hour . . . The deathbed in the Eisleben inn had become a stage; and straining their ears to catch Luther's last words were enemies as well as friends."[40] Once one speaks out of one's deepest convictions, people eventually listen, either to cheer or jeer. Once one steps a foot on the path of a conscience that is captive to truth, one chooses a side, and from then on, the path leads on through trials and tribulations as well as occasional hope and joy. While on the path, however, one must choose whatever door presents itself, whatever theses demand to be written, and whatever way leads to the good of humanity and a clear conscience that one has lived life as best as one can. Luther was far from perfect, he made many errors of judgment in his life; as he said, he is human and humans make mistakes. He spoke too harshly, too often; at times, he became a problem that needed to be solved, such as was the case with his stance on the Jews. Still, he also spoke out against abuse and became a catalyst for change that all started with a thunderbolt, a simple niggling question, a piece of paper and pen, and a door upon which to seek public debate. What is your door?

ENDNOTES

1 Heiko Oberman, *Luther: Man Between God and the Devil* (New Haven: Yale University Press, 1982), 13. One caveat: this paper is an exploration of the idea of how Luther's conscience came to be formed. This work re-evaluates modern scholarship on Luther in order to develop a thesis about how Luther's conscience developed over time and as a result what we ourselves might learn from Luther's life. A special thanks to Dr. Richard Chapman for his expert editorial help, and Dr. Ernest Simmons for his suggestions in developing this text.

2 Oberman, 13.

3 Oberman, 14.

4 Oberman, 14.

5 Oberman, 15-16.

6 Oberman, 16.

7 Walther von Loewenich, *Martin Luther: The Man and His Work* (Minneapolis: Augsburg Publishing House, 1982), 36-37.

8 WATR 3, no. 2888 in *D. Martin Luthers Werke, Kritische Gesamtausgabe: Tischreden*, 6 vols. (Weimar: Verlag Hermann Böhlaus Nachfolger, 1912-21).

9 For more on the archeology of Luther's upbringing see *Martin Luther: Treasures of the Reformation*, 2 volumes (Dresden: Sandsten Verlag, 2015).

10 WATR 2, no. 2756a; Loewenich, 40.

11 WATR 1, no. 119; LW 54:14-15; Loewenich, 52.

12 WATR 2, no. 1559; LW 54:157; Loewenich, 39.

13 WATR 2, no. 2756a; Loewenich, 40.

14 WA 40 I:531; LW 45:369; Loewenich, 44.

15 Oberman, 95.

16 Loewenich, 54-55.

17 WABr 2:238; LW 48:300-301; Loewenich, 56.

18 Loewenich, 56.

19 Diarmaid MacCulloch, *The Reformation* (New York: Penguin Books, 2005), 115.

20 Loewenich, 61-63.

21 Loewenich, 54, 72ff.

22 Oberman, 137.

23 WA 41:690; Loewenich, 72.

24 Oberman, 101.

25 Oberman, 102.

26 Oberman, 136f.

27 WATR 2, no 2255a; Loewenich, 80.

28 Oberman, 58.

29 Roy Hammerling, "Martin Luther: The Reformed Augustinian Beggar" in David C. Mengel and Lisa Wolverton, eds., *Christianity and Culture in the Middle Ages: Essays to Honor John Van Engen* (Notre Dame, IN: University of Notre Dame Press, 2015), 481.

30 Roy Hammerling, "Martin Luther: The Reformed Augustinian Beggar" in David C. Mengel and Lisa Wolverton, eds., *Christianity and Culture in the Middle Ages: Essays to Honor John Van Engen*, (Notre Dame, IN: University of Notre Dame Press, 2015).

31 Oberman, 134.

32 Oberman, 147.

33 Oberman, 147.

34 Augustine, *De Sermone Domini in Monte*, 2.8; Augustine, Sermon 56.

35 Oberman, 147ff.

36 Oberman, 149.

37 Loewenich, 92.

38 Loewenich, 83ff.

39 Loewenich, 84.

40 Oberman, 3

SUSTAINABILITY AND THE TRANSFORMATION OF EDUCATION

DR. KENNETH FOSTER
Associate Professor of Political Science,
Program Director, Global Studies

> Our challenge is to ensure that the ecological systems on which we depend remain healthy even as we seek to thrive economically and in community. This is the vision set out by the concept of sustainability, which recognizes the interdependence of ecological systems, economic systems, and social communities. It is a vision based fundamentally on hope and a sense that we now have the opportunity to rethink current practices and to build a better world for ourselves, other people, and future generations.
>
> —Concordia College's "Vision for Sustainability"[1]

Can we learn to live in ways that promote human thriving while preserving the integrity and beauty of the Earth? Might we discover ways of organizing economic and social life that create and support both thriving human communities and the vibrancy and health of the Earth's biosphere? Is it possible to eliminate the unjust patterns of environmental harm that are in evidence across the globe today? These are some of the questions raised by the concept of sustainability. The sustainability framework calls on individuals, organizations, and societies to re-imagine human interaction with the Earth and to re-create economic and social systems so that they support a shared and just prosperity within healthy natural ecosystems. The sustainability challenge is an ethical, intellectual, and practical challenge *par excellence*. It calls us to marshal all of our resources and creativity to determine how we can develop a notion of *planetary citizenship*, to use the phrase in the title of this book, in a time when some argue we have entered a new and dangerous era called the Anthropocene. The fact that humans are shaping the planet to a degree unfathomable even 50 years ago is a source of great concern, but it can also give us hope: we do have the ability to use our power to create sustainable and resilient ways of living.

Over the past 20 years, the sustainability movement has entered into a wide variety of spheres of life. It is a powerful framework for understanding our current predicament—and for spurring future-oriented action. Sustainability can also provide the basis for a transformation of education. One of the key questions of this book concerns how education should be reformed to prepare students to thrive and to be agents of positive change in a century defined by increasingly damaging human impacts on the Earth and its ecosystems. More specifically, what would Lutheran education for planetary citizenship look like? The sustainability framework and the education for sustainability movement, can help us answer these questions.

This chapter will first sketch out briefly the environmental problems that have spurred the development of the sustainability framework. It will then turn to examine how a variety of scholars and other writers have approached the idea of sustainability, providing a sense of the development of the concept and the hopeful visions that emerge out of it. The third section will explore some of the main components of what practitioners call the education for sustainability movement. The chapter ends with a review of how sustainability has been understood at Concordia College and a call to move further in putting sustainability at the center of the educational enterprise.

I. Our Unsustainable Trajectory

The concept of sustainability emerged out of concerns that the path of economic development that humans have pursued since the beginning of industrialization is damaging the Earth systems on which life depends. That is, people increasingly became concerned that humanity had embarked on an unsustainable trajectory, that the gains in socioeconomic development were being made through the unsustainable use of nature's resources and degradation of ecosystems. The sustainability idea formed around the insight that economic, social, and environmental (ecological) systems must be understood as fundamentally interrelated. Yet the core problem that was identified was that human activities are damaging the Earth, raising the specter that human advances will prove to be short-lived as the Earth is transformed into a less hospitable and less life-giving environment. To put this another way, the Earth provides humans with a variety of "ecosystem services," the healthy functioning of which are essential for human life and prosperity—and as these are impaired, humanity's future becomes less promising.[2]

At the most macro level, the problem of unsustainability is effectively illustrated by a set of empirical observations that capture what is called the Great Acceleration.[3] Around 1950, the rate of growth of global population and GDP (gross domestic product) began to accelerate dramatically. After centuries of minimal population growth and negligible increases of global GDP, from 1950–2000 population increased by over 200 percent while real GDP increased by over 700 percent. Since most of this increase in GDP was driven by putting more and more of Earth's resources through production systems which then generated waste products, the result was a correspondingly rapid acceleration of human impacts on the Earth. Negative human impacts on the planet during this continuing era are unprecedented, severe, and cumulative.

The most ambitious project to measure environmental conditions and the health of global ecosystems, the Global Environmental Outlook project overseen by the United Nations Environment Programme, quantifies the secular degradation of Earth's environmental health.[4] The GEO-5 report, issued in 2012, finds that "the 7 billion humans alive today are collectively exploiting the Earth's resources at accelerating rates and at intensities that surpass the capacity of its systems to absorb wastes and neutralize the adverse effects on the environment."[5] The report further argues that from an earth system perspective, "it is clear that thresholds have been or are being reached, beyond which abrupt and irreversible changes occur . . . These changes will affect the basic life-support functions of the planet."[6] The report's findings include: an alarmingly high deforestation rate, an air pollution crisis in many developing countries, increasing water scarcity and contamination of water sources, a decline in biodiversity coupled with an increase in extinction rates, and a rapid increase in the amount and toxicity of human-generated waste.

Of course, the largest and trickiest problem caused by human activity is global warming, also referred to as the problem of climate change.[7] As the planet warms due to the unprecedented amounts of greenhouse gases being put into the atmosphere by the burning of fossil fuels (and certain other human activities), changes to the climate system are expected to have a variety of impacts on ecosystems and to put severe stress on the systems humans have developed to try to achieve prosperity and a high quality of life for all.[8] Some of the impacts on natural systems include changes in precipitation patterns, more frequent extreme weather events (such as drought and large storms), warming and acidification of the oceans, rising sea levels, increases in variability of river flows, and negative pressures on flora and fauna as their habitat changes.[9] Just as plants and animals will find it difficult to adapt to rapidly changing conditions, so also will human societies struggle to adapt as the natural patterns around which they were built begin to change significantly.

While the precise impacts of a warming climate are difficult to predict, scientific organizations across the globe are in agreement that rising CO_2 levels due to the burning of fossil fuels is driving a rapid increase in global temperatures—an increase of a magnitude that will inevitably have serious impacts. Whereas for at least the past 600,000 years CO_2 levels had fluctuated regularly between 180 and 280 parts per million (ppm), after the beginning of the industrial revolution (circa 1750), the level began to rise beyond 280 ppm. By 2017, the level had exceeded 400 ppm, representing an extraordinarily rapid 40 percent increase in a mere 267 years. Even more striking, the level in 1950 was 311 ppm, meaning that most of the increase has happened only over the past 67 years.[10] As would be expected, global temperatures have risen as a result, increasing by 1.0 to 1.5 degrees Celsius over a pre-industrial baseline level.[11] This is 10 times faster than the most rapid warming seen in past millennia, when it generally took 1,000 years to warm by one degree.[12] Most governments have accepted these findings and are actively working to determine how to reduce carbon emissions so as to slow down and eventually reverse the warming trend. Unfortunately, current policies and trends will not prevent the global temperature from rising by another 2 to 5 degrees Celsius. With each degree increase, the impacts become increasingly severe, and there is broad agreement that even an increase of another 2 degrees will be extremely disruptive and damaging to societies across the globe.[13]

Overall, then, humanity is currently living beyond its means. While the Earth provides bountiful resources and wondrously productive ecosystems that can sustain a rich diversity of life, prevailing ways of living and modes of development are failing to create a synergistic relationship between humans and the Earth. The unsustainable current situation is illustrated plainly by the Global Ecological Footprint metric: today humanity uses the equivalent of 1.6 Earths to provide the resources we use and absorb our waste.[14] And this is the case even though three billion people currently live on less than $2.50 per day. If prosperity for all is to be achieved, significant changes to reduce the per capita ecological footprint must be made. The concept of sustainability organizes efforts to figure out how to do this.

II. Sustainability: Contested Concept and Hopeful Vision

Sustainability is a classic example of what is known as a "contested concept." These are concepts and ideas that are foundational and ubiquitous in debates about contemporary life and about the future. Many of these involve deep ethical questions, multi-faceted diagnoses of complex problems, and controversial methods for achieving a desired outcome—and the outcome often has to do with creating "a good society" or some near-utopian state in which all is well in the world. That is, concepts such as sustainability contain an expansive vision of what is possible with the application of a set of ethical and problem-solving principles. One prime example of a contested concept is "democracy." With both sustainability and democracy, there never will be full agreement on what exactly they are and how to define them. Nevertheless, both concepts have grown to serve as touchstones in vitally important debates about how to organize and govern human activity and in conversations about the kind of society we hope to create.

The concept of sustainability emerged out of a fear that human activities and human progress are *un*sustainable due to the deleterious ecological consequences of prevailing modes of generating economic growth. In 1972, the landmark book *The Limits to Growth* argued that the world was on a path to an ecological collapse that would be catastrophic for humanity.[15] This led to ferocious debate along with efforts to understand how to respond to the growing ecological/environmental crisis, epitomized by Lester Brown's book *Building a Sustainable Society*.[16] While some people followed Brown in arguing that fundamental changes to economic and social systems were needed, others latched onto the idea of *sustainable development*, constructing arguments about how the world can continue to undertake economic development even while safeguarding the health of the Earth on which life depends. Working in this strand of thinking, in 1987 the Brundtland Commission published what became the most widely quoted definition of sustainable development: "Humanity has the ability to make development sustainable—to ensure that it meets the needs of the present without compromising the ability of future generations to meet their own needs."[17]

Since then, however, advocates of sustainability have preferred not to privilege development as a goal. They have also moved beyond the environmental movement's traditional focus on safeguarding the health of the earth's natural systems. Instead, sustainability has come to center on analysis of the interrelationships among what are often called the three pillars, or legs, of sustainability: society, environment, and economy. In this broad framework, we can only thrive as human communities if we simultaneously pursue economic prosperity, ecological health, and social justice/inclusiveness, attaining a dynamic balance among the three areas. Achieving this balance will result in communities in which all people live well as part of healthy natural ecosystems. The "three pillar" formulation of course leaves a lot of room for interpretation. The rest of this section provides a sample of current perspectives on sustainability.

One of the best recent treatments of the subject of sustainability is provided by Leslie Paul Thiele. He suggests that "to practice sustainability is to manage change such that civilization does not undermine the conditions that allow it to flourish within a supportive web of life." He further says that ". . . sustainability is not an ideology . . . It is more of an art that skillfully grounds moral commitments in, and adapts its practices to, the best available science." And he offers this definition:

> Sustainability is an adaptive art wedded to science in service to ethical vision. It entails satisfying current needs without sacrificing future well-being through the balanced pursuit of ecological health, economic welfare, social empowerment, and cultural creativity.[18]

Note that Thiele adds a fourth leg, cultural creativity, on the conviction that this is both essential for addressing the crisis of unsustainability and a core feature of a thriving human society.

One of the most influential figures in global development, Jeffrey Sachs, chooses to maintain the sustainable development frame but tries to bring it closer to broader conceptions of sustainability by introducing the notion of holistic development. He argues that "sustainable development is both a way of understanding the world and a method for solving global problems."[19] Intellectually, it "tries to make sense of the interactions of three complex systems: the world economy, the global society, and the Earth's physical environment."[20] As a normative outlook, "sustainable development envisions four basic objectives of a good society: economic prosperity; social inclusion and cohesion; environmental sustainability; and good governance by major social actors, including governments and business."[21] (Note, again, that a fourth leg is introduced.) For Sachs, as for others in the field of sustainability, embracing complexity and focusing on the interactions of complex systems is critical to the success of the project to carve out a path to a better world.

Robert Engelman, president of the Worldwatch Institute, laments that sustainability is being defined too broadly and argues that in order for humanity to survive, we need to focus in on defining *environmentally sustainable*, developing metrics that we can use to develop practical measures to can move us towards sustainability.[22] Indeed, since the core challenge of sustainability is reversing the accelerating degradation of Earth's natural systems, many in the field view the environmental/ecological part of the framework as foundational rather than as one of three (or four) equal pillars (or legs). This seems in keeping with the original impetus behind the creation of the concept. Without moving quickly to stop environmental degradation and to allow healthy ecosystems to flourish, economic and social goals will be impossible to achieve. After all, even amidst all of our technologies, our lives still depend on well-functioning and dependable Earth systems. Large-scale problems such as climate change call out for changes to our ways of living just to maintain any progress that humanity has achieved to date.

While not disagreeing that stemming ecological decline is important, others have proposed that achieving this requires that we pay more attention to the social or economic systems than to the biological/physical (ecological/environmental) systems. For example, Agyeman, Bullard, and Evans (quoting Haughton) argue that "the social dimension is critical since the unjust society is unlikely to be sustainable in environmental or economic terms in the long run."[23] Their approach flows out of engagement with the environmental justice movement, which is based on the observation that poor and marginalized communities shoulder a disproportionate share of the negative consequences of environmental degradation. In this frame, the root problem is injustice caused by power imbalances—unjust social, economic, and political systems are driving the ecological crisis at the expense of the poor and marginalized. Achieving sustainability, then, requires attacking injustice in human communities, and the emphasis in the vision of sustainability is on creating societies that are deeply just, equitable, and inclusive.

Others working on sustainability issues elevate economics to the prime position. For these scholars and observers, the core problem is that modern economies are based on the continuous promotion of growth, with growth is defined as increasing the flow of material through the economic system. Since modern economic growth is precisely what is causing ecological degradation (rich people cause far more ecological harm than poor people), changing our economic systems is of paramount importance. As Tim Jackson argues, "there is an urgent need to develop a resilient and sustainable macro-economy that is no longer predicated on relentless consumption growth."[24] For Jackson, enabling humanity to flourish in the context of ecological limits requires a reshaping of our economic assumptions and models. The field of ecological economics has already produced considerable research on understanding how an alternative economic system might work and be organized.

The endeavor to change economic systems—and indeed the entire project to create a more sustainable world—raises important questions about changing human consciousness and behavior. Discussions of sustainability inevitably lead to debates about how to encourage people to live differently and to adopt new assumptions about nature, prosperity, and justice. In a nutshell, three basic methods of doing this tend to surface: 1. change people's consciousness and values, which leads to behavioral change; 2. introduce incentives to encourage people to behave differently; 3. enforce social and governmental policies that cause people or groups to behave differently. In her recent book, Francis Moore Lappe sets out a manifesto of how we need to change our thought patterns and consciousness. She argues that we need to create an "eco-mind," that (as the book's subtitle puts it) by changing the way we think, we can create the world we want.[25] By contrast, other roadmaps to achieving sustainability ignore values and consciousness completely, focusing instead on techniques and policies that can change behavior and turn a society in a different direction.[26] The interplay of ideas centered on ethics, values, and consciousness with those centered on policy instruments, technologies, incentives, and large-scale policy interventions is a dynamic and fascinating aspect of sustainability research.

And so, speaking of policies—what about politics? One of the curious features of the wide-ranging literature on sustainability is that politics—as in the struggle over resources and power that takes place everywhere—is often given scant attention. Instead, much of the analysis is about the technologies or policies that are needed to address a problem, or about the ethical stances or economic principles that should be adopted, without due consideration of how, politically, to make things happen. Moreover, in the world in general people have a troubling tendency to focus on individual actions that can support sustainability—recycle, use less water, turn off the lights, and so on—even though a few behavioral changes by some enlightened individuals has a negligible impact on the overall situation. To be sure, those within the field of environmental justice often put politics and collective action front and center. Yet this is still (unfortunately) a relatively minor part of the sustainability conversation. As mentioned earlier, Sachs does include governance as a fourth pillar, but offers little discussion of the political challenges and contradictions that make good governance difficult.[27] On the other hand, Thiele takes up the issue forcefully, arguing that "sustainability demands political activity and legislation because politics and law are often the cause, or at least the all-too-willing accomplices, of unsustainable economies and lifestyles."[28] Moreover, sustainability is challenging because "there is no shortage of people who actively oppose the social, economic, cultural, political, and legal changes that the practice of sustainability demands."[29] To achieve sustainability, collective action is needed, which necessitates engaging in the tumultuous world of politics, whether at local, regional, national, or global levels. How to achieve political success remains a pressing and daunting issue among those seeking to promote sustainability.

One of the most serious obstacles to achieving movement towards sustainability appears to be, somewhat ironically, that discussions of sustainability are often dominated by a negative message: if we do not take significant action to stop ecological decline soon, there will be catastrophic consequences. Information about the seriousness of ecological degradation and climate change initially motivated action and of course started the whole sustainability movement, but in fact negative messages often turn people away from the message and reduce motivation to take action.

As a result, there is now a strong emphasis on fully developing and articulating hopeful visions of what our world could be like if we were to embrace sustainability principles and practices. As Robert Costanza and Isa Kubiszewski put it in their book *Creating a Sustainable and Desirable Future: Insights from 45 Global Thought Leaders*,

> Creating a shared vision of a sustainable and desirable future is the most critical task facing humanity today. This vision must be of ... a world that provides permanent prosperity within the Earth's biophysical constraints in a fair and equitable way to all of humanity, to other species, and to future generations.... In this future, living in harmony with nature is recognized as enhancing everyone's quality of life....[30]

The 46 chapters in *Creating a Sustainable and Desirable Future* provide a rich exploration into what the future could look like, specific elements of a desirable future, and strategies to create the world that we envision. Somewhat utopian, yes; but not unreachable. Yet perhaps sustainability is best thought of not as a destination, but rather as a process—a process of continually renewing our ways of living so as to maintain a dynamic balance of healthy Earth systems, economic systems that create shared prosperity, and inclusive and just social systems. The sustainability conversation calls us to envision how we can live in harmony with each other and in deep symbiosis with the Earth systems and nonhuman species that give us life. And it calls us to work hard on learning how to enter, with all kinds of people, into respectful dialogue about the future and about what we need to do. At the same time, advocates also need to engage in political and social struggles to ensure that life-giving sustainability prevails over destructive unsustainability. In these conversations and struggles, positive visions of the future coupled with practical steps that can be taken now will likely prove more effective than doom-and-gloom scenarios of impending catastrophe.

III. Sustainability in Higher Education

While the environmental movement has influenced higher education for many decades, primarily through the creation of environmental studies majors and programs, the sustainability movement's influence is more recent. As sustainability has spread across the broader landscape of organizations and groups, the importance of education in the project to promote sustainability has led to a great deal of activity at colleges and universities. In the 2000s a new push for institution-wide sustainability efforts began, aimed both at reducing the environmental impact of university operations and at education for sustainability. Since then, over a thousand universities and colleges have conducted campus-wide sustainability assessments, issued sustainability plans, and created a full-time sustainability coordinator or director position. Created in 2006, the Association for the Advancement of Sustainability in Higher Education now has nearly 1,000 member institutions, and its annual conference attracts over 2,000 attendees.[31] Sustainability is now firmly ensconced in the higher education ecosystem.

As noted above, sustainability in higher education has two main goals: 1. making campus operations more sustainable (primarily through reducing environmental impacts); 2. educating all students about sustainability and for sustainability leadership. The first goal has proven easier to pursue, as resource-saving changes to campus operations are not difficult to do in a piece-meal fashion and usually generate financial savings for the institution. Of course, most institutions still have much work to do in this area, and progress is hampered by the fact that they operate within an overall system and culture guided by assumptions, principles, and practices that continue to carry us down an unsustainable path.

Progress on the second goal, educating all students about sustainability and for sustainability leadership, has lagged operational improvements. In 2011, the authors of *The Education for Sustainability Blueprint* concluded that "progress is greater in 'greening' campus buildings, grounds and operations than in actual teaching and learning, resulting in few if any indicators that this generation of college graduates on average is any more literate about sustainability than its predecessors."[32] Implementing education for sustainability reforms entails confronting established curricular structures, entrenched ways of organizing knowledge in the disciplines, and conventional pedagogical approaches. These make the goal of ensuring that *all* students graduate equipped with the knowledge, understandings, consciousness, and skills needed to work for sustainability in the wider world especially difficult to achieve. Our collective understandings of how and why contemporary economic and social systems—and our ways of living—are damaging the Earth's natural systems and undermining the chances of enabling all humans to thrive in the future has developed relatively recently. Most academic disciplines, and the curriculums found at most institutions, have not adapted to incorporate these new understandings. Instead, theories and frameworks in most disciplines either obviously or subtly continue to teach *unsustainability*, by reinforcing the very ideas that have led us to the current predicament. At the most basic level, when the relationship between human activity and the Earth's natural systems and nonhuman life is ignored, students learn that this relationship is simply not very important. As a result, their analysis of issues leaves out a critical consideration, and their consciousness remains firmly within the dominant unsustainable paradigm. At the same time, if a key challenge of our day is to work actively to create a truly sustainable world (whether in one's own life or in the broader community), and if this is a challenge that everyone must take up, students need to acquire the skills required to take on this challenge effectively and with an attitude of active hope.[33] The sustainability movement argues that how and what we teach and learn must change in fundamental ways. Given the natural conservatism (as in reluctance to change) built into the disciplines and most institutions of higher education, this is a tall order.

Those promoting education for sustainability have focused on endeavoring to integrate sustainability into all parts of the curriculum rather than simply trying to get new sustainability-focused programs created. Sustainability is expansive enough, and has enough discreet themes and areas, so that nearly anyone in any discipline can authentically infuse sustainability-related content, perspectives, issues, activities, or skills into a course—and do this in a way that dovetails with existing student learning outcomes. With this in mind, considerable work has been done to identify the key themes, concepts, competencies, and pedagogical approaches that seem to be at the core of education for sustainability.

Sustainability calls for the adoption of new ways of thinking. In particular, the education for sustainability community agrees on the need for students to become skilled in taking an integrated systems approach to issues. This approach is grounded in systems thinking,[34] which calls for a focus on interconnections and the ability to view phenomena and issues from multiple perspectives.[35] This approach contrasts with the dominant approach in the academy, which generally divides knowledge into narrow, discrete categories (disciplines and sub-disciplines), and privileges specialization over the ability to cross boundaries. In a brief but powerful essay, Stephen Sterling reviews the problems with currently dominant ways of thinking and makes the case for moving towards an "ecological sensibility—supporting a culturally shared ecological intelligence" based on the lessons taught to us by the Earth's systems.[36]

While disciplinary knowledge remains important, sustainability education generally pushes in the direction of multi-, inter-, and trans-disciplinarity. It has become somewhat of a truism that the complexity of the various issues wrapped up in the sustainability challenge requires the breaking down of traditional disciplinary boundaries. Environmental studies has remained a fully interdisciplinary field from its inception, and practitioners in the field of education for sustainability endeavor to push this even further, arguing that the academy must embrace inter- and trans-disciplinarity in much more transformative ways that it has to date.[37]

Also at the core of sustainability education is, not surprisingly, environmental and ecological understanding. In a modern world that enables us, through technology, to live as if we do not rely upon the Earth for life, education about the biosphere and how natural systems support life is more important than ever. Back in 1992, David Orr argued forcefully that "the failure to develop ecological literacy is a sin of omission and of commission . . . Not only are we failing to teach the basics about the Earth, and how it works, but we are in fact teaching a large amount of stuff that is simply wrong . . . By failing to include ecological perspectives in any number of subjects, we are teaching students that ecology is unimportant to history, politics, economics, society, and so forth."[38] Even beyond this, the Earth (and what is often called *nature*) is a fascinating, beautiful, and infinitely complex place. The more students engage with it, the more they tend to appreciate and even love it, and so want to take care of it.

The focus on complexity and relationships that is found in education for sustainability calls also for the constant juxtaposition of the global with the local. The systems approach shows us how chains of causation stretch from small local actions to vast global systems, and vice versa. To comprehend and learn how to address sustainability issues, students need to understand and perceive global systems and changes.[39] At the same time, engagement with one's local place seems to be a critically important part of education for sustainability.[40] Place-based education enables students to develop a connection with the ecosystems in which they live while engaging with the local community on real-world issues.

As for the kinds of pedagogies that seem most effective in sustainability education, there is broad agreement that experiential, inquiry-based, and problem-solving approaches need to be utilized much more than is currently the case. Since sustainability as a concept centers on the need to experiment, to be creative, and to re-imagine how we do things, this is not surprising. The vast constellation of real-world issues and challenges that are part of the sustainability challenge offers endless opportunities for faculty and students alike to "get their hands dirty," so to speak, jumping into the fray to tackle problems and learn through trial and error. Moreover, collaborations and partnerships with community organizations commonly occupy a foundational place in programs and curricula focused on sustainability education.

The large and diverse set of substantive issues that need addressing makes teaching and learning about sustainability endlessly interesting and exciting. Engaging in education for sustainability most often means taking one's areas of expertise and infusing it with new relevance and energy by linking it to our collective need to build more sustainable systems and ways of living. Whether this linkage runs through the investigation of food justice, renewable energy, the psychology of climate change, or one of hundreds of other issue areas, students and faculty alike find that the rewards far outweigh the challenging work needed to step beyond disciplinary boundaries, venture out of comfortable intellectual frameworks, and experiment with new pedagogies that call for deep engagement in the community beyond the classroom. This has certainly proven to be true at Concordia, and the next section reviews the college's experience in embracing sustainability as a key framework for college operations and education.

IV. Education for Sustainability Leadership and Planetary Citizenship at Concordia

Over the past 10 years, Concordia has made remarkable progress in conceiving and implementing sustainability initiatives. In 2006, a group of faculty and students succeeded in convincing President Pam Jolicoeur to establish, for the first time, a group charged with promoting sustainability across the campus. Following President Jolicoeur's untimely death in 2010, the task force lobbied Interim President Paul Dovre to create a full-time sustainability coordinator staff position at the college. Essential for any college desiring to make real progress in sustainability, this position was created in 2011 and filled in January 2012.

President William Craft arrived in 2011 with a deep interest in seeing the college embrace sustainability to an even greater degree. Following consultation with task force members and his cabinet, in October 2011 he created the President's Sustainability Council to replace the task force as a long-term consultative body, consisting of the sustainability coordinator, three faculty members, four staff members, and two students. President Craft then signaled the seriousness of his intentions by immediately engaging with the long-standing dream of students to establish a residential house devoted to ecologically-friendly living. In November 2011 the president's cabinet approved the renovation of a college rental property into the Concordia EcoHouse.

Part of the council's initial work was to develop, in broad consultation with various campus constituencies, a statement expressing the college's distinctive understanding of and approach to sustainability. On December 6, 2012, Concordia College's "Vision for Sustainability" was issued by the president.[41] The vision, in part:

> Concordia College will embrace a concern for sustainability that is rooted in the responsibility to ensure the environmental, economic, and social health of the college and of our global community. Concordia College's sustainability vision is interwoven with our commitment to global learning, with our faith tradition and abiding commitment to ethical deliberation, and with the values and practices of the liberal arts.
>
> More specifically, we envision Concordia as a place where:
>
> - The principles of sustainability—environmental, economic, and social—are fundamental in all decision-making processes.
> - Conversations about sustainability are a regular part of community life.
> - Insights into the sustainability challenge and ideas about creating sustainable ways of living are constantly generated and explored.
> - Students, faculty, and staff develop the perspectives and skills needed to work for sustainability in the wider world.
> - College operations have as little negative ecological impact as possible.
>
> As a global liberal arts college of the church, Concordia can have a distinctive approach to fulfilling its commitment to sustainability. Most fundamentally, since we are an institution of higher education, everything that we do to advance sustainability should involve the promotion of learning and student success. . . . This vision of a sustainable Concordia is profoundly consistent with our established identity and will allow us to achieve a new level of scholarly excellence, global engagement, moral

deliberation, and ongoing relevance.

This vision is expansive and ambitious. Moreover, it is distinctive in how it asserts strongly that the pursuit of sustainability at Concordia is fundamentally about enhancing our ability to carry out our educational mission. This is different than the approach taken at many other institutions, where the "greening of operations" is emphasized. While work has begun on making this vision a reality, much more work is needed, and this work requires imagination, flexibility, innovation, and a willingness to take risks.

The opportunity, in 2013, to apply for a large grant from the Margaret A. Cargill Foundation enabled us to elaborate further on Concordia's approach to sustainability. The title of the proposed grant program elucidated what we are aiming to do: *Preparing Students for Globally-engaged, Justice-driven, and Ecologically-minded Citizenship and Leadership*. The grant provided $550,000 to use from 2014 to 2017. Initiatives supported by the grant included a multi-pronged faculty development program, the creation of a new sustainability science faculty position, the addition of an innovative high tunnel facility at the campus garden, the development of student internships at local organizations, an effort to include sustainability considerations in study abroad programming, the creation of a Fargo-Moorhead Sustainability Network, and the installation of a solar array on the new science facility. The grant program centered on education and engagement in the community, enabling the pursuit of sustainability to serve as a catalyst for other key strategic initiatives at the college. In particular, sustainability work has run ahead of the integrative learning initiative, demonstrating the power of this approach to education while providing examples for others to examine and ready-made opportunities to engage students in integrative learning. The imagination shown by faculty members, staff members, and students as they have engaged in sustainability work testifies to the capability we have as a community to pursue a robust vision of integrative learning.

On April 11, 2017, Concordia entered a new phase of its sustainability work when President Craft signed the Integrated Climate Commitment (ICC), enabling the college to join the Climate Leadership Network run by the organization Second Nature.[42] As President Craft wrote in an email to the campus, the commitment calls on Concordia "to respond to climate change by working to reduce carbon emissions and by integrating consideration of the impacts of climate change into our curriculum and decision-making processes." It also directs us "to work with community partners to increase our ability to manage changes generated by climate change, to become a more resilient college in a more resilient community." In becoming a signatory to the ICC, Concordia commits to developing a Climate Action Plan that sets out measurable goals and practical strategies for reducing carbon emissions, enhancing climate change education, and improving community resilience. This work, while challenging, will open up further opportunities to enhance student learning and to fulfill the college's mission as a global liberal arts college of the church.

V. Towards a Future of Human Thriving on a Vibrant Earth: Putting Sustainability at the Center of the Educational Enterprise

> We stand at a critical moment in Earth's history, a time when humanity must choose its future. As the world becomes increasingly interdependent and fragile, the future at once holds great peril and great promise. To move forward, we must recognize that in the midst of a magnificent diversity of cultures and life forms, we are one human family and one Earth community with a common destiny. We must join together to bring forth a sustainable global society founded on respect for nature, universal human rights, economic justice, and a culture of peace. Towards this end, it is imperative that we, the peoples of Earth, declare our responsibility to one another, to the greater community of life, and to future generations.
>
> —From the preamble of The Earth Charter[43]

How many of us would sign on to this statement from The Earth Charter? How many of our students would give their signature to signal their agreement with it? To what extent do we and our students comprehend the implications of the statement? (It sounds nice, but the implications are tough and vast.) If we agree with most, if not all of this statement, what then is to be done "to bring forth a sustainable global society?" How could education change to facilitate achievement of this goal? How might Concordia College adapt to put itself at the forefront of a global movement to educate for sustainability and for planetary citizenship?

Concordia has made tremendous progress in adopting sustainability as a core part of its ethos and in infusing sustainability concerns into campus operations and the curriculum. Yet if Concordia College is to be a responsible social institution and serve its students well, it needs to do more to put sustainability themes and practices into the very center of the educational enterprise. Those who are ignorant of the crises of ecological decline and climate change, and who lack the analytical perspectives and personal skills necessary to respond to these crises, are not truly thoughtful and informed. Today, becoming responsibly engaged with the world must involve engagement with the whole world—the nonhuman world, the Earth's natural systems, the interrelationships that cause ecological harm to ricochet across the globe, the unjust distribution of environmental harm that disproportionately affects the poor and marginalized members of society.

Over 25 years ago, David Orr gave an address entitled "What is Education For?" In this classic text, he argued that "all education is environmental education" and that education has to focus on enabling people to live within and work with the ecological mechanisms that bind us to the Earth.[44] Similarly, Frank H. T. Rhodes, former president of Cornell University, has proposed that "the concept of sustainability could provide a new foundation for the liberal arts and sciences."[45] As most fundamentally an exercise in exploration and discovery (as good liberal arts has always been), curricula grounded in sustainability may, in Rhodes' view, "form the basis for a new kind of global map—a policy blueprint—that would allow us to set a common course for all the people of our rare, beautiful, and benevolent planet." Mitchell Thomashow, in his provocative and far-reaching book, *The Nine Elements of a Sustainable Campus*, suggests that the sustainability movement has "the potential to transform higher education, but only if it [can] reach into every corner of the campus community."[46] Indeed, such a move seems imperative if society is to successfully address the crisis of unsustainability. For this task requires a paradigm shift and the adoption of new priorities and frameworks that can prepare students to live in harmony with the Earth's systems and survive on a changing planet.[47] Closer to home, we need to make sustainability part of the DNA of Concordia College and an anchor of the curriculum— not as an add-on, but as a frame that helps animate the curriculum and makes the college an engine of exploration into complex issues, for the good of students and the world.

It seems appropriate to end with the final paragraph of Concordia College's "Vision for Sustainability," which elegantly sets out why the embrace of sustainability is so important:

Given who we are as an institution and a community, recent global trends compel us to articulate a vision for the future that embraces sustainability as a core principle and value. Most fundamentally, our concern for sustainability stems from the simple yet profound observation that the earth is our home. It arises from the conviction that we have a sacred duty to protect the earth's vitality, diversity, and beauty. In so doing, we work for the well-being of all of humanity, for the good of people living now as well as future generations.[48]

ENDNOTES

1 "Vision for Sustainability," for Concordia College, Moorhead, MN, accessed at https://concordiacollege.edu/files/resources/sustainvisiondec12.pdf on April 21, 2017.

2 Millennium Ecosystem Assessment, *Ecosystems and Human Well-Being: Synthesis* (Washington, DC, 2005) and http://www.wri.org/publication/ecosystem-services (accessed on April 21, 2017)

3 Developed by the International Geosphere-Biosphere Programme, http://www.igbp.net/globalchange/greatacceleration.4.1b8ae20512db692f2a680001630.html (accessed April 21, 2017). The empirical tables are reproduced in Larry L. Rasmussen, *Earth-honoring Faith: Religious Ethics in a New Key* (Oxford: Oxford University Press, 2013), 56-57.

4 http://web.unep.org/geo/.

5 United Nations Environment Programme, *Global Environment Outlook 5: Environment for the Future We Want* (NY: United Nations, 2012), xviii, available at http://web.unep.org/geo/assessments/global-assessments/global-environment-outlook-5. Production of a GEO-6 report is currently underway.

6 Ibid., 210.

7 See resources provided by the Intergovernmental Panel on Climate Change for the most comprehensive and widely accepted information on climate change: http://www.ipcc.ch/.

8 Comprehensive data is found in reports of the Intergovernmental Panel on Climate Change, http://www.ipcc.ch/report/ar5/wg2/.

9 In addition, reports on the impacts of climate change note that there are further risks associated with climate change that are not well understood but that fit with existing models. For example, melting of the arctic permafrost and ice cover could lead to accelerated warming, while specific ecosystems could rapidly collapse (as appears to be happening with coral reefs).

10 Scott Waldman, "Atmospheric Carbon Dioxide Hits Record Levels," in *Scientific American*, reprinted from *Climatewire* (March 14, 2017) with permission from E&E News, accessed at https://www.scientificamerican.com/article/atmospheric-carbon-dioxide-hits-record-levels/; National Oceanic and Atmospheric Administration data accessed at https://climate.nasa.gov/climate_resources/24/ on April 22, 2017.

11 Climate Central, "Earth Flirts with a 1.5 Degree Celsius Global Warming Threshold," April 20, 2016, in *Scientific American*, accessed at https://www.scientificamerican.com/article/earth-flirts-with-a-1-5-degree-celsius-global-warming-threshold1/.

12 The Earth Observatory, "https://earthobservatory.nasa.gov/Features/GlobalWarming/page3.php accessed on April 22, 2017.

13 William Brangham, "Why 2 Degees Celsius Is Climate Change's Magic Number, on *PBS Newshour*, (December 2, 2015) accessed at http://www.pbs.org/newshour/bb/why-2-degrees-celsius-is-climate-changes-magic-number/. Temperature increases beyond 2 degrees will have devastating impacts and eventually the world would be completely transformed.

14 Global Footprint Network, *Ecological Footprint*, accessed at http://www.footprintnetwork.org/our-work/ecological-footprint/ on April 22, 2017.

15 Donella Meadows, Jorgen Randers, and Dennis Meadows, *The Limits to Growth* (New York: Universe Books, 1972).

16 Lester R. Brown, *Building a Sustainable Society* (NY: W.W. Norton, 1981).

17 World Commission on Environment and Development, *Our Common Future* (Oxford: Oxford University Press, 1987), 8.

18 Leslie Paul Thiele, *Sustainability* (Cambridge: Polity Press, 2013), 4-5.

19 Jeffrey Sachs, *The Age of Sustainable Development* (New York: Columbia University Press, 2015), 1.

20 Ibid., 3.

21 Ibid., 4.

22 Robert Engelman, "Beyond Sustainabable," in *State of the World 2013: Is Sustainability Still Possible*, ed. The Worldwatch Institute (Washington: Island Press, 2013), 13.

23 Julian Agyeman, Robert D. Bullard, and Bob Evans, "Joined-Up Thinking: Bringing Together Sustainability, Environmental Justice, and Equity," in *Just Sustainabilities: Development in an Unequal World*, eds. Agyeman, Bullard, and Evans

(Cambridge, MA: MIT Press, 2003), 9. Quoting George Haughton, "Environmental Justice and the Sustainable City," *Journal of Planning Education and Research* 18, no. 3 (1999): 64.

24 Tim Jackson, *Prosperity Without Growth: Economics for a Finite Planet* (London: Earthscan, 2009), 185.

25 Francis Moore Lappe, *EcoMind: Changing the Way We Think, to Create the World We Want* (New York: Nation Books, 2011).

26 For example, Peter P. Rogers, Kazi F. Jalal, and John A. Boyd, *An Introduction to Sustainable Development* (London: Earthscan, 2008).

27 Sachs.

28 Thiele, 140.

29 Ibid., 116.

30 Robert Costanza, and Ida Kubiszewski, "Why We Need Visions of a Sustainable and Desirable World," in Robert Costanza and Ida Kubiszewski, eds., *Creating a Sustainable and Desirable Future: Insights from 45 Global Thought Leaders* (New Jersey: World Scientific, 2014), 1.

31 The Association for the Advancement of Sustainability in Higher Education, found at www.aashe.org.

32 EfS Blueprint Network, *Education for Sustainability Blueprint* (Boston, Second Nature, 2011), 4.

33 Joanna Macy and Chris Johnstone, *Active Hope: How to Face the Mess We're in Without Going Crazy* (Novato, CA: New World Library, 2012).

34 An introduction to this by one of its most ardent proponents is found in Diana Wright, ed., *Thinking in Systems –A Primer* / Donella H. Meadows (White River Junction: Chelsea Green Publishing, 2008).

35 Wheeler, Keith, "Introduction," in *Education for a Sustainable Future*, edited by Keith A. Wheeler and Anne P. Bijur (New York: Springer, 2013), 1.

36 Stephen Sterling, "Ecological Intelligence: Viewing the World Relationally," in Arran Stibbe, ed., *The Handbook of Sustainability Literacy* (Devon: Green Books, 2009), 77-83.

37 The path-breaking School of Sustainability at Arizona State University, created 11 years ago, placed trans-disciplinarity at the core of its approach. See www.schoolofsustainability.asu.edu.

38 David Orr, "Ecological Literacy," reprinted in David W. Orr, *Hope Is an Imperative* (Island Press, 2011), 251.

39 A fascinating book that discusses this is Mitchell Thomashow, *Bringing the Biosphere Home: Learning to Perceive Global Environmental Change*, (Cambridge, MA: MIT Press, 2002).

40 For example, in Wendy Peterson Boring and William Forbes, eds., *Teaching Sustainability: Perspectives from the Humanities and Social Sciences* (Nacogdoches, TX: Stephen F. Austin State University Press, 2013).

41 "Vision for Sustainability," Concordia College.

42 Second Nature found at www.secondnature.org.

43 www.earthcharter.org/discover/the-earth-charter.org (accessed July 9, 2016).

44 David W. Orr, "What is Education For," reprinted in David. W. Orr, ed., *Hope Is*

an *Imperative* (Washington, DC: Island Press, 2011).

45 Frank H.T. Rhodes, "Sustainability: The Ultimate Liberal Art," *The Chronicle of Higher Education* 53, no. 9 (2006): B24.

46 Mitchell Thomashow, *The Nine Elements of a Sustainable Campus* (Cambridge, MA: MIT Press, 2015), 13. Tom Kelly likewise argues for "Sustainability as an Organizing Principle in Higher Education," in John Aber, Tom Kelly, and Bruce Malloy, eds., *The Sustainable Learning Community: One University's Journey to the Future* (Durham, NH: University of New Hampshire Press, 2009). Also see Neil B. Weissman, "Sustainability and Liberal Education: Partners by Nature," *Liberal Education* 98, no. 4, (2012).

47 Worldwatch Institute, *EarthEd (State of the World): Rethinking Education on a Changing Planet* (Washington, DC: Island Press, 2017).

48 "Vision for Sustainability," Concordia College.

ASSUMING RESPONSIBILITY FOR THE COMMONS

Lutheran Higher Education in a World of Unscripted Problems

DR. PER ANDERSON

Associate Dean for Global Learning and Professor of Religion

No previous ethics had to consider the global condition of human life and the far-off future, even existence, of the race.

—Hans Jonas, *The Imperative of Responsibility: In Search of an Ethics for the Technological Age*[1]

The purpose of a twenty-first-century education is to produce graduates who recognize themselves to be of the world and who also assume responsibility for the world. Such graduates respect the specificities of particular cultures as well as the need for a global commons. As stewards of such cultures and commons, they draw upon multiple disciplines and viewpoints to address the world's problems, and they work collaboratively with others to solve them.

—Douglas C. Bennett, Grant H. Cornwell, Haifa Jamal Al-Lail, and Celeste Schenck, "An Education for the Twenty-First Century: Stewardship of the Global Commons"[2]

I. Introduction

The reforming movement of Martin Luther and his colleagues disrupted dominant powers through retrieval of ancient truth and public debate about its meaning and authority. It produced remarkable change in the convictions and practices of Christians. The most radical and consequential concerns the social location of discipleship, what the philosopher Charles Taylor terms the "affirmation of ordinary life."[3] For Luther and his colleagues, all Christians—clergy and laity—are equal before God and serve vital needs of this world in joyful response to God's unmerited grace. Disciples of Christ participate in the loving agency of God through their places of responsibility in society. These callings are fully of the world and for the world. They include the work of civil righteousness which fosters the constitutive goods of life—the commons. The dignity of worldly agency was profound for Luther and his colleagues.

This essay explores the civic purpose of Lutheran higher education in conversation with contemporary convictions about responsibility for new planetary times, what the theologian Dietrich Bonhoeffer termed a "world come of age."[4] A "world come of age" denotes the advent of collective and novel human powers that Luther could not have imagined and that call for adaptation—reformation—of received beliefs and values about human being and doing for an agency of resilience and responsibility.

Our current institutions of understanding and practice originate from life worlds where "the human" exercised far less autonomous and effective power to control (know, invent, reproduce, consume, extend, resist) and where the forces and communities of nature largely resisted control. Today, the capacity of humans to exercise phenomenal control and even to influence planetary systems common to all life are beyond question and have triggered debate among scientists as to whether the scale, scope, and permanency of "anthropogenic" cause and effect merit recognition as the dawning of a new epoch in planetary history, the "Anthropocene."[5]

Since Bonhoeffer and other late twentieth century observers of modern human power, an adaptive discourse of resilience and responsibility has emerged across various and many societies. Still, adequate changes in patterns of thinking and practice continue to lag across all sectors of human being and doing—including higher education. The causes are many. Manifold adaptations are needed. Among these responses, we need what the ethicist Larry Rasmussen terms "anticipatory communities" dedicated to examining received traditions and seeking creative revisions for a new and consequential historical moment.[6] A Lutheran liberal arts college can be an anticipatory community (among others, religious and secular) that examines rigorously what planetary conditions and needs require from higher education.

As a response to the quincentenary of the Lutheran Christian movement, Lutheran higher education should embrace the teaching of the Evangelical Lutheran Church in America and engage the best human thought about responsible education. In particular, Lutheran educators should claim the ELCA pledge "to sustain, renew, and where need be, reform our calling in education for this time and place so that we will be a stronger, livelier, and more faithful teaching and learning church."[7] What, then, do our time and place call us to do as educators, particularly as collegiate educators?

To answer the question of integrity and responsibility, we must inquire about context and need. What is going on today? What is new about our world? Do changes in human understanding and planetary conditions warrant major revision of current norms, practices, and contents of higher education? What does human responsibility require of education to be adequate to what we know and can expect about twenty-first century life?

This essay addresses questions of purpose and aim in Lutheran higher education and argues for a shared quest to see institutions of higher education as anticipatory communities and to formulate educational norms that enable humans to assume new responsibility for the world commensurate with new human powers. After addressing the question of new human powers, this essay examines the "new academy" proposal of the American Association of Colleges and Universities (AAC&U), which seeks to revise the goals and pedagogy of higher education in the United States across the spectrum of institutional types. This essay offers an affirmative appraisal of the new academy and calls for its adoption and development, because the hour is late for responsible higher education.

This proposal grounds its claims for responsibility in Lutheran convictions about the moral life. Consistent with Lutheran understandings of moral realism and reciprocity, it seeks to be an exercise in public discourse that engages all people of good will.[8] Humans across time and culture discern that teaching and learning are constitutive of human existence and flourishing and enact normative commitments. All humans must grapple with normative questions of formation and development. How serious should we be about learning? What should we seek to learn, and why? We live in a moment when people across cultures sense that new societal and planetary times require new learning and that responsible humans are called to construct new conceptions of the educated person and new structures for learning.

II. Lutheran Christian Morality in Outline

Confessing the Apostle's Creed, saying the Lord's Prayer, and observing the Ten Commandments are core Christian commitments across the ages. Assuming responsibility for the commons is not. Until only recently, such a claim would have been unthinkable for reasons to be discussed below. Before considering what responsibility for the commons might mean and how this norm should guide higher education, we need a basic framework of the Christian life for Lutherans, the what and why of living faithfully.

The Christian life seeks to imitate and cooperate with the benevolent and gracious agency of God in the world. Life is god-centered—as God relates to the world, so humans relate to the world. Christians bear witness to the unconditional love of God and participate in God's providential care for the world through faithful service to the "neighbor" (increasingly understood to be the community of life, human and other kind). God calls and empowers people to serve the neighbor in the affairs of ordinary life. To serve the neighbor, Christians must be in conversation with others about the needs of God's world. Today, many Christians believe they are called to membership in a public church that works corporately and with all people of good will in various ways to respect and enhance a global commons.

Christians bear witness to God by loving the neighbor in response to grace. Trusting God's promises of unmerited giving and forgiveness, people of faith are freed in Christ from the sinful condition of securing and justifying themselves. Through the work of the Holy Spirit in Word and Sacrament, God empowers believers to reject sin, death, and evil and to embrace and depend upon God's love alone. In joyful response to God's creation and redemption of the world, people of faith glorify and please God by following the double commands to love God with heart, soul, and mind and to love the neighbor as equal to themselves. Liberated from devotion to self, Christians live beyond themselves—in Christ through faith and in the neighbor through love. These neighbors share in the steadfast generosity and mercy of God as beloved creatures worthy of respect and care.[9]

When Christians live in loving mutuality with others, they anticipate the fulfillment of God's promises. They live today as if sin, death, and evil do not exist and God's will reigns. As witnesses to grace and promise, Christians communicate in word and deed a love that proclaims the coming rule of God. Confident in God's future, Christians bear witness to love in a world of brokenness, injustice, and violence—even as they remain sinners who must practice continual repentance, forgiveness, and amendment of life. Considered righteous by God, faithful people see a world that need not and should not be broken, unjust, and violent. They live in holy restlessness and discontent with the way things are. Through awareness of God's commands, Christians see how God restrains a broken world from collapse and preserves the commons despite the harms of sin. They are called to cooperate with God in the promotion of the many goods that constitute life.

As recipients of abundant grace, Christians seek to glorify and please God by imitating the love of God in Christ. God came into the world in Christ and dwells continually as the Holy Spirit. God affirms the world and invites people of faith to participate in its affairs as a gift and task to be embraced with gratitude, confidence, and courage. God calls humans into existence to live out various social roles and places of responsibility that participate in divine providence. These callings offer different ways to serve the community of life and to practice civic righteousness with other people of good will. God works through all humans to create, redeem, and sustain the world. Through the callings, Christians do holy work by participating in God's love and care for the world. They understand their lives and actions to be accountable to God according to the double-love command and the work of Jesus Christ.

For Martin Luther in *The Freedom of a Christian*, doing the work of Christ means Christians should undertake radical love of neighbor ("serve and help the neighbor in every possible way") in reciprocity for the radical love of Christ ("the very manner in which God in Christ acted and continues to act toward us"). In Christ, God values and dignifies selfless service to the needs of the neighbor. As Luther says for himself, "I will therefore give myself as a Christ to my neighbor, just as Christ offered himself to me."[10] Christians, then, love the neighbor in imitation and gratitude to God in Christ by attending to the neighbor's every need. This summary of the moral life prompts key questions for these reflections. Should Lutheran higher education embody the love of Christ? If so, what does such radical service and help mean for twenty-first century education?

III. New World of Technology

Ethical reflection in the Lutheran tradition begins by asking about the needs of the neighbor and the community of life. What is going on? Lutherans ask this question because ethical action takes the form of response to God and response to the needs of the neighbor and the community of life. Christian action seeks to undertake a fitting response to particularity. Accordingly, we turn now to the cultural and moral analysis of Hans Jonas, a twentieth century philosopher whose insight into modernity provides durable guidance for the turn to social responsibility in contemporary American higher education. Writing in the late 1970s, Jonas begins his groundbreaking study in the ethics of responsibility with prescient observations about the novel dimensions of modern human power:

> Modern technology, informed by an ever-deeper penetration of nature and propelled by the forces of market and politics, has enhanced human power beyond anything

> known or even dreamed of before. It has a power over matter, over life on earth, and over [humanity]; and it keeps growing at an accelerating pace. Its unfettered exercise for about two centuries now has raised the material estate of its wielders and main beneficiaries, the industrial "West," to heights equally unknown in the history of mankind. Not even the ravages of two world wars—children of that overbrimming power—could slow the upward surge for long; it even gained from the spin-off of the hectic technological war effort in its aftermath. (The decades after World War II may well denote the high-water mark of technologic-economic ebullience.) But lately the other side of triumphal advance has begun to show its face, disturbing the euphoria of success with threats that are as novel as its welcomed fruits. Not counting the insanity of a sudden, suicidal atomic holocaust, which sane fear can avoid with relative ease, it is the slow, long-term, cumulative—the peaceful and constructive use of worldwide technological power, a use in which all of us collaborate as captive beneficiaries through rising production, consumption, and sheer population growth—that poses threats much harder to counter. The net total of these threats is the overtaxing of nature, environmental and (perhaps) human as well. Thresholds may be reached in one direction or another, points of no return, where processes initiated by us will run away from us on their own momentum—and toward disaster.[11]

For Jonas, these convictions back two major claims about our common moral situation. First, Jonas argues that because the dominant moral traditions of humankind have their origins in pre-technological societies, they do not serve adequately to guide the new moral realities and questions of a technological era. Second, Jonas argues that because the nature of human action has changed with modern technology, humans must create and practice new conceptions of moral responsibility commensurate with new power. The responsibilities humans have assumed since the emergence of *Homo sapiens* for daily social interactions continue and require moral attention. For example, people should tell the truth. The rich should share power and wealth with the poor. "But this sphere," argues Jonas, "is overshadowed by a growing realm of collective action where doer, deed, and effect are no longer the same as they were in the proximate sphere, and which by the enormity of its powers forces upon ethics a ᵔw dimension of responsibility never dreamed of before."[12]

Vhat does Jonas mean by these claims? If valid, what implica-
ᶠollow for a socially responsible higher education? For Jonas,
ᶦived moral traditions work with assumptions about humanity
responsibility for the world. The human has a fixed nature
e known and that makes discernment of the human good
nowledge of the right and the good is not problematic.
ht and the good is the problem. Morality is about confor-
n moral order that all people know and should respect
b habits that form virtues and reduce vices. Moreover
an portantly, the "moral" is limited to direct and daily dealings of the self with others and with oneself. These ethical norms can therefore be termed "anthropocentric" in character.

Consider, for example, the Decalogue, which Luther understands as middle axioms of the double love command and as a biblically-revealed reminder of innate moral knowledge that corresponds to a divinely ordered creation.[13] The commandments not only limit morality to inter-human affairs, they situate doing the right and the good in the immediate present and the local. Matters of the distant future involving remote planning are absent. "Ethics accordingly," Jonas observes, "was of the here and now, of occasions as they arise between [people], of the recurrent, typical situations of private and public life."[14] The good person dealt with these situations according to social norms of wisdom and virtue. As for the long-run consequences of action, these were not judged to be morally relevant. The future belongs to forces beyond human control. People are responsible for contemporaries who live near at hand and not far away. Human agency has no connection with those living at a distance and therefore no responsibility. Humans informed by traditional ethics are responsible individually for a world that is local, in present time, human constituted, normatively intelligible, and readily manageable.

For Jonas, this sense of responsibility no longer matches the lives most humans live today and the societies that define and dominate the global situation. Until the rise of modern technology, human interactions with the realm of *techne*—the material and natural spheres of life such as farming, crafting, and healthcare—were viewed (with the exception of medicine) to be ethically neutral endeavors. Pre-modern technology did not wield enough power and control to harm or to put the human or natural good at risk of harm. It did not command attention as a sphere of ethical challenge and achievement. Since *techne* was not a matter of moral achievement, humans could do as they please with the material and natural sphere. There were no right or wrongs when interacting with the material or with nature.

For Jonas, the value system of modernity has long ago rejected the ethically neutral character of traditional technology. Modern technology "assumes ethical significance by the central place it now occupies in human purpose." Instead of being something humans are forced to do to survive in this world, technology has become a basic value commitment of modern societies and even a "calling" says Jonas, "Now, *techne* in the form of modern technology has turned into an infinite forward-thrust of the race, its most significant enterprise, in whose permanent, self-transcending advance to ever greater things the vocation of [humanity] tends to be seen, and whose success of maximal control over thing and [self] appears as the consummation of [one's] destiny."[15]

Jonas is not alone in viewing technology as a collective form of life, a common lifeworld and shared way of being in the world, that distinguishes and defines the modern era. The philosopher Leon Kass defines technology as a "way of thinking and believing and feeling, a way of standing in and toward the world. Technology . . . is the disposition rationally to order and predict and control everything feasible, in order to master fortune and spontaneity, violence and wildness, and to leave nothing to chance, all in the service of human benefit."[16] There are others who agree with Jonas' analysis of the dominant role of technology and the need for a new ethics of responsibility commensurate with the new scale, objects, and consequences of modern technology.[17]

IV. Collective Practice, Vulnerability, and Knowledge

If Jonas's analysis of human action and power today is correct, what implications follow for higher education? In this section, we consider three that should define education for a technological era. First, higher education must take due account of the altered nature of human agency. With the advent of modern technology, humans have undertaken a new kind of human action, which Jonas terms "collective technological practice." Jonas is struck not only by the novel objects of this action (the genetic modification of life forms) but equally by the scale of activity (the Internet) and its indefinitely cumulative effects (extension of life span). Collective action means humans make things happen through coordinated joint agency that invests responsibility in the group and not the individual actor. This group also undertakes actions whose consequences often extend in time and space beyond the life of the group. People are responsible for actions they themselves do not experience. As noted, traditional ethics do not consider and do not hold agents accountable for the long term and non-local consequences of actions undertaken by the group. Yet, these collective, daily, technologically empowered actions have reached levels of power and consequence that call for normative reflection and thus for new ethical norms. The concept of "sustainability" is a norm of recent moral awareness that seeks to address the ethical void that Jonas notices with concern.

The concept of sustainability assumes a moral obligation to future generations and human capacity to shape and guide the actions of billions of persons. It also assumes a second implication of Jonas' analysis, namely, the vulnerability of nature, which went unappreciated until certain unforeseen effects of technological intervention began to appear and at a level of disruption and danger that demanded a new precautionary way of thinking, as evidenced in the emergence of ecology as a scientific field. The study of ecology reflects for Jonas the nascent recognition that human power over the whole biosphere of the planet is a fact that requires new knowledge to extend the reach and the complexity of human intentions. Responsible agency, for Jonas, requires good will and intention. Human participation in collective technological action complicates action with good intention. In the absence of the capacity to predict future outcomes, there can be no responsible technology. Thus, the new vulnerability of nature requires a new morality informed by the long-term, subtle, and cumulative consequences of technological practice. Nature has become a matter of moral concern across the world because of the influence humans have collectively over the biosphere.

The advent of the science of ecology points to a third implication of Jonas' thought for higher education, namely, the new role of knowledge in moral agency. For pre-modern ethics, there was no need for predictive knowledge because morality was understood to occur in the immediate and short-term context. There was no need for special or expert knowledge to discern right intention and right action. What people were expected to do in a given social situation was usually obvious. People had to form intentions. They needed to apply a norm believed to be knowable and absolute. The moral context was immediate and near-term. The outcome of action was present, visible, and subject to public judgment. People with common sense and good will could be morally competent.

In a technological society, knowledge has become an essential trait and a "prime duty," says Jonas.[18] This knowledge should be commensurate with the scope and scale of human action. In fact, technical knowledge typically arises and proceeds toward applications that outpace human ability to predict consequences. This gap is itself a moral problem. How much ignorance should society accept? How much precautionary action should be undertaken in response to unknown consequences of actions aimed to benefit humanity? These are new moral questions without obvious answers for an era where expert knowledge produces power to act effectively in novel ways.

Pursuit of knowledge can be commended as an intrinsic good. Humans have cognitive capacities, and pursuit can fulfill human potential. For Jonas, pursuit of knowledge in general and development of predictive knowledge about human action in particular are consequences of human potential to act in the world and to construct things, systems, and worlds. Humans in the modern era have expanded the need for knowledge, both in terms of the scope and scale of what people should know and who should know. Almost all members of a technological society participate in and benefit from the fruits of technological power. Yet, as the philosopher Albert Borgmann has noticed, the core values of technology, particularly what Borgmann terms "the experience of availability," mitigate against engagement with and deep understanding of the devices and systems that allow us to control our worlds as we please.[19] Most citizens are consumers who allow technical experts to define and enact our technology civilization. For Jonas, this is precisely the social reality that must change. In the United States, this means participatory democracy must be invigorated by appropriate knowledge.

To be responsible wielders and consumers of technology, Jonas' philosophy implies an imperative of higher knowledge for all with curricula correlated with the current state and expected future of collective technological practice. People can no longer be responsible reasoning with common sense alone. Across the callings, both public and private, persons must be knowledgeable about collective technological practice, its manifestations and questions. In the United States today, there is debate about the necessity of higher education for all. Some who advocate for universal higher education see need for an educated workforce to be competitive in the global economy. For Jonas, the debate about higher education for all should engage the imperative of responsibility and consider whether society through its educational institutions cultivates knowledge attuned to new human power.

V. Citizenship in American Higher Education

Jonas first called for an ethics of responsibility to match the radical extension of human power over thirty years ago. During this time, public awareness of human power has grown. Developments in global civil society have produced movements and compacts such as the Earth Charter, which affirm human obligations for the community of life and for its future.[20] Questions of new duties to the future garner mass awareness today. The long debate over climate change has tacitly been about human power and responsibility. The sense that the moral life must be enacted on a global stage needs no defense. And many are willing to accept, what the Anthropocene thesis holds, that human activities now have a significant impact on planetary systems. But such developments do not mean global values, practices, systems, and institutions have adapted adequately or will respond soon.

In the next section, we explore the adequacy of response in theory and practice of liberal education in the United States. This analysis considers sophisticated revisionist thinking proposed by the American Association of Colleges and Universities (AAC&U). From Jonas, we now have a framework for interpreting the purpose of a higher education systems and a standard for evaluating the adequacy of a system. The adequacy question is timely because the American system is negotiating societal change prompting searching debates about the next paradigm.

These debates matter because humans now live in a context of complex, rapid, and consequential change where time itself matters morally, as Jonas argues. The pace of change in institutions may lag behind needs of humanity and the planet, which require urgent collective response before they reach crisis proportions or even escape control. The novelty and complexity of these needs challenge the work of predictive knowledge and fitting response. Human actions during the first half of the twenty-first century are believed by many to be critical to long term conditions of planetary life that follow.[21] The imperative of responsibility calls upon higher education and other formative institutions to be cognizant of their social role and confident they are doing their best based upon learning fitted to the new shape of collective activity.

The proposal of AAC&U embodies a movement termed by UNESCO as "global citizenship education," which marks a shift in the purpose and aim of public education to include moral formation toward international cooperation and societal change.[22] People are enacting universal values based upon a common humanity, both present and future. Global citizenship education goes beyond cognitive knowledge and skills to advance values, attitudes, and skills that promote a more just, peaceful, tolerant, inclusive, secure, and sustainable world.

Before considering the AAC&U proposal, we should note the significance of this turn to formation for social responsibility in the

American context, where for much of the twentieth century the purpose of higher education was generation of specialized knowledge through scientific research and value-free inquiry to serve the autonomous individual, the market economy, and the technological society. According to the analysis of Robert Bellah and colleagues in *The Good Society*, the beginnings of higher education in the eighteenth and nineteenth century saw formal education in school as one of several institutions designed to develop character and capacity for democratic citizenship. As a pre-technological society, the polis did not require citizens with advanced knowledge. The economy did not require a highly-skilled workforce. Society did require participatory powers, especially those of public discourse. American higher education until the dawning of the twentieth century sought mainly to educate public leaders for the commons.

With the rise of the research university and scientific investigation in the twentieth century, the university quickly became a "multiversity" of disciplines and departments that abjured shared moral vision and social purpose save pursuit of free inquiry. Bellah notes that with the advent of the technical university, knowledge as the accumulation of tested facts about the objective world becomes the dominant learning, displacing experiential and participatory education of family, job, and church, and assumes its integral role in creating the technological society of power and control. The pursuit of technological progress advanced the rise of utilitarian and expressive individualism and the consumer society by giving students what they needed to get ahead in the world. The communicative reason that liberal arts colleges cultivated for democratic citizenship gives way to instrumental reason, as the production and dissemination of technical knowledge becomes the dominant purpose of higher education. Community of moral discourse for democratic citizenship all but disappears within higher education. "Ethical reflection," says Bellah, "about the good life and the good society, drawing on the religious, philosophical, and literary heritage of the West, was no longer at the center of higher education. Indeed, it survived only precariously in the interstices of the research university conceived as a collection of specialized disciplines."[23]

For Bellah, writing 25 years ago, higher education as an institution needs "to recover an enlarged paradigm of knowledge, which recognizes the value of science but acknowledges that other ways of knowing have equal dignity."[24] Such change will be basic to the recovery of moral reason in higher education and must position education for citizenship as essential learning for free people in a complex modern world. With Jonas, Bellah affirms specialized knowledge as a dimension of moral reason for citizenship formation. The polis needs people who understand the details and dimensions of human power. This knowledge class must also serve the commons. The knowledge required for the renewal of democratic citizenship must include other valued ways of knowing and communal practices that engage them constructively.

VI. The Anticipatory Academy for a World of Unscripted Problems

Democratic citizenship upholds civil society in the United States and must be a fundamental aim of education in societies constituted by democratic norms. In its 2012 report, *A Crucible Moment: College Learning and America's Future*, a national task force advances a landmark case for new civic learning and democratic engagement.[25] The report addresses widespread dissatisfaction with U.S. civic health. It responds to workforce development interests and argues convincingly that the learning needed for the modern workplace and for diverse democracies overlaps significantly given common environments. These shared worlds of cultural diversity and global interdependence engender problems of novel scale and scope, problems sure to persist in the future. Addressing such problems requires significant expansion of civic education toward a rigorous, pervasive, and extended curriculum that goes beyond factual knowledge to skills and capacities such as effective communication, critical thinking and problem-solving, collaboration with others in understanding and action, ethical discernment for complexity, and intercultural competence. In addition to proposing more and new learning, the report challenges the system to serve all college students to strengthen democracy.

A Crucible Moment makes a massive claim on American higher education and points to a great awakening among leadership of the civic engagement sector to realities and conditions requiring a new paradigm both more comprehensive in content and inclusive in participation. Perhaps most important and as can be expected in an era of global connectivity and interdependence, this awareness of need for a new citizenship shares much with other voices for change in American higher education. For these voices, our "crucible moment" extends to all learning for the commons. The service higher education renders to individuals and society needs to address unanticipated challenges and threats that cannot be ignored and that require deeply-settled, still socially-constructed, conventions to be reformed. This vision looks to a novel future that education for the commons must address. Because of the magnitude of change imagined by these thought leaders and their sense of moral accountability for the future, we can call this vision a new "anticipatory academy." These educators are critically examining received traditions and seeking creative revisions for a new and consequential historical situation.

A Crucible Moment builds upon and reinforces a larger paradigm shift in American higher education under the leadership of AAC&U. Beginning with a 2002 national panel report, *Greater Expectations: A New Vision for Learning as a Nation Goes to College*, AAC&U has sought to persuade stakeholders in learning (academy, government, business, civil society, students, families) that liberal education, an approach to learning that prepares people to deal with complexity, diversity, and change, must execute a number of turns to benefit all students in every discipline at all institutions.[26] *Greater Expectations* finds numerous features of American secondary and collegiate education to be inadequate and calls for a new "intentional learner" engendered by a "new academy" that advances both qualitative change in human knowledge and expanded access for a knowledge-intensive world.

Before we examine this new paradigm, we should consider briefly the context that warrants change. While AAC&U thought could say more about the forces reshaping communities and individuals, it works with assumptions about present and future environments that evidence sound understanding of our historical moment with its novel features and trajectories. This text in *College Learning for the New Global Century* captures key environmental realities:

> In recent years, the ground has shifted in virtually every important sphere of life—economic, global, cross-cultural, environmental, civic. The world around us is being dramatically reshaped by scientific and technological innovations, global interdependence, cross-cultural encounters, and changes in the balance of economic and political power. Only a few years ago, Americans envisioned a future in which this nation would be the world's only superpower. Today it is clear that the United States—and individual Americans—will be challenged to engage in unprecedented ways with the global community, collaboratively and competitively.

Such are the dynamics of the present world. As for the future, AAC&U expects:

> These seismic waves of dislocating change will only intensify. The world in which today's students will make choices and compose lives is one of disruption rather than certainty, and of interdependence rather than insularity. To succeed in a chaotic environment, graduates will need to be intellectually resilient, cross-culturally and scientifically literate, technologically adept, ethically anchored and fully prepared for a future of continuous and cross-disciplinary learning.[27]

Constant and accelerating change with unforeseen and unwelcome features on a global scale—this is a daunting account of our times. It backs AAC&U's summary—and striking—proposal that American higher education should prepare all students for "a world of unscripted problems," problems consistently described as urgent and complex.[28] Here we should note the critical but tacit judgment that dominant norms and arrangements of the American educational system advance a contemporary world of massive and uncoordinated power. The system contributes to the chronic chaos that troubles thought leaders. Global interdependence and change make societies vulnerable. Complexity overtaxes individual agency. People, educated and uneducated alike, are increasingly powerless to govern environments of human making, hence, the call for system change with a problem-solving aim.

AAC&U thought leaders understand that some stakeholders will contest a new academy that embraces a common dedication to forming students who can solve real-world problems. The American system is about pluralism and choice and specialization. Common mission is almost unthinkable. While twenty-first century education requires a diversity and multiplicity of educational goods, they must no longer be ensconced in narrow independent disciplines. The many should be woven through common aim and structure to engender responsible learners capable of addressing together challenges that beset the global commons. As Jonas argues, problems rooted in collective human action require collaborative and intentional response. Twentieth century confidence that modern power will lead to worldly wellbeing for all has long been questionable. Education for the unscripted problems of a common future cannot be dismissed given credible possibilities and risks.[29] The new anticipatory academy comes with a hard premise—that a powerful educational system is not good enough for its world.

VII. A Turn to Responsibility, Perhaps in Time

For Jonas, the current system is not responsible—to the extent it fails to prepare students to be accountable for important negative consequences of human agency—the urgent and complex problems that AAC&U calls higher education to engage. For Jonas, responsibility includes the imperative of higher education for all that forms human agency commensurate with the current state and expected future of "collective technological practice." The new academy of AAC&U proposes basic change in college (and secondary) learning commensurate with the astonishing power, plasticity, complexity, and dynamism of the human community. This anticipatory academy is a responsible academy in Jonas' terms because its problem-solving intention assumes accountability for collective human finitude and moral failure. The new academy embodies Bonhoeffer's "world come of age," which has learned that modern projects of control and enhancement are often insufficiently attentive to the novel, complex, unpredictable, and immense dimensions of human agency and their future consequences.

What, then, are the main turns of the new academy toward a responsible liberal education? Since the articulation of four essential learning outcomes and seven principles of excellence in *College Learning for the New Global Century* in 2007, AAC&U has proposed a curricular framework suitable for all forms of higher education to advance a real-world, problem-solving paradigm. A 2011 vision document coupled with a 2013-17 strategic plan make clear "integrative liberal learning for the global commons" provides an interpretive key to the outcomes and principles. The principles represent a bold revision of quality in American higher education that supports landmark inclusion of practical learning in the outcomes. While the outcomes continue to call for basic literacy and knowledge to explore the great questions that humans and societies engage, they announce a new liberal learning that focuses upon a complex skill set providing enduring capacities for worlds of change. The outcomes include a strong account of personal and social responsibility for worlds of diversity, which supports learning for the wicked problems of the present and beyond.

The essential learning outcomes and principles of excellence advance a real-world agenda through attention to inclusivity, inquiry, innovation, intercultural competence, collaboration, application, complexity, and other realities and norms. Second, this new academy is relational, communal, global, and committed to access for all. Problems of collective power require pluralistic and participatory interventions. Third, AAC&U decenters specialized knowledge (the discipline, the major) and deploys it for urgent and complex challenges. The new academy must be interdisciplinary, cross-cultural, dialogical, and collaborative to prepare students for an interdependent world arising from the novel reach of collective human power in a technological age. Helping students to work with and benefit from multiple perspectives is integral to solving complex and far-flung problems, because responsible power cannot be wielded by individuals working in isolation. The collective and interactive power of human diversity (noetic, cultural, experiential, biological) must be practiced to exercise responsibility for modern agency.

The new anticipatory academy of AAC&U exhibits two kinds of responsibility. First, it calls upon human adaptability and ingenuity to re-imagine higher learning to limit and avoid problems of our making. To be human is to learn. What do humans know today about effective learning that they did not know 50 years ago? AAC&U founds its case on recent human learning about effective education. The responsible humans that Jonas seeks are possible. AAC&U calls these students "intentional learners."[30] Humans can reduce problems of their own making. Second, higher education should respond quickly and seriously to forming agents to address problems of irresponsible human power—like climate change or extreme poverty. The fact that these problems have their origins in the decisions of previous societies does not negate contemporary obligation. Humans today are complicit in these legacy problems. The moral standing of the future applies to current problems no differently than possible problems.

The new academy of AAC&U promotes responsible learning for a world of unscripted problems. Lutheran higher education should embrace this agenda as a new pathway to civic righteousness. It merits adoption by colleges and universities that seek to educate students for service to the neighbor—the global commons—through liberal learning. This new academy will differ significantly from the status quo. It is an unknown form in human history. Institutions that embrace it must have courage to fail and confidence in human resilience and good will. The new academy seeks to educate for a world that changes quickly. The hour is late for system change. The problems that need to be addressed are urgent and complex. Responsibility calls Lutheran educators to act now.

ENDNOTES

1 Hans Jonas, *The Imperative of Responsibility: In Search of an Ethics for the Technological Age*, trans. Hans Jonas with David Herr (Chicago: University of Chicago, 1984), 8.

2 Douglas C. Bennett, Grant H. Cornell, Haifa Jamal Al-Lail, and Celeste Schenck, "An Education for the Twenty-First Century: Stewardship of the Global Commons," *Liberal Education* 98/4 (Fall 2012): 37.

3 Charles Taylor, *Sources of the Self: The Making of Modern Identity* (Cambridge: Harvard, 1989), 211-233.

4 For original insight into Bonhoeffer's use of this phrase regarding modern human power and responsibility, see Larry Rasmussen, "Lutheran Sacramental Imagination," *Journal of Lutheran Ethics* 14/2 (February 2014), accessed May 3, 2017, http://www.elca.org/JLE/Articles/42.

5 Christian Schwägerl, *The Anthropocene: The Human Era and How It Shapes Our Planet* (Santa Fe: Synergetic, 2014).

6 Larry Rasmussen, *Earth-honoring Faith: Religious Ethics in a New Key* (New York: Oxford, 2013), 121, 223-224, 226-227, 364-365.

7 Evangelical Lutheran Church in America, "A Social Statement: Our Calling in Education," 2007, accessed May 3, 2017, http://www.elca.org/education/, 11.

8 Martin Luther, "Temporal Authority: To What Extent It Should Be Obeyed," in *Luther's Works*, ed. Walther Brandt (Philadelphia: Fortress, 1962), 45:127-128.

9 Martin Luther, *The Freedom of a Christian*, trans. Mark Tranvik (Minneapolis: Fortress, 2008).

10 Luther, *Freedom*, 82. For further development of this account of Lutheran ethics, see Per Anderson, "Luther, Martin," in The International Encyclopedia of Ethics, ed. Hugh LaFollette (Hoboken: Blackwell, 2013): 3093-3101.

11 Jonas, *Imperative*, ix.

12 Jonas, *Imperative*, 6.

13 Martin Luther, "How Christians Should Regard Moses," in *Martin Luther's Basic Theological Writings*, ed. Timothy Lull (Minneapolis: Fortress, 1989): 135-148.

14 Jonas, *Imperative*, 5.

15 Jonas, *Imperative*, 9.

16 Leon Kass, "Introduction: The Problem of Technology," in *Technology in Western Political Thought*, eds. Arthur M. Melzer, Jerry Weinberger, and M. Richard Zinman (Ithaca: Cornell, 1993): 4-5.

17 The key thinker in Christian and religious ethics today is William Schweiker. See *Responsibility and Christian Ethics* (Cambridge: Cambridge, 1995) and *Power, Value, and Conviction* (Cleveland: Pilgrim, 1998).

18 Jonas, *Imperative*, 7.

19 Albert Borgmann, *Technology and the Character of Contemporary Life* (Chicago: University of Chicago, 1984), 41-48.

20 Earth Charter Initiative, "The Earth Charter," (2001), accessed May 3, 2017, http://earthcharter.org.

21 For an influential statement of the critical role of current action in the long-term wellbeing of the planet, see Bill McKibben, "A Special Moment in History," *The Atlantic Monthly* 281/5 (May 1989): 55-78.

22 United Nations Educational, Scientific and Cultural Organization (UNESCO), *Global Citizenship Education: Preparing Learners for the Challenges of the 21st Century* (Paris: UNESCO, 2014), 14.

23 Robert N. Bellah, Richard Madsen, William M. Sullivan, Ann Swidler, and Steven Tipton, *The Good Society* (New York: Vintage, 1991), 163

24 Bellah, *Good Society*, 177.

25 The National Task Force on Civic Learning and Democratic Engagement, *A Crucible Moment: College Learning and Democracy's Future* (Washington: Association of American Colleges and Universities, 2012).

26 Greater Expectations National Panel, *Greater Expectations: A New Vision for Learning as a Nation Goes to College* (Washington: American Association of Colleges and Universities, 2002).

27 The National Leadership Council for Liberal Education and America's Promise, *College Learning for the New Global Century* (Washington: American Association of Colleges and Universities, 2007), 15. See also The National Leadership Council for Liberal Education and America's Promise, *The LEAP Vision for Learning: Outcomes, Practices, Impact, and Employers' Views* (Washington: American Association of Colleges and Universities, 2011), 6

28 AAC&U's problem-solving vision begins with Greater Expectations in 2002 and develops with each succeeding publication to the present. The two most recent reports are clear and compelling: see AAC&U Board of Directors, "Strategic Plan 2013-17: Big Questions, Urgent Challenges: Liberal Education and Americans' Global Future," accessed May 3, 2017, https://www.aacu.org/about/strategicplan, and American Association of College and Universities, "The LEAP Challenge: Education for a World of Unscripted Problems," accessed May 3, 2017, https://www.aacu.org/leap-challenge.

29 See James Howard Kunstler, *The Long Emergency: Surviving the End of Oil, Climate Change, and Other Converging Catastrophes of the Twenty-first Century* (New York: Grove, 2009); James Lovelock, *A Rough Ride to the Future* (London: Allen Lane, 2014); Jorgen Randers, 2052: *A Global Forecast for the Next Forty Years* (White River Junction: Chelsea Green, 2012).

30 Greater Expectations National Panel, *Greater Expectations*, 21-26.

WHOLE SELF

INTRODUCTION

> "Whole Self: Lead students into life-long reflection on their identity, purpose, and engagement in the world."[1]

The chapters in this section took different perspectives in exploring how we aim to teach the whole self, yet certain common threads emerged to link them together. Larry Papenfuss argues that the foundational tenets of our identity as a Lutheran liberal arts college of the church should continue to shape our campus culture. In doing so, we will prepare students who not only embody our mission and achieve the goals of Concordia's most current strategic plan (developing the whole self, in order to lead whole lives, for the sake of the whole world), but also prepare students for planetary citizenship.

Mark Krejci, writing about a focus on sustainability, argues for a move away from a consumerist worldview where goods, services, energy, even marriage are to be consumed to a view of life as a gift. He further argues that we participate in God's gift through our vocation. Papenfuss and Krejci's chapters are linked by the common thread of viewing life as a gift—a gift that we hold in humble stewardship rather than rampant consumerism.

Faith Ngunjiri's chapter focuses on how she infuses the themes of vocation and values in her course Ethics and Leadership, enabling her students to articulate their own values and begin the process of understanding vocation as the nexus of one's gifts and the world's needs. Thus the thread of vocation links the Papenfuss, Krejci and Ngunjiri chapters.

Finally, Erika Claire Strandjord interrogates the idea of teaching the whole self by arguing for a view of our students that sees our students as "whole-broken," a view that demands that we engage compassionately and become an inclusive campus for different kinds of students. Seeing students as whole-broken demands that we "affirm their wholeness even as we see their brokenness and work with them in our classrooms and campuses." Strandjord and Ngunjiri's chapters are linked by the theme of identity—where Strandjord explores identity in terms of whole-broken or different abilities, Ngunjiri's focus is on student's identity in relation to their deeply held values as well as their spiritual identity.

Together, these four chapters argue for a view of whole self that is embodied/physical as well as spiritual, a whole self that is imbued by a sense of humility and stewardship in living this life that we and our students have been given as a gift from God.

—Dr. Faith Ngunjiri,
Associate Professor of Ethics and Leadership,
Director of Lorentzsen Center for Faith and Work

ENDNOTES

1 "Whole Self, Whole Life, Whole World: The Plan for Concordia College 2012-2017," Concordia College, Moorhead, MN, last modified October 12, 2012, https://concordiacollege.edu/files/resources/strategicplan.pdf.

THE HUMBLE SELF

DR. LARRY PAPENFUSS
Gift Planner and
Co-Director of the Dovre Center for Faith and Learning

October 31, 2016, marked the 125th anniversary of Concordia College. Our mission statement, which grew out of an effort to chart our strategic path over 50 years ago, states:

> The purpose of Concordia College is to influence the affairs of the world by sending into society thoughtful and informed men and women dedicated to the Christian life.[1]

In 2017, we begin a year-long observance of the 500th anniversary of the Reformation. It is fitting that we, as a Lutheran liberal arts college, ask how we will continue to reform in order to best serve our students and society. Like the church itself, our Lutheran colleges must continue to reform, to be active co-creators with God, to ask how we can continue to *influence the affairs of the world* as we face the challenges of today; not the least of which is the looming environmental crisis. I submit in this paper that the foundational tenets of our identity as a Lutheran liberal arts college of the church should continue to shape our campus culture. In doing so, we will prepare students who not only embody our mission and achieve the goals of Concordia's most current strategic plan (developing the whole self, in order to lead whole lives, for the sake of the whole world),[2] but also prepare students for planetary citizenship.

To borrow a frequently quoted maxim from organizational leadership, "culture eats strategy for breakfast." So if one believes, as I do, that an institution's culture is the most indelible aspect of its curriculum, then what about Concordia's culture can help us achieve our goals? I begin with three foundational tenets of our Lutheran identity that help shape our campus culture: 1. understanding salvation as a gift and the resulting sense of **humility** that comes from this realization; 2. the commitment to **dialogue** and debate that acknowledges limitations in our understanding, cultivates wisdom, and encourages us to speak truth to power; and 3. the centrality of the Lutheran concept of **vocation**.

I. Humility

Many people have shaped my own perspective on Lutheran liberal arts education, and Concordia's particular flavor of it. Names like Sittler, Forrell, Schwehn, Benne, Christianson, Jodock, and our own Simmons and Dovre, have all significantly informed my views. Each has, for me, made a case for the distinctive features of the kind of education that we seek to provide—an education that is rooted in Luther's inspiration that we are saved by grace through faith. As passive recipients of God's righteousness, we recognize that there is nothing we can do to earn salvation. Rather it is, a gift from God, a gift that then frees us to serve others. Benne expounds upon Luther's *The Freedom of a Christian* when he says:

> In Christ, God stoops to gather us up for communion with him, in spite of our sin. We are made "free lords of all, subject to none," by God's mercy. The human response to this is one of grateful joy and renewed faith in the promises of God. . . At the same time that we are free lords of all, subject to none, we are paradoxically, "dutiful servants of all, subject to all." The love that we have received from God in Christ moves through us toward our neighbor. Our incurved wills are warmed by the Spirit so that they spontaneously move outward toward others." [3]

Thus this theological foundation that we are saved by grace, rather than our own doing, fosters both a personal and intellectual humility. Benne alludes to what Augustine, Luther, and later Karl Barth, described as our greatest sin; that is, our own self-centeredness—*incurvatus in se*—or being turned in on oneself. Our human nature causes us to focus on our own needs and desires, ultimately leading us to sin against others and the creation. Society and market-driven economies are powerful advocates for this self-centeredness within our greater culture.

Many students come to campus focused on how a college degree will help them become more successful, often with little thought about how what they choose to do in life will help them serve others. They are part of what author David Brooks refers to as a generation of the "Big Me."[4] Brooks points to generational shifts of increasing narcissism and a preponderance of societal messages encouraging young adults to seek meaning by turning to one's inner self. In turn, this produces a drive to seek external validation of one's own self-worth resulting in ceaseless striving to do more, accomplish more, and attain success. It is this preoccupation with self that forms the predominant values of the Anthropocene era: me first, convenience first, and profits first. Understanding salvation as a gift on the other hand, allows us to accept ourselves despite our limitations and weaknesses. Helping our students understand that they are worthy and worthwhile, even when they can't do everything, accomplish it all, or even when they fail in some endeavor, is central to instilling humility. As Brooks concludes; "Humility is freedom from the need to prove you are superior all the time."[5]

The Earth Charter provides an environmental perspective. The charter was the culmination of a project initiated by the United Nations involving a decade-long, world-wide and cross-cultural conversation. It is an ethical guide for achieving a sustainable future; in the preamble it states: "The spirit of human solidarity and kinship with all life is strengthened when we live in reverence for the mystery of being, gratitude for the gift of life and humility regarding the human place in nature."[6] The Earth Charter recognizes the threat that self-centeredness poses and affirms the need for cultivating an attitude of humility as important in promoting sustainability.

At their heart, Lutheran liberal arts colleges seek to offer an antidote to this self-centeredness by developing empathy for others. This call comes from both spiritual and intellectual perspectives. Joseph Sittler describes the task as "complicating lives open."[7] William Cronon in his landmark article, "Only Connect," provides an intellectual correlate to Luther's *Freedom of a Christian* when he says; "Liberal education nurtures human freedom in the service of human community, which is to say that in the end it celebrates love."[8] Liberal arts apologist, Martha Nussbaum also acknowledges the role of religious values when she writes; "Love of neighbor is a central value in all major American religions. These religions call us to a critical examination of our own selfishness and narrowness, urging more inclusive sympathy."[9] It is an education, according to Jodock, that frees us from our unexamined views and beliefs and fosters "responsible participation in the world"[10] or, as the theme of the Concordia College core curriculum states, to "become responsibly engaged in the world."[11] This type of education diminishes self-interest, produces empathy for others and fosters humility.

II. Dialogue

There is a correlate of *incurvatus in se* that manifests itself in intellectual arrogance, or the certainty that one's view is so singularly right or true that it excludes, or dismisses, any credible critique. Contrast this with the wisdom found in accepting the paradoxical nature of truth; in acknowledging the complexity of the world with all its uncertainty; and in embracing our limited understanding. By doing so, we honor the mystery of God. In a quote attributed to the British philosopher, writer and activist, Bertand Russell on bigthink.com: "The whole problem with the world is that fools and fanatics are always so certain of themselves, and wiser people so full of doubts." Wisdom is, of course, a much greater commodity than knowledge. Jodock identifies the cultivation of wisdom as one of the key features of the Lutheran tradition.[12] That is why the Lutheran commitment to dialogue is so important. Ideas matter and, through dialogue, discussion and debate, the best ideas are honed and ignorant views abandoned. Consider, for example, those who deny global warming. Without the willingness to subject one's views to empirical evidence or criticism by others, ignorance can reign. Wisdom then is communal in nature; and it is through our interactions with others (particularly those different from ourselves and with different views than our own) that truth emerges. Any commitment to reforming should continue to demonstrate a willingness to expose our ideas to debate and speak truth to power.

III. Vocation

Ultimately, what is perhaps most unique about Lutheran higher education is the constant engagement with the topic of vocation. It begins with the big questions: "Who are you called to be?" and, "What will you choose to do with your life?" It goes on to explore one's understanding of faith and the role it plays in one's sense of purpose. Here, Luther's understanding of vocation as service on behalf of the neighbor creates opportunities for discovering meaning, purpose and deeper spiritual fulfillment in life. "Since each and every person thus thrives through their own faith—so that all other works and the sum total of life flows out from that very faith—by these works each may serve and benefit the neighbor with willing benevolence."[13] Lutheran liberal arts education provides a gadfly by reminding students (and one another) that because we are gifted with salvation, we are now free to transcend our own self-interest. The interest of the neighbor becomes more important. This is a spiritual endeavor that helps students think beyond themselves and care for the other. As Simmons says; "Spirituality consists in self-transcending selfhood connected with the life of the body and the material world."[14]

Bobby Fong, former president of Butler University and Ursinus College, sees faith values, like empathy for others, as important to both secular and religious institutions. For religious institutions, he claims: "The challenge here is to renew the language of faith for a generation for whom it is a legacy but not one personally examined and claimed as one's own."[15] Of course, vocational dialogue need not be restrictively Lutheran. Indeed service to the neighbor is a worthy goal for all, regardless of religious affiliation or background.

A primary task of our Lutheran colleges then, is to create an environment where students are constantly asked to consider how their faith informs their learning and how their learning informs their faith. It should be an environment that encourages questioning, dialogue and engagement with those that are different from oneself. It should encourage vulnerability and taking risks in the pursuit of learning who I am and who I wish to be. In short, it should be an education for more than just a career; rather, it should be an education for a meaningful life.

Creating a culture that fosters empathy for others and the creation cannot be the sole responsibility of a single person, course, program or area of study, but must be operationalized in a variety of experiences that are part of the four-year conversation that we carry on with students. It entails every opportunity that we have to engage students with questions of identity, purpose, and faith from orientation through graduation and beyond. The Concordia culture has multiple entry points for "becoming responsibly engaged in the world," mediating self-interest and promoting humility, some of which are:

- Beginning in the first week of orientation, students participate in a service project (Hands for Change) as a way to introduce them to the discussion of vocation.
- The dialogue is operationalized through the theme of the curriculum—Becoming Responsibly Engaged in the World (BREW), a theme addressed throughout the four-year experience.
- The liberal arts education helps students see the inter-relatedness of disciplines and subject matter, which creates an understanding that wisdom is cultivated through community and complexity.
- Students are engaged—they write, they present, they serve, they assume leadership roles. They participate in experiences where the life of the mind intersects with the habits of the heart.
- They explore faith—intellectually in the academic study of religion and in a wide variety of faith formation activities through campus ministry.
- The Forum for Faith and Life, The Lorentzsen Center for Faith and Work, The Dovre Center for Faith and Learning, and Campus Ministry keep the discussion of faith and learning alive on campus among students, faculty and the community.

- We promote numerous opportunities for participation in a wide variety of service–from walking across the street to serve a meal at the Dorothy Day House, to travelling to another part of the country or world to participate in Justice Journey, Habitat for Humanity or May Seminar experiences.
- We are blessed with faculty mentors who exemplify care for students, embrace the mission of the college, and who humbly live out their own vocations.
- Finally, I want to also acknowledge that not all of our students come to us as stereotypical self-absorbed millennials. Indeed many come with a strong sense of empathy for others that plays out in, and outside of, our classrooms. They come to us because they are attracted by an understanding of our mission. In turn, they help reinforce our culture of humility and are among the greatest influences on their classmates.

So then, how must we think of re-forming for planetary citizenship? I'd like to think that it will be in sustaining our culture—a culture that promotes self-acceptance and humility—a culture that embraces dialogue and debate as a means of seeking truth—and a culture that continually engages students in the discernment of vocation. By re-committing ourselves to these tenets of our Lutheran liberal arts identity, while embracing greater diversity, we can help create thoughtful and humble leaders who demonstrate love for neighbor and care for creation.

ENDNOTES

1 "Whole Self, Whole Life, Whole World: The Plan for Concordia College 2012-2017," Concordia College, Moorhead, MN, last modified October 12, 2012, https://concordiacollege.edu/files/resources/strategicplan.pdf.

2 "Whole Self, Whole Life, Whole World," Concordia College.

3 Robert Benne, *The Paradoxical Vision: A Public Theology for the Twenty-first Century* (Minneapolis: Fortress Press, 1995), 66.

4 David Brooks, *The Road to Character* (New York: Random House, 2015), 6-8.

5 Brooks, *The Road to Character*, 8.

6 The Earth Charter last modified in 2016, http://earthcharter.org/discover/the-earth-charter/.

7 Joseph Sittler, "Church Colleges and the Truth," in *Faith, Learning and the Church College: Address by Joseph Sittler* (Northfield, MN: St. Olaf College, 1989).

8 William Cronon, "Only Connect . . . The Goals of a Liberal Education," *The American Scholar* (Autumn 1998): 73-80.

9 Martha Nussbaum, *Cultivating Humanity: A Classical Defense of Reform in Liberal Education* (Cambridge: Harvard University Press, 1997), 292.

10 Darrell Jodock, "Vocation of the Lutheran College and Religious Diversity," *Intersections*, no. 33 (Spring 2011): 6.

11 "BREW (Becoming Responsibly Engaged in the World)," website of Concordia College, Moorhead, MN, last modified 2017, https://www.concordiacollege.edu/academics/brew/

12 Jodock, *Vocation of the Lutheran College.*

13 Martin Luther in Timothy J. Wengert, *The Freedom of A Christian 1520: The Annotated Luther Study Edition* (Minneapolis: Fortress Press, 2016), 521.

14 Ernest Simmons, *Lutheran Higher Education: An Introduction for Faculty* (Minneapolis: Augsburg Fortress, 1998), 48.

15 Bobby Fong, "Cultivating 'Sparks of the Divinity:' Soul-Making as a Purpose of Higher Education," *Liberal Education* 100, no. 3 (Summer 2014).

SUSTAINABILITY THROUGH THE HERMENEUTIC OF THE GIFT

DR. MARK KREJCI
Professor of Psychology

As Concordia prepares students to "influence the affairs of the world . . ." we engage in dialogue concerning the state of the world to which our students will be sent. We seek to have our students be prepared for the variety of ways in which they will responsibly engage in the world. This type of engagement, guided by an ethos of responsibility to the neighbor, is being considered in this publication's chapters, within a context of the sustainability of the world set within the age of the Anthropocene.

Sustainability is most commonly thought of as a concept referring to the environment given the reality of climate change. In addition to this challenge, the United States is also faced with questions about the sustainability of many aspects of society. Federal government spending is outpacing the growth of our economy. According to the Congressional Budget Office, the federal deficit is projected to be $544 billion this year (FY 2016), an increase of $100 billion over the previous year.[1] Set within the context of the yearly GDP, the amount of federal debt is more than double what it was 10 years ago and could climb as high as 125 percent of GDP by 2025.[2] In spite of the growing deficit, tax revenues will remain at 18.3 percent of GDP given the apparent lack of political will to either decrease spending and/or increase taxes. How can we engage our students on the sustainability of our federal government in a way that avoids political posturing and presents the need to make adjustments now in order to avoid a worse situation in the future?

Another area of sustainability that we should consider is the state of marriage and the family. The divorce rate is often stated to be at "50 percent" but in reality about 40 percent of marriages that occurred in the 1970s and 1980s end in divorce.[3] The divorce rate of those who were married in the 2000s is lower than those married in previous decades, however, this is offset by an increasing number of this age group living together and not marrying. When these relationships end there are no divorce proceedings and thus the dissolution of these relationships is not accurately measured.[4] Further evidence of the overall decrease in marriage was reported by the Pew Research Center in 2011 when it reported that less than half of U.S. adults were married, a record low percentage.[5] These data call into question the sustainability of the nuclear family given the present social circumstances in our society. While this paper does not allow for the adequate review of scholarship on how children are impacted by the loss of a nuclear family environment, the state of marriage and family life should be a point of discussion if Concordia is to engage our students in this aspect of sustainable society. The challenge is: how do we engage students in this discussion while recognizing that they will have a range of expectations about what family life should entail?

Climate change is another aspect of sustainability that the world faces. The political nature of this debate has often resulted in a retreat from the discussion at a scientific level of analysis, but the overwhelming scientific consensus is that our current climate change is significant and has been created by humans.[6] Even when the scientific data is known and accepted, there are great individual differences in whether people modify their behavior to decrease their energy footprint. The challenge in behavior modification regarding energy use is that the external reinforcement or punishment for behavior either does not occur or is so remote (i.e. in the future) that it fails to impact daily behavior. The use of energy is experienced by people as an abstract, non-immediate experience involving multiple behaviors and has various degrees of personal relevance for people especially given the context of the relatively low cost of energy in the U.S.[7] Those who have a high intrinsic motivation are more willing to take steps to limit energy use however there are a lack of societal incentives to create a robust change in behaviors.[8] In other words, people are not personally impacted to the point where they are motivated to change even if they believe that global warming is real and caused by humans.

When people are confronted with the growing federal deficit, the decline in marriage, and the rising global temperature, there is typically consensus that something must be done, but at the same time there is wide disagreement on what steps should be taken and even less political and/or personal will to address the issues. Might the basic philosophical approach that we have when we approach these issues create difference and what could be an alternative?

Consumerism, referred to as ". . . an organizing principle of American life"[9] is defined as "the theory that an increasing consumption of goods and services is economically desirable; a preoccupation with and an inclination toward the buying of consumer goods."[10] Set within a consumer approach to life, energy is something to be consumed, marriage is focused on what is personally gained from the relationship, and government is expected to provide for an increasing range of citizens' needs preferably at a low price (i.e. taxes). Such an approach to life creates a worldview that is self-centered and based on one's more immediate wants rather than the greater good.[11]

As an alternative to consumerism, the Christian tradition offers a hermeneutical approach to life focused on "the gift." In short, from both Catholic[12] and Protestant[13] traditions, approaching life as a "gift" focuses on God's creative act as a free gift given to humanity originating in God who is love. An approach to a "gift" hermeneutic of life versus a "consumerism" approach to life radically changes our understanding and practice of sustainability.

Darrell Jodock writes that, "according to the Lutheran tradition, being right with God and having dignity as a human are free gifts, for which there are no prerequisites."[14] While this understanding of life as gift should decrease our anxiety, Jodock holds that our unsustainable economic, environmental, and political structures are creating a deep anxiety that is preventing society from adequately addressing these issues. When life is understood in light of consumerism, the things of the world—goods, services, relationships, environment—are meant for our use in ways that will make us happy. When life is understood in light of "gift," what emerges is an understanding of a life well lived when it is focused on responsibility to the neighbor lived through vocation.

God's generosity is provided to all without merit or preconditions. God freely gives to all because God loves the world and created the world as a gift.[15] But this gift is not meant to be governed by the philosophy of consumerism (humans own the earth and have a right to consume it) but rather through an understanding that with a gift comes responsibility for the caring of what is freely given.

In his exegesis on the parable of the prodigal son, Robert Barron[16] explains that the prodigal son's demand of the inheritance is akin to Adam and Eve's eating the forbidden fruit. The son will eventually receive his inheritance when his father dies but instead demands that it be immediately given to him. Rather than a gift to be received in the father's time, the inheritance becomes a possession the son demands. Similarly, Adam and Eve have everything they need including the opportunity to stroll with God, and even though the forbidden tree is part of their inheritance, they are impatient and in their own way demand that they are able to consume the fruit right away. In both cases, demanding the possession results in consumption of what was meant to be a gift. The result of the consumption: hunger and the loss of contact with the Father. Barron draws towards his conclusion by stating that the gift from God is not something to be possessed but something in which we are to participate. As with Jodock, Barron writes that we cannot earn nor do not merit this gift: "We can only be embraced by it."[17]

We participate in God's gift through our vocation. God's free gifting is ongoing because "God" (is) "down here," amid the ordinary, amid the suffering and the chaos as well as the order and beauty, deeply involved in delivering good gifts to anyone and everyone through the agency of other humans and creatures."[18] This agency, this role that we play in God's creation, is our call to vocation, ". . . a calling to serve the neighbor and the community . . ."[19] by sharing the gift. Thus the gift that we are freely given and are called to embrace is meant to be shared through our vocation. Barron describes Pope John Paul II's *hermeneutic of the gift* in a similar way. ". . . Pope John Paul II, speaks of the centrality of the law of the gift in the Christian tradition; one's being increases and is enhanced in the measure that one give it (the gift) away. To achieve the ultimate end of the moral life is not to attain a prize that gratifies the ego; rather it is to enter into the gracious way of being characteristic of God."[20]

If Concordia is to help our students responsibly engage the world, a world with a myriad of sustainability challenges, understanding life through a hermeneutic of gift can be offered as a moral and intellectual contrast to consumerism. With consumerism, if energy is cheap and one can afford it, why not take extra trips or raise the thermostat in the winter. With consumerism, if one tires of a marriage, why not go out and look for another that would better satisfy. With consumerism, one wants the government to provide more and more and should do so with low taxes.

In contrast, by understanding life as our participation in the divine gift through vocation we live to serve the neighbor. We recognize that our energy use impacts everyone's life around the world and through future generations. Our spouse is meant to be someone we love and the experience of love is in reflecting God's love to our spouse rather than demanding the love we want. We approach our country following John F. Kennedy's advice to "ask not what your country can do for you, but what can you do for your country."[21] Thus, a hermeneutic of life as a gift can be presented as a framing view, rooted in a vocation of responsible engagement in the world, through which we can consider with our students the topic of sustainability in all of its many forms.

ENDNOTES

1 *Updated Budget Projections: 2016 to 2026* (Washington DC: Congressional Budget Office, 2016), accessed May 15, 2016.

2 Ibid.

3 Rose M. Kreider and Renee Ellis, *Number, Timing and Duration of Marriages and Divorces: 2009* (Washington DC: United States Census Bureau, 2011), https://www.census.gov/prod/2011pubs/p70-125.pdf.

4 Casey E. Copen, Kimbery Daniels, Jonathan Vespa and William D. Mosher, *First*

Marriages in the United States: Data from the 2006-2010 National Survey of Family Growth, (Washington DC: U.S. Department of Health and Human Services, Center for Disease Control and Prevention, and National Center for Health Statistics, 2012).

5 D'Vera Cohn, Jeffrey S. Passel, Wendy Wang, and Gretchen Livingston, *Barely Half of U.S. Adults are Married—A Record Low*, (Washington DC: Pew Research Center, 2011), accessed at http://www.pewsocialtrends.org/files/2011/12/Marriage-Decline.pdf.

6 John Cook et al., "Quantifying the Consensus on Anthropogenic Global Warming in the Scientific Literature," *Environmental Research Letters* 8 (2013). doi:10.1088/1748-9326/8/2/02402 and *Climate Change: How Do We Know?* (Washington DC: NASA, 2017), accessed at http://climate.nasa.gov/evidence.

7 Beth Karlin, Joanne F. Zinger, Rebecca Ford, "The Effects of Feedback on Energy Conservation: A Meta Analysis," *Psychological Bulletin* 141, no. 6 (2015): 1205-1227.

8 Ibid.

9 Amitai Etzioni, "Consumerism and Americans," in *Social Problems: Readings with Four Questions.*, eds. J.M. Charon and L.G. Vigilant (Belmont, CA: Cenage Learning, 2012), 41-46.

10 Merriam-Webster (2016), "Consumerism," accessed May 15, 2016, https://www.merriam-webster.com/dictionary/consumerism.

11 John Paul II, Encylical Letter 'Sollicitudo Rei Socialis' (1987), paragraph 28, accessed May 4, 2014. http://w2.vatican.va/content/john-paul-ii/en/encyclicals/documents/hf_jp-ii_enc_30121987_sollicitudo-rei-socialis.html ("the treachery hidden within a development that is only quantitative, for the 'excessive availability of every kind of material goods for the benefit of certain social groups, easily makes people slaves of "possession" and of immediate gratification.'").

12 John Paul II, *Man and Woman He Created Them: A Theology of the Body* (Boston: Pauline Books, 2006).

13 Darrell Jodock, "Vocation of the Lutheran College and Religious Diversity," *Intersections* 33 (2011): 5-12.

14 Ibid.,7.

15 Genesis 1:26 refers to human "dominion" over the earth.

16 Robert Barron, *The Priority of Christ: Toward a Postliberal Catholicism* (Grand Rapids, MI: Baker Academic, 2016).

17 Ibid., 80.

18 Jodock, (2008), 8.

19 Ibid.

20 Robert Barron, *Exploring Catholic Theology: Essays on God, Liturgy, and Evangelization* (Grand Rapids, MI: Baker Academic, 2015), 43.

21 John F. Kennedy, "Inaugural Address," (January 20, 1961), speech in Washington, DC, http://www.presidency.ucsb.edu/ws/index.php?pid=8032&

VOCATION AND VALUES IN THE ETHICAL LEADERSHIP CLASSROOM

DR. FAITH NGUNJIRI
Associate Professor of Ethics and Leadership and Director of Lorentzsen Center for Faith and Work

According to Lee Shulman in his foreword to the book *Rethinking Undergraduate Business Education: Liberal Learning for the Profession*, a good business education ought to prepare students to "dig deeply, critically, and analytically when confronted by a problem; to be able to see that same problem analytically from different points of view, and perhaps most important, to develop a sense of self and of personal identity in which these capacities and dispositions are well integrated."[1]

This, I believe, ought to be true of a well-educated business student, especially one who has had the benefit of a liberal arts education. The typical business ethics coursework is, however, unlikely to include concepts such as personal values, calling, vocation, and spirituality that would be germane to developing that well-integrated identity. However, at Concordia College's Offutt School of Business, with our commitment to educating "the whole self," students have engaged with these concepts in our 200-level ethics and leadership course since fall 2013. We assume that whole self-education involves the critical and purposeful formation of personal identity, which must include giving students the opportunity to clarify their personal values, helping them entertain the idea that work should be more than merely a means to earn a living, and inculcating in them the desire to bring their whole selves to their work life—including their spiritual or religious identity.

The mission of Concordia College—the idea that we want our students to become responsibly engaged in the world—is a big reason why I work here. Indeed, I am convinced that part of preparing students to be responsibly engaged must involve sharpening their *moral muscle* so that they can not only make ethical decisions themselves, but also influence others into behaving ethically. The goal then is to help our students develop and strengthen their moral muscle memory—that is, the sensitivity for ethical issues and the character to act morally— in order to become ethical leaders who can positively "influence the affairs of the world" as our mission statement requires. Incorporating the discussion of values and a view of work as a vocation is integral to that effort.

I. Values and Vocation

As a course offered within a business school context, Ethics and Leadership introduces our students to the notions of vocation and values early in the semester. It serves as a foundation for articulating personal moral responsibility as students and future leaders. The concept of vocation is of great importance within Lutheran higher education, as I learned soon after joining the Concordia community and participating in the annual Vocation of a Lutheran College conference. Understanding vocation ought to help us and our students because we live in a context that is "framed by a narrow preoccupation with efficiency, measurable outcomes, and careerist thinking."[2] Dawson argues that vocation is both the practice of the educator—that is, viewing my own job as a calling— as well as the aspiration of the students that we teach; the desire to do meaningful work. In this regard, my goal is to help students see work as both a social good, as well as a source for personal meaning. Since the term vocation has deep religious roots, we engage students in discussions about work in various religious traditions, in order to understand that every major religion does have views of work related to it being more than merely toil or for paying the bills. In the Christian tradition, we talk about how some viewed work as mere toil/curse, while "vocation" was seen in terms of leaving that toil to serve God, "calling away from daily productive activity to dedicate one's life to prayer and contemplation."[3] Instead, we talk about how Luther redeemed vocation from this religious garb so that all of daily life is sacred before God. By the end of our discussions on vocation, we focus on that idea of work as both a way to meet our material needs and a way to find personal meaning by contributing to the common good. Thus the definition informing our discussion:

> Typically, the terms calling and vocation are used to refer to a sense of purpose or direction that leads an individual towards some kind of personally fulfilling and/or socially significant engagement within the work role...A vocation is an approach to a particular life role that is oriented toward demonstrating or deriving a sense of purpose or meaningfulness and that holds other-oriented values and goals as primary sources of motivation.[4]

My own understanding of vocation prior to becoming a part of this Concordia community was deeply influenced by the work of Parker Palmer, particularly his book *Let your Life Speak*.[5] Students engage with a selection from the book, as it also provides a basis for understanding the theme of our primary textbook, that leaders can either cast light or shadows within their spheres of influence.[6]

II. Enhancing Moral Imagination Through Giving Voice to Values

I am convinced that students need to clarify their own values early in their educational journey, so that those values can act as a guide for their behavior moving forward. In order to raise students' moral awareness about what happens when business leaders "preach water but drink wine," our ethics and leadership class actually begins with the movie *Enron: The Smartest Guys in the Room*. Most of our students have not heard about Enron as it was before their time, and they are often shocked to see the disregard for ethics and human values that are displayed in that documentary movie, which exposes one of the greatest business frauds of all time. Beginning with a negative example, a case of unethical leadership, I believe helps to lay the foundation for "what we do not want you to become." Similarly, our textbook by emeritus George Fox University Professor Craig Johnson starts off the first two chapters talking about toxic and bad leadership. Johnson argues that we need to understand "dark (bad, toxic) side of leadership as the first step in promoting good or ethical leadership."[7] Johnson's is the only textbook that I am aware of that takes this approach of dealing with the negative first before proceeding to discuss positive approaches that result in ethical leadership. Considering how little work experience our undergraduate students have, I think this is a wonderful approach to help raise their moral imagination—that is, their "sensitivity to moral issues and options," which enhances students "ethical reasoning" and recognition of the "moral elements of events."[8] Without an active moral imagination, it is possible for students, and leaders alike, to fail to recognize when an issue has an ethical dimension that they need to engage with.

I also appreciate Johnson's text because he dedicates an entire chapter to the leader's character, where he explores an Aristotelian approach of virtue ethics and offers several ways through which students can build their moral character—including the need to clarify their own values, and then ensure that they live up to those values.

From an Aristotelian perspective, "the purpose of business activity is to create wealth in a way that makes a manager a better person and the world a better place . . . it is possible to simultaneously create wealth, while being ethical and happy"[9] My goal, should I be successful, is to get students to understand that character matters, that the failures of moral imagination that result in people ending up on the front page of the newspaper for fraud or other white color crimes can be subverted through character development and through ethical leadership development. We talk about the fact that leaders should not only be focused on developing their technical job skills, but also their ethical reasoning capacities.

In a further effort to enhance students' moral imagination, I use a behavioral ethics approach called Giving Voice to Values (GVV). Mary Gentile who developed the approach argues that:

> It's not that ethical theory and high level strategic dilemmas are not important; they are. But they don't help future managers and leaders figure out what to do next—when

> the boss wants to alter the financial report, or their sales team applies pressure to misrepresent the capabilities of their product, or...the near term skills needed to deal with these kinds of challenges concern knowing what to say, to whom, and how to say it when a manager knows what he or she thinks is right in a particular situation—but doesn't feel confident about how to act on his or her convictions. This overlooked but consequential skill is the first step in building the ethical muscle. [10]

Indeed, GVV aims at helping students develop the moral courage to speak up, to influence peers and those above or below them in a hierarchy, in order to get people to do the right thing. Gentile argues that, often, it's not that managers and leaders cannot figure out the right thing to do. Rather, it's that they often don't know how to get that right thing done by influencing others around them. Our class aims at helping students develop their awareness of ethical issues; it also provides them with the tools (i.e. various step-by-step approaches) that they can employ to analyze those ethical situations in order to figure out the right thing to do. In order to complete the loop, we then utilize the GVV approach to help students get to action, which we do by practicing and rehearsing how to respond to the most commonly heard "reasons and rationalizations" that people most often give for their unethical behavior. Working in groups, students practice delivering those scripts in response to case studies. Thus, GVV provides students the chance to practice voicing their values. As Gentile argues, GVV is about "building the skills, the confidence, the moral muscle, and frankly, the *habit* of voicing our values. It begins with the assumption that most of us want to bring our whole selves to work —skills, ambitions, and values."[11]

While in no way an empirical measure, I recently heard from a student who took my class about three years ago, who commented that "whenever an ethical question is raised, I remember the 'voicing your values' exercises." This is indeed what I would hope for, that when students are faced with ethical dilemmas on campus or in their future work roles, they would be able to recall and be motivated to act on their values, to do the right thing and influence others to do the right thing, as well. Empirically, perhaps this provides a great avenue for a future research goal, to survey alumni who have experienced our revised ethics and leadership curriculum, and find out how they resolve ethical issues. One would hope that more of them would be able to say they are able to, more often than not, voice their values. That assumption mentioned by Gentile that we all want to bring all of whom we are to work, including our values, is what guides me in and inspires me to teach this class in a way that helps students start by clarifying their values, and proceed by practicing how to voice those values—particularly the values that we all share of honesty, integrity and respect. In this way, I hope I am helping to educate the students as whole selves.

III. Implications for Teaching Practice

To quote Professor Roy Hammerling in his convocation speech delivered on August 31, 2006:

> The great Latin poet Ovid (43 BC- 18 AD), who lived at the time of Jesus said, ". . . a faithful study of the liberal arts humanizes character and permits it not to be cruel."[12]
>
> The Liberal Arts came to mean those studies which were able to set people free to look at their own lives so that they could dig up and root out bad moral and intellectual habits and replace them with virtuous and noble ones. This free life was believed to have the great advantage to mold into more compassionate people.

So, if our goal is to "humanize character" and to "root out bad moral and intellectual habits," replacing them with "virtuous and noble ones," I want to believe that every course at Concordia College would benefit from educating the whole self. What I have offered here is my approach, for my one class on ethics and leadership. But I do believe that there are lessons here for others. I want to believe that my colleagues in various disciplines can find resources that are relevant to their particular courses that enable them to incorporate teaching the whole self—a whole self consisting in not just the brain/intellect, but also the soul or spirit and the character of our students. After all, don't we all want the same thing: students who are empowered to be wholly human with hands, hearts, and heads living in integrity?

I cannot dictate what those resources might be since I mostly know my own interdisciplinary world of leadership and management studies. However, I suspect that, like the conferences I attend in my disciplines, all disciplines have sessions on teaching where such resources might be found.

Beyond your own particular disciplines, I want to suggest that it is possible to learn from and incorporate ideas and techniques from other disciplines that can facilitate your own teaching to the whole self. I am aware of colleagues in religion who incorporate meditation into their classes to reach the spiritual/soul of our students and, as an amateur meditation practitioner myself, I know that this actually bridges soul/spirit with character too. So what are the activities, resources, practices that you can incorporate that would work in your own courses to teach to the whole self?

ENDNOTES

1 Anne Colby et al., *Rethinking Undergraduate Business Education: Liberal Learning for the Profession* (San Francisco, CA: Jossey Bass, 2011), ix.

2 J. Dawson, "A History of Vocation: Tracing a Keyword of Work, Meaning, and Moral Purpose," *Adult Education Quarterly* 55, no. 3 (2005): 220-231. doi:10.1177/0741713605274606.

3 Ibid., 223.

4 B.J. Dik and R. D. Duffy, "Calling and Vocation at Work: Definitions and Prospects for Research and Practice," *The Counseling Psychologist* 37, no. 3 (2009): 424-450. doi:10.1177/0011000008316430.

5 P. J. Palmer, *Let Your Life Speak: Listening for the Voice of Vocation* (San Francisco, CA: Jossey-Bass, 2000).

6 Craig Johnson, *Meeting the Ethical Challenges of Leadership: Casting Light or Shadow* (Thousand Oaks, CA: SAGE Publications, 2015).

7 Ibid., 2.

8 Ibid., 53.

9 Charles Wankel and Agata Stachowicz-Staunch, Agata, *Management Education for Morality in the Era of Globalization* (2011), 3.

10 Mary C. Gentile, *Giving Voice to Values: How to Speak Your Mind When You Know What's Right*, Kindle Edition (New Haven, CT: Yale University Press, 2010), Kindle locations 123-125.

11 Ibid., locations 135-137.

12 Ovid, Publius Ovidius Naso, Ex Ponto, II, ix, 47.

EDUCATING THE WHOLE, BROKEN SELF

DR. ERIKA CLAIRE STRANDJORD
Assistant Professor of English

In the strategic plan for Concordia College 2012-2017, the authors lay out the parameters of what "whole self" means: "In a time of constant distraction and clashing ideals, we will lead our students into a lifelong habit of reflection on their identity, purpose, and leadership in a deeply interconnected world."[1]

Education for the whole self, then, is ultimately a thought process, an ongoing reflection on "identity, purpose, and leadership." The rest of the strategic plan goes into more detail, suggesting additional dimensions of (inter)faith, vocation, and a "practice of time that puts the examined life at the center."[2] I find it interesting that the description of "whole self" dances around the idea of the self as a body with distinct experiences and needs—perhaps not surprising at an institution of learning. However, for my purposes I am going to deliberately misread "whole self" as indicating our students (and ourselves) as entire people with complex pasts and differing levels of preparation, and as people we place on a continuum of belonging in our classrooms.

I also want to break away from the framework laid out in the strategic plan because educators around the nation are having discussions of students as whole selves in ways that presume a "whole self" student is self-reliant and without physical, mental, or psychiatric disability. This national conversation revolves around a number of terms, but the one I am most interested in interrogating is *resilience*, which is part of this book's title. Originally a way to discuss how ecosystems adapt to catastrophic change, resilience has been narrowed to the individual level in conversations about students. These students are usually judged as lacking resilience when they fail to behave in ways we expect or want.[3] When we diagnose students as lacking resilience, we implicitly tell them that they are broken, and thus currently unfit for academia.

The Lutheran liberal arts have something to offer to this conversation by presenting a view of human beings (and thus our students) that is more nuanced than a whole/broken dichotomy. Rather, I suggest, we can use a Lutheran lens and play off of Martin Luther's insistence that Christians are simultaneously justified and sinners to view our students as paradoxically and simultaneously whole *and* broken. By acknowledging that our students already come to us as whole people and as broken people, we can affirm their wholeness even as we see their brokenness and work with them in our classrooms and on campus.

This paradoxical view is both a disposition toward our students and a set of practices that we can put in place. The whole-broken paradox as a disposition shapes our beliefs about and attitudes toward our students. While the implications of the paradox extend beyond what I have room to discuss, acknowledging our students as whole-broken asks at least these things of us:

1. It asks us to look at our students as always-already whole people. We do not need to diagnose them as lacking.
2. It asks us to look at all of our students as always-already broken, no matter their outward appearances or successes.
3. It asks us to acknowledge that brokenness is part of human existence, and that narratives of overcoming are fundamentally oppressive. In other words, this disposition asks us to face brokenness, rather than hiding, fixing, or rejecting it.

4. It asks us to acknowledge that brokenness does not preclude wholeness, to believe that we and our students are whole. In other words, this disposition asks us to not fixate on brokenness but to presume competence and wholeness.

The first two points lay out the basic principles of the whole-broken paradox, but the third and fourth are especially important, and so I want to tease out their implications.

While we should always acknowledge the brokenness of the people in our classrooms and offices, we must also always affirm wholeness. Similarly, while we should approach students as whole and competent, we must also not use that wholeness to gloss over or deny students' experiences of brokenness. Both are damaging, but forcing students to perform wholeness even when they are struggling and suffering is particularly inhumane. To illustrate: at a prior institution, a colleague mentioned that a student of theirs had done all of the work for the course and turned everything in on time even though the student had missed many classes because his father had been murdered during a random carjacking. "I told my other students that none of them had an excuse if this student had gotten all of the work done," the colleague told me. Like this colleague, we tell stories about students (or about ourselves) overcoming depression or physical disability to succeed in academia or other arenas. When we do this, we implicitly or overtly tell our students that doing anything less is failure, that wholeness is the only option.

In disability studies, scholars have taken up the term "super-crip" to describe how we fetishize overcoming. Robert Murphy describes the "super-crip" as a disabled person who "works harder than other people, travels extensively, goes to everything, and takes part in anything that comes along. This is how he shows the world that he is like everybody else, only better."[4] More recently, disability activist Stella Young has dubbed these stories of overcoming "inspiration porn," which she argues exist so that non-disabled people can say "Oh well if that kid who doesn't have any legs can smile while he's having an awesome time, I should never, EVER feel bad about my life."[5] When we as educators tell these stories of overcoming to each other and to our students (both disabled and non-disabled), we are reinforcing the idea that struggle is unacceptable if it does not result in success, or that students we have deemed "normal" have no right to reveal their brokenness to us.

The Luther-inflected disposition to see our students as whole-broken, in contrast, expects all of our students to struggle without imposing on them the need to overcome in order to be acceptable to us. This is not a defeatist position; we can simultaneously see our students as whole selves who are capable of taking on the challenges we set for them.

To be clear, I am not saying that I perfectly embody this disposition—I am just as guilty or more so than anyone of focusing so much on what I perceive as a student's lack that I forget their abilities. I am also not suggesting that we as educators take on the roles of counselors (the perennial cry of the professor, "I'm not a therapist!" is ringing in my ears as I type this). However, I am suggesting that we should not use our lack of credentials as counselors to avoid the responsibility of approaching our jobs with compassion and understanding.

As we cultivate a disposition to see our students as whole-broken, we can implement practices that make the college more open to the whole-broken student. What follows is far from exhaustive, but I see it as a way to start a discussion rather than the final word.

1. Listen to students and take their concerns seriously. We are already doing this in classrooms, offices, and elsewhere on campus. But this is a commitment we need to strengthen, because as busy people with many responsibilities, it can be easy to respond to students' revelations of struggle and brokenness with annoyance or the simple claim that they need to become more resilient. When students trust us with their brokenness, listening deeply to what they have to say and responding with acceptance and kindness is one of the most powerful things we can do. We do not need to fix them or tell them what to do, but we do need to listen.

2. Acknowledge the importance of uncertainty and struggle in our own learning processes and give students low-stakes opportunities to fail.

   Accurately modeling the process of inquiry and learning means being honest about failure and struggle. Many students come to us feeling that only success is acceptable and assuming that we have always succeeded. One way I attempt to debunk this assumption in my writing classes is that I bring in examples of my own writing at various stages in my drafting process. When students see how messy, recursive, and sometimes painful my writing process is, they are more likely to believe me when I tell them that it is okay to try something in a draft, decide it's not working, and start again. We also need to think seriously about the place that failure has in our courses and how we can incorporate chances for students to make mistakes, try different approaches, and start over without them feeling like they will be penalized.

3. Think in terms of accessibility rather than accommodations in order to focus on structural change rather than individual remediation.

   We have probably all had the experience of getting a piece of paper from the Counseling Center that lists accommodations a student is entitled to in a class or at work. These are important and ensure that students with documented disabilities have the same educational opportunities as their non-documented peers. However, this is a reactive system—instructors and supervisors are expected to change something to accommodate a single student. Accommodations also miss students who do not have a documentable disability. Focusing on designing classes and a campus that are accessible to as many people as possible, on the other hand, can help us rethink pedagogy, classroom setup, and even building design from the ground up. Changes to improve accessibility often benefit everyone (e.g. curb cuts, closed captioning, audiobooks), and so this work could benefit everyone on campus. Of course we cannot anticipate every single student we will work with, but the more ways to engage with classes and work that we create, the easier it will be for us and our students to work together.

4. When appropriate, be honest about our own experiences of brokenness without turning our own stories into stories of overcoming.

I hesitated about putting this last suggestion in because it asks a lot of us. We do not always want to be vulnerable to our students or even to each other. But when our students speak to us about their struggles and challenges, it can be comforting for them to know that they are not alone and that they do not need to always act like everything is all right. One of my most vivid memories of being a student in college was sitting in Dr. Richard Simon Hanson's Psalmody of the Bible class. One day, when we were talking about lament psalms as prayers, he shared with the class that one of his children had been killed in a car accident when he had been driving the car. He did not draw a simple moral lesson from it or lecture us about perseverance, but instead spoke honestly about his own experience of lament as prayer. Not only did this help me encounter the psalms as if real people had spoken and sung them for real reasons, but it also helped me understand that sorrow can have a real place in my life without me needing to get over it or turn it into a positive.

If we are going to educate the whole self, we need to acknowledge the complexities of the human beings in our classrooms and work with them as whole people, not as disembodied intellects that exist outside of the troubles, sorrows, and joys of life. This means that we cannot only judge students as able or lacking in our classrooms. Instead, we need to take the time to understand their concerns, respond compassionately, and make the institution more open to different kinds of people. Seeing our students this way can also encourage us to see ourselves in a more compassionate light. We are whole-broken people too, and we are not always successful at treating ourselves as such. What it means to make an institution accepting of and responsive to human beings as broken and whole people is outside the scope of a single chapter, but I hope we can use this as a starting point for conversation, experimentation, and change.

ENDNOTES

1 "Whole Self, Whole Life, Whole World: The Plan for Concordia College 2012-2017," Concordia College, Moorhead, MN, last modified October 12, 2012, https://concordiacollege.edu/files/resources/strategicplan.pdf.

2 Ibid.

3 There is too much literature in this vein to cite here, but Peter Gray summarizes the general attitude that students lack resilience very well, writing, "So now, here's what we have: Young people, 18 years and older, going to college still unable or unwilling to take responsibility for themselves, still feeling that if a problem arises they need an adult to solve it." Peter Gray, "Declining Student Resilience: A Serious Problem for Colleges," *Psychology Today*, https://www.psychologytoday.com/blog/freedom-learn/201509/declining-student-resilience-serious-problem-colleges, September 22, 2015.

4 Robert Murphy, *The Body Silent* (New York and London: W.W. Norton, 1990), 95.

5 Stella Young, "We're Not Here for Your Inspiration," Australian Broadcasting Corporation, last updated July 2, 2012, http://www.abc.net.au/news/2012-07-03/young-inspiration-porn/4107006.

WHOLE LIFE

INTRODUCTION

We are truly at the crossroads of a new age. We face today numerous, seemingly insurmountable issues which challenge our sense of self, the very fabric of what constitutes our identity, and the way in which we function in the world and towards one another. Racism, poverty, environmental degradation, gender dysphasia, a seemingly dysfunctional political system, and mass immigration, to name but a few, provide a context for our students' experiences even before they enter Concordia College, to say nothing of the challenges that await them afterwards. These are not just issues which affect individuals and communities in the United States. The paradigms which once informed us, the worldview of our parents, are no longer relevant in the face of these global issues.

The question before the authors in this Whole Life section of the Luther anthology is how we provide a framework for recognizing, understanding, and critically thinking about the many challenges that we face today. According to Concordia's strategic plan, we are called to develop for our students, and guide them through, "a coherent and increasingly challenging experience to build competence, creativity, and character."[1] Now more than ever, these traits are essential if we are to surmount these challenges. At the same time, the core requires that the courses we teach provide the basis for students to become responsibly engaged in the world. Given the enormity of the issues with which we are faced, this does not seem sufficient. We have to choose our paths wisely and equip ourselves to meet unforeseen challenges along the way. This collection of essays attempts to understand what those challenges may be and provides recommendations as to how one can overcome these hurdles.

Joseph Whittaker argues in his essay, "Accepting Science into Our Community, Naturally," for an examination of the way in which science is taught to our students and presented to the public in order to counteract increased skepticism of scientific research, particularly around controversial issues like climate change. He suggests, first, that instructors be more purposeful in how students learn the process of science and, second, that scientists must do a better job in communicating their research with the public: "As scientists we must make a greater effort to explain why our research is important." With these changes he seeks common ground for a healthier, reasoned debate.

In her essay, "Power Relationships in Education: Cultivating Leaders," Susan Larson looks at the importance of developing ethical leaders and understanding how the use of power, beginning in the classroom, is fundamental to responsible leadership throughout one's life: "Direct attention to the ways in which we educate students to effectively and ethically understand and use power in their lives is generally lacking from literature on leadership development." Ethical leadership begins in the classroom through exposure to and responsible dealing with power. She writes that "as we educate our students to be leaders I believe we should pay more attention to helping students understand power. Further, I believe that college professors have an important role to play in educating students about power and its effective uses."

In "Engagement in a Fast-Paced World," Ronald Twedt considers the degree to which this fast-paced world influences the decisions we are being asked to make. Quick decisions may be a hallmark of effectiveness, but decision-makers must still process huge amounts of information and judge the efficacy and value of information. How do we best prepare students to engage quickly and act decisively, discerning what is relevant and what is extraneous in order to make the right choices in a rapidly changing world?

Laura Probst is also interested in power relationships found at the undergraduate level. In "Building Voice: Understanding Changing Perceptions of Authorship and Audience in the Digital Environment," Probst challenges us to consider how we are best able to teach students "about their own agency, their audiences, and their rights and responsibilities as authors" in a world in which the boundaries of communication are blurred and the influence of communication is expanding. Technology has redefined the relationship between authorship and audience, and educators are tasked with "teaching the critical thinking and communication skills that will allow [students] to navigate our new world of sharing authorship, where relationships to and among audiences are complex and where individual responsibility lies in both the creation and consumption of ideas, knowledge, and culture."

In "Contextualizing a Whole Life: Luther, Islam and Mission," Jonathan Clark strikes a different tone by questioning the need to make excuses for things we hold dear and admonishes us to be more critical of our own traditions in order to provide a context for a healthy whole life. He takes aim at Luther himself by investigating Luther's attitudes towards Islam (and Judaism), especially given today's mass migration of individuals from predominantly Muslim countries, and questions the effectiveness of Concordia's mission, the core and other courses in providing a sound context for a whole life.

We are wrestling with the realities of massive social change caused by complex factors that we may not fully control or even yet understand. Our challenge in these essays and as faculty in Lutheran higher education is to help our students develop the capacities to be successful in navigating this change and to develop the skills they will use in their adult lives and workplaces rather than the skills that make them successful students. We acknowledge that our current educational practices reinforce a disconnect between college life and what follows. Our challenge going forward is to reform our teaching practices to more effectively model the elements of learning that we describe in these essays and approach our curriculum and co-curricular activities through the lens of work-life expectations rather than those of the classroom.

—Dr. Jonathan Clark, Associate Professor
of German World Languages and Culture, and
Ms. Laura Probst, Director of Carl B. Ylvisaker Library

ENDNOTES

1 "Whole Self, Whole Life, Whole World: The Plan for Concordia College 2012-2017," Concordia College, Moorhead, MN, last modified October 12, 2012, https://concordiacollege.edu/files/resources/strategicplan.pdf.

ACCEPTING SCIENCE INTO OUR COMMUNITY, NATURALLY

DR. JOSEPH WHITTAKER
Assistant Professor of Biology

> Scientists may depict the problems that will affect the environment based on available evidence, but their solution is not the responsibility of scientists but of society as a whole.
>
> —Mario Molina[1]

As I enter my second half-century of life, I am still full of curiosity. I am no longer that person who hikes in nature, naively marveling at everything I see. Well, I still marvel, but on different levels and with less naiveté. As I matured intellectually, I went through many stages of asking questions, and the level of sophistication with which I searched for answers deepened. I often turned to science. I relied on observation and evidence before I made decisions. Now I form and test rejectable hypotheses. I question explanations and evaluate them based on evidence. I acknowledge exceptions to most "rules" in the world. I do not reject faith, but I see science as a way of seeking answers and faith as a way to put those answers into a moral context. Both are important to me in seeking answers.

As I reflect on the anniversary of the Reformation, my passion is stirred with one issue I see in need of a modern reformation. In recent years science has been increasingly cited and dismissed as opinion, dismissed as mere unproven "theories" or hypotheses, or cited as political tools (hoaxes perpetrated by foreign governments to mislead). The general public often seems to dismiss science as well. To truly reform the public's mistrust and lack of scientific understanding, we must begin science education as early as possible, in the primary years, and build on that foundation through adulthood. We must teach science as a process of inquiry and acknowledge its strengths and weaknesses.

Scientific research must always be examined critically. Results can be misinterpreted or misused, purposely or through honest misinterpretation. Scientists are as fallible as are those who interpret their findings. While complicated variable relationships can occur in any study, it is especially true in ecological field experiments where there can be lack of control for confounding variables. This inherent lack of control can make it difficult to identify or understand the relationships among complex variables.[2] It is the job of scientists themselves to critically evaluate studies through the peer review process. While imperfect, this process ensures experts in a particular field are able to vet research and question conclusions while examining the research in context of established knowledge.

Unfortunately, there have been some big, and very public, errors and misconceptions that have shaken the general public's trust of science. One example is Woodward and Dawson's 1912 discovery of "Piltdown Man" in England.[3] The fossil became an immediate sensation and much of the scientific community supported their conclusion about this fossil. Unfortunately, this fossil was a hoax that shook the scientific community and the public trust. It should be noted that it was the scientific process that ultimately uncovered the hoax and self-corrected. A more recent and damaging hoax was the study which reported a link between childhood vaccinations and autism.[4] The potential importance of this research finding saw the paper rushed through peer review and published. Unfortunately it was a hoax, but even worse, it represented a deliberate falsification of data,[5] apparently for financial gain.[6] In this case, a single fabricated, and subsequently retracted, study gained public support, and has had the potential to negatively impact hundreds of thousands of people.[7]

There are also very important cases in which scientists were eventually vindicated through the process of science when their conclusions were considered radical or impossible given the current state of knowledge.[8] Thus, scientists walk a thin line and need to be critical, but be open to results of credible studies and flexible enough to revise concepts as more information becomes available, even when that information challenges our views.

Climate change represents one of the greatest threats to the planet but received essentially no coverage in the 2016 election. In spite of recent polls indicating that 59 percent of Americans believe global climate change is occurring, that 65 percent believe human activities contribute to climate change, and that 57 percent feel it is a serious threat,[9] there were no policy discussions, and President Trump stated that it was a plot by the Chinese to disrupt our economy.[10] How can we, or can we at all, reach out to educate climate change deniers on the science behind climate change?

Teaching people to understand science has to happen early, well before they are adults engaged in their careers. Eshach lists and discusses justifications for the need of scientific explorations in, or even prior to, elementary school.[11] Early exposure to science can lead to positive attitudes towards science in general, enjoyment and interest in nature, and the ability to develop scientific concepts and reason scientifically.[12] Additionally, he advocates for using problem based-learning to develop investigative and collaborative skills and apply previously learned concepts.[13]

If science education needs to happen early, how are we doing regarding teaching science in elementary school? According to Wilson et al.,[14] students need to move beyond content knowledge and to focus on the process of science. Science learning needs to integrate knowledge with hands-on activities, to engage in the process or practice of science, and to build on previous experience and allow revision of thought. However, the committee acknowledges that currently this vision is not what students are exposed to. There is disparity between communities and within schools for students with varying abilities. Additionally there is wide variation in facilities between schools with lower grades, in particular, often lacking necessary resources to teach science. Science is given little time in most elementary schools and even when addressed, activities are often loosely related to scientific concepts and more likely selected to keep student attention. To align practice with goals would require science teachers to adjust teaching practices. However, for teachers to re-align their teaching, they would need support to learn and practice new methods and resources to make relevant educational practices possible.[15] This would also require a realignment of some teachers' cynicism about science in early education and convincing them that science education at a young age is germane.[16]

As scientists, it has to be part of our mandate to summarize our research and engage the public. As scientists we must make a greater effort to explain why our research is important. One of the most exciting parts of science for many of us scientists is how research often leads to more questions and at times may be contradictory. The lack of certainty is often contrary to human nature. In particular, modeling of complex systems can lead to vastly different scenarios (e.g., climate change). While those scenarios may seem at odds, we must communicate that the models are only as good as the predictive information we have available and will provide different outcomes depending on a number of factors about which scientists must make assumptions.[17]

If the vast majority of publications provide evidence for one conclusion, for instance with vaccines and climate change, why then are these conclusions not universally accepted? The clash appears to be largely between science and violation of people's deeply held beliefs. Roseneau argues that the disconnect is not so much about a problem with science itself, but with the inability for people to accept science that challenges their sense of identity and/or induces fear regarding their perceptions of the world.[18] For instance, deeply religious people may fear the idea of evolution because they equate it to immorality (and conversely creationism as morality). If evolution is true, why would people need to behave in a moral manner? The fear becomes concern about whether society can survive without the morality provided by religion. Vaccination may be seen as governmental control over people's right to choose. Additionally, vaccines play on fear of chemicals (preservatives, heavy metals, and/or antigens) causing autism and overtaxing the bodies of children. Likewise, regulations aimed at curbing climate change are seen as governmental regulation of business. With this challenge to their core belief system, people are more likely to grasp onto any source that justifies their belief system, even if it is overwhelmingly contraindicated. Unfortunately, the people doing this are often selecting pseudoscientific sources or sources deliberately attempting to mimic science sources.[19]

To combat this selection of questionable sources that support personal belief-systems, it is important for people to understand the peer review process and what constitutes actual science. That harkens back to scientific training from an early age and the willingness and ability for people to view sources critically, including both sources that are supportive of and ones that challenge them. Additionally, Roseneau points out the importance of community leaders and religious leaders speaking out on issues and supporting established science.[20] The Catholic Church has offered support of scientific views on evolution, climate change, resource use and population control. Some prominent evangelical Christians have also spoken out supporting the science behind evolution and climate change. This continued participation of community leaders will be crucial to seeing the eventual acceptance of good science and ultimately to our ability to have a chance to continue the progress of human society.

For generations we scientists have diligently worked, and published, assuming our work was having an impact. But now it appears much of our work goes unheeded or ignored, especially outside the scientific community.[21] How do we scientists become more mainstream and influence the public's perceptions? One key thing we scientists need to do is to work on communication. Many scientists I know are introverts and shun public attention. Without seeking public engagement, however, we will not be able to advocate for our findings and discuss the relevance of our research projects. We also need to be prepared to discuss in potentially hostile or critical settings, and where possible to defuse hostility. While this is often uncomfortable and stressful, it is our obligation to take this information out to the public and to do everything we can to put it out to discuss and debate.

We also have to understand the stakeholders involved. We scientists need to learn to empathize with the public and to listen to concerns. I was once asked to sit in on a panel discussing mountaintop removal and valley-fill for coal extraction. In my best science-speak, I described how polluting of streams results in loss of salamanders and I described why salamanders are important bio-indicators of water quality. I remember a coal miner telling me he couldn't care less about a bunch of salamanders when to him it was a matter of being able to feed his family. I tried to make clear that by worrying about salamanders, I was also worrying about his family and the toxins in the water he and his family were drinking.

The primary goal with regard to effective science communication is to connect with your audience.[22] Bowden interviewed several leading science communicators, and their advice included relating your research to everyday life and making it relevant.[23] Minimize jargon and keeps terms simple. Allow the audience to see your enthusiasm for your research and entertain them with personal stories. Bernstein related how some science communicators are turning to improvisation skills, a technique often used in comedy.[24] The idea is to notice when the audience is not understanding you and adjust your presentation before you lose them. Improvisation allows you to receive instantaneous feedback and adjust accordingly. These skills can help replace memorization and mechanical delivery with enthusiasm that will engage your audience. Offit and Coffin, describing communication of science to the media, state the importance of making your research "informative, personal, emotional, and compelling."[25] They recommend a strategy of conveying to the media what is at stake if the study is not communicated to the public.

In order to make scientific studies more comprehensible, Offit and Coffin also explain the necessity of explaining to the public the difference between coincidence and causality.[26] For instance, if people notice that following introduction of a factor you seem to get a result (e.g., a vaccination is given and autism symptoms appear) they might imply causation. This is not enough to indicate causation without also considering the number of cases where the factor is present but that the result does not occur (vaccine but no autism).

Additionally, you need to consider the rate of the result when the factor is not present (rates of autism without vaccinations). Only when all these options are considered together statistically, can you determine causation.

A discussion of coincidence and causality should be coupled with a detailed explanation of the scientific method.[27] As scientists, we know that hypotheses are framed with regard to the null hypothesis (negative hypothesis). We collect data, conduct our statistical analyses, and then either reject or fail to reject the null hypothesis. Technically speaking, we do not ever "support" the null hypothesis, only fail to reject. It is widely accepted that often for climate change science, the null hypothesis is "humans have no influence." We must as scientists be able to explain that if we do reject this null hypothesis, thus supporting humans do have an influence, that it does not mean that other non-human factors cannot also contribute to climate change (as obviously they have since the beginning of time and well before the evolution of humans). Thus rejecting the null hypothesis should stimulate further testing.[28] If we fail to reject this null hypothesis, it does not mean the null hypothesis is supported, but simply that we were not able to reject it (thus we cannot support that humans do influence). Researchers, and those interpreting it, must consider potentially biased samples, magnitude of random variation, and statistical power.[29] Thus we may fail to reject the null hypothesis even when the alternative hypothesis is not false. (Statisticians call this a Type II error). This should not make the public distrustful, but hopefully make them look more closely at the study and seek further research.

As scientists, we must push ourselves to leave the comfort of our labs and engage the public, effectively communicate, and enlist support from community leaders. We need to move outside our communities, look at larger issues of poverty and inequality, encourage the education and elevation of disadvantaged groups (frequently including women in the developing world), and reach out to indigenous communities in the United States and abroad. Without equality and the ability to provide education and opportunity for people to care about and understand science, we will not be able to reform our societies in a way that will sustain us on this planet.

ENDNOTES

1 Bonnie Denmark, "Mario Molina: Atmospheric Chemistry to Change Global Policy," *Visionlearning*, last modified 2015, http://www.visionlearning.com/en/library/Inside-Science/58/Nobel-Prize-recipient-Mario-Molina/211.

2 See Kevin McGarigal and Samuel Cushman, "Comparative Evaluation of Experimental Approaches to the Study of Habitat Fragmentation Effects," *Ecological Applications* 12 (2002): 335-345.

3 Chris Stringer, "The 100-year Mystery of Piltdown Man," *Nature* 492 (December 2012): 177-179.

4 Andrew J. Wakefield et al., "Ileal-Lymphoid-Nodular Hyperplasia, Non-Specific Colitis, and Pervasive Developmental Disorder in Children," *The Lancet* 351 (1998): 637-641.

5 See Robert T. Chen and Frank DeStefano, "Vaccine Adverse Events: Causal or Coincidental?" *The Lancet* 351 (1998): 611-612; Brent Taylor et al., "Autism and Measles, Mumps, and Rubella Vaccine: No Epidemiological Evidence for a Causal Association," *The Lancet* 351 (1999): 2026-2029; N. Sengupta et al., "Does the MMR Triple Vaccine Cause Autism?" *Evidence-Based Healthcare & Public Health* 8 (2004): 239-245; Frank DeStefano, Cristofer S. Price, and Eric S. Weintraub, "Increasing Exposure to Antibody-Stimulating Proteins and Polysaccharides in Vaccines is Not Associated with Risk of Autism," *The Journal of Pediatrics* (2013): 561-567; Luke E. Taylor, Amy L. Swerdfeger, and Guy D. Eslick, "Vaccines are Not Associated with Autism: An Evidence-Based Meta-Analysis of Case-Control and Cohort Studies," *Vaccine* 32 (2014): 3623–3629.

6 Brian Deer, "How the Vaccine Crisis was Meant to Make Money," *BMJ* 342 (2011): 136-142.

7 Daniel Jolley and Karen M. Douglas, "The Effects of Anti-Vaccine Conspiracy Theories on Vaccination Intentions," *PloS One* 9, no. 2 (2014): 1-9; Eugene J. Gangarosa et al., "Impact of Anti-Vaccine Movements on Pertussis Control: The Untold Story," *The Lancet* 351 (1998): 356-361.

8 See Sven Hernberg, "Lead Poisoning in a Historical Perspective," *American Journal of Industrial Medicine* 38 (2000): 244-254; Mario J. Molina and F. Sherwood Rowland, "Stratospheric Sink for Chlorofluoromethanes: Chlorine Atom-Catalysed Destruction of Ozone," *Nature* 249 (1974): 810-812.

9 Lydia Saad and Jeffery M. Jones, "U.S. Concern about Global Warming at Eight-Year High," *Gallup*, last modified March 16, 2016, http://www.gallup.com/poll/190010/concern-global-warming-eight-year-high.aspx.

10 Edward Wong, "Trump has Called Climate Change a Chinese Hoax. Beijing Says It Is Anything But," *The New York Times*, November 18, 2016, https://www.nytimes.com/2016/11/19/world/asia/china-trump-climate-change.html?_r = 0.

11 Haim Eshach, *Science Literacy in Primary Schools and Pre-Schools* (Dordrecht: Springer, 2006), 1-28.

12 Ibid., 6

13 Ibid., 31-35.

14 Committee on Strengthening Science Education Through a Teacher Learning Continuum, *Science Teachers' Learning: Enhancing Opportunities, Creating Supportive Contexts*, eds. Suzanne Wilson, Heidi Schweingruber, and Natalie Nielsen (Washington DC: The National Academies Press, 2015), 47-58.

15 Ibid., 57.

16 See Eshach, *Science Literacy*, 86, 91-96; Tarik Tosun, "The Beliefs of Preservice Elementary Teachers Toward Science and Science Teaching," *School Science and Mathematics* 100, no. 7 (2000): 374-379.

17 See McGarigal and Cushman, "Comparative evaluation," 335-345; Michael E. Gilpin, "Do Hares Eat Lynx?" *The American Naturalist* 107, no. 957 (1973): 727-730.

18 Joshua Rosenau, "Science Denial: A Guide for Scientists," *Trends in Microbiology* 20, no. 12 (2004): 568.

19 Ibid., 568.

20 Ibid., 568-569.

21 Savo Heleta, "Academics Can Change the World—If They Stop Talking Only to Their Peers," *The Conversation*, last modified March 31, 2017, https://theconversation.com/academics-can-change-the-world-if-they-stop-talking-only-to-their-peers-55713.

22 Rachel Bernstein, "Spontaneous Scientists: Some Think That Researchers Can Improve Their Communication by Flexing Their Improvisation Skills," *Nature* 505 (2014): 121-123; Rachel Bowden, "FameLab: Secrets of Successful Science Communicators," *Naturejobs Blog*, June 10, 2011, http://blogs.nature.com/naturejobs/2011/06/10/famelab-secrets-of-successful-science-communicators/.

23 Ibid.

24 Bernstein, "Spontaneous scientists," 121-123.

25 Paul A. Offit and Susan E. Coffin, "Communicating Science to the Public: MMR Vaccine and Autism," *Vaccine* 22 (2003): 3.

26 Ibid., 3-4.

27 Ibid., 4.

28 Mathilde G. E. Verdam, Frans J. Oort, and Mirjam A. G. Sprangers, "Significance, Truth and Proof of p Values: Reminders about Common Misconceptions Regarding Null Hypothesis Significance Testing," *Quality of Life Research* 23 (2014): 6.

29 Ibid, 6.; Robert R. Sokal and F. James Rohlf, *Biometry* 3rd ed. (New York: W.H. Freeman and Company, 1995), 158-160.

POWER RELATIONSHIPS IN EDUCATION

Cultivating Leaders

DR. SUSAN LARSON
Chair of Division of Sciences and Mathematics, and Professor of Psychology

Lutheran liberal arts colleges seek to develop students into ethical leaders who engage responsibly in their personal, professional, and civic lives. Concordia College embraces Luther's notion of vocation, a calling to "lead a useful and meaningful life in service to the wellbeing of one's neighbors,"[1] and it is central to Concordia College's educational mission. Concordia provides for student developmental opportunities to help them discern their vocation and emphasizes the importance of responsible engagement in the world in our core curriculum and in co- and extra-curricular activities. Faculty at Lutheran colleges are called to "model for and to teach their students the value of a life lived in relationship with others and in service to one's neighbor."[2] Ernest Simmons challenges us further by suggesting that Lutheran liberal arts education must prepare students "to become leaders for a sustainable, interfaith society."[3] In light of the current environmental state of the world, he suggests it is not enough that our students are leaders, in service to the neighbor in their professional and civic lives. Their understanding of vocation should include service to the natural world and Concordia must embrace education for sustainability leadership. Key to this is the development of our students into *leaders*.

Patricia King suggests that "helping students develop the integrity and strength of character that prepare them for leadership may be one of the most challenging and important goals of higher education"[4] Fortunately, Concordia College, like many institutions, values leadership development and seeks ways to infuse curricular, co- and extra-curricular experiences with opportunities for student leadership development. A scan of liberal arts college websites reveals that many have regularly offered leadership programming, typically facilitated by the student affairs division of the college. Many of these programs adopt a social change model of leadership development and some, like the College of William and Mary, even suggest that it is the leadership model for the twenty-first century.[5] Focusing on individual, group, and community engagement, a social change model of leadership emphasizes equity, social justice, self-knowledge, personal empowerment, collaboration, citizenship, and service. All of these components would be suitable for leadership in many personal, professional and civic domains, including leadership for sustainability. Research has demonstrated students can and do increase their leadership potential in college[6] and leadership development is associated with the enhancement of various personal and civic engagement variables. Positive outcomes of leadership development in college provide support for Jensen's contention that leadership should be an important learning outcome for sustainability education.[7]

Much like higher education, professional organizations and work environments provide leadership development training and encourage employee empowerment; however, it is suggested that few organizations actually teach people how to use power.[8] I contend this is also true in higher education. Direct attention to the ways in which we educate students to effectively and ethically understand and use power in their lives is generally lacking from literature on leadership development. While this is a component of leadership development and is implied in some leadership training programs, as we educate our students to be leaders, I believe we should pay more attention to helping students understand power. Further, I believe that college professors have an important role to play in educating students about power and its effective uses.[9]

Much of the research on the role of power in the classroom has assessed the kinds of power faculty have and employ in the classroom, the perceptions by students of faculty power use, and the ways in which faculty use of power influences student behavior.[10] McCroskey and Richmond, leaders in this work, have identified and defined five typologies of power used by instructors: coercive power (the ability to punish students), reward power (the ability to grant rewards to or remove punishments from students), legitimate power (the power an instructor possesses due to authority), expert power (the possession of knowledge and competence in a subject area), and referent power (the ability to be deemed likable). Research repeatedly shows that coercive and legitimate power are perceived negatively by students; however, expert, referent, and reward power are positively correlated with student learning, motivation to study, and better student-faculty communication. Types of power used in the classroom also influence students' behavior and satisfaction with the learning environment. Instructors using more pro-social forms of power, such as expert and referent power are perceived as being fair and this, in turn, fosters less student resistance and aggression.[11] Taken together, these data suggest that students are sensitive and responsive to faculty use of power.

Given the power relationships that exist between faculty and students, and given that students are sensitive and responsive to faculty use of power, if careful attention is paid to how faculty ethically and deliberately use power in their classrooms, faculty have the potential to positively impact their students' leadership development and their future uses and understanding of power. Additionally, faculty mentoring is a predictor of student leadership outcomes suggesting that faculty may play an important role in helping students understand their leadership capacity and how to ethically and effectively use their power.[12] This should lead us to ask: how can we construct our classrooms and attend to uses of power in our teaching so that we model appropriate use of power, encourage and support our students to be engaged learners and contribute to their leadership development? Luechauer and Schulman[13] suggest that learning environments in which students are engaged and empowered learners will better prepare students to be leaders in their post-collegiate lives. This can take many forms, but one example of a significant course restructuring to empower students was undertaken by Costello, Brunner and Hasty, who used student-centered instruction to prepare their management students for an empowered workforce.[14] Students engaged in a group process simulation, which was open-ended, required student ownership, and cooperative learning and had minimal instruction from the professor. The goal was learning about group development and required students to study and reflect on behavior as it happened. While some concerns were initially expressed by students about this pedagogical approach, ultimately students developed a greater sense of personal responsibility and it is the contention of Costello et al. that the empowered classroom better prepares students to transition to an empowered workforce.

While whole-scale pedagogical reform, like the student-centered environment introduced by Costello and colleagues might contribute to student leadership development, there are other ways we can use the classroom to educate students about power and its uses without detracting from course goals and student learning outcomes. Class assignments in which students are encouraged to develop leadership characteristics and explore their own power and ability to influence is one such strategy. Assignments can provide an opportunity for instructors to discuss ethical use of power and for students to exercise their own power as they meet course-related learning outcomes. One example is a multi-stage civic engagement exercise in my Drugs and Behavior course. Students research a current drug policy in their community, broadly defined (city, county, state, country, or global issue), form an opinion about the policy based on research, and demonstrate civic engagement by communicating with elected officials or civic employees in their community. In their civic engagement communication, students argue for a change in the drug policy. Throughout this exercise, students gain practice using their democratic power by participating in the civic process. They develop an understanding of how policy is developed and are empowered to have a voice in changing the policy. This experience allows the professor to integrate a conversation about power into the classroom.

In addition to assignments and pedagogical approaches, one way to share power with students and facilitate open discussion about use of power in the classroom is allowing students to be partners in setting the course agenda and expectations.[15] For instance, professors can use the first day or two of class to discuss the expectations for the professor and student and set the course schedule and assignments. Although this prevents the professor from setting the entire schedule before the start of the course, these conversations may help minimize use of legitimate or coercive power in the classroom and immediately make students feel ownership over their course experience. Discussing rationale behind certain policies (e.g., reporting plagiarism violations to the dean's office, rather than dealing with them "behind closed doors" gives power to students to appeal the charge) can also be a way of having students reflect on power. If we use the development of college and classroom policy as a way to discuss power and justice, students may see faculty as role models making ethical use of the power they have. In addition to being exposed to a positive professor-student power dynamic, students who experience the collaborative development of course policies and expectations may feel they have a voice in their learning and are thereby more empowered and effective learners.

Given the number of ways faculty can model and provide instruction about power, institutions of higher learning should, in professional development programs, attend to issues of power in the classroom. At the very least, faculty should know that students are aware of power messages in the classroom and that these messages influence student behavior. This information can go a long way in ensuring faculty make use of pro-social forms of power in the classroom.

The approaches offered by faculty in their courses should supplement other ways, such as formal student development programs, in which college students develop their leadership capacity and understanding of power. As the world faces environmental crises and many other significant challenges, we must ask ourselves: *how do we educate for a society of continuous change and increasing complexity?* The current Concordia strategic plan sets forth the goal of educating our students for the *whole of life* through the building of competence, creativity, and character.[16] In doing so, our students will be prepared to influence the affairs of the world and to be leaders throughout their whole lives. As students live out their vocation in service to their neighbor, they need to understand power. By ensuring that faculty help students develop leadership capacity and provide an understanding of ethical uses of power; by being role models who, with awareness and reflection, utilize pro-social forms of power; by designing courses in ways that appropriately share power with students and/or engage in reflection on decision making; and by creating empowered student-centered learning environments, we will all contribute to educating our students for the whole of life and to respond to complex and challenging problems.

ENDNOTES

1 R. Guy Erwin, "Lutheran Higher Education in Global Context: Called to Serve the World," *Intersections* 27 (2008): 13.

2 Ibid., 13.

3 Ernest Simmons, "Lutheran Liberal Arts Education: Nurturing Vocation for Planetary Citizenship," in *Reformation and Resilience: Lutheran Higher Education for Planetary Citizenship*, eds. Ernest Simmons and Erin Hemme Froslie (Minneapolis: Lutheran University Press, 2017), 19.

4 Patricia M. King, "Character and Civic Education: What Does It Take?" *Educational Record*, 78: 87

5 The Office of Student Leadership Development, "Engaging, Exploring and Elevating Student Leadership Development at the College of William and Mary," https://www.wm.edu/offices/studentleadershipdevelopment/documents/StudentLeadershipDevelopmentUpdate_December2013.pdf.

6 John P. Dugans and Susan R. Komives, "Developing Leadership Capacity in College Students: Findings from a National Study," *A Report from the Multi-Institutional Study of Leadership* (College Park, MD: National Clearinghouse for Leadership Programs, 2007).

7 Jon Jensen, "Learning Outcomes for Sustainability in the Humanities" in *Teaching Sustainability: Perspectives from the Humanities and Social Sciences*, ed. Wendy Peterson Boring & William Forbes (Nacogdoches, Texas: Stephen F. Austin University Press, 2014): 34.

8 Vidula Bal and others, *The Role of Power in Effective Leadership*, (N.p.: Center for Creative Leadership, 2008): 14, https://www.ccl.org/articles/white-papers/the-role-of-power-in-effective-leadership/.

9 Many definitions of power exist, and for this purpose, we do not need to settle on a single one. However, to ensure a shared understanding, I will use the definition offered by James C. McCroskey and Virginia R. Richmond ("Power in the Clasroom I: Teacher and Student Perceptions," Communication Education 32, no.2 (April 1983), 175-184) of power as "an individual's potential to have an

effect on another person's or group of persons' behavior" and acknowledge that both position and personal power are important.

10 Virginia R. Richmond, "Communication in the Classroom: Power and Motivation," *Communication Education* 39 (1990), 181-195; Virginia R. Richmond and James C. McCroskey, "Power and the Classroom II: Power and Learning" *Communication Education*, 33 (1984): 125-136; Paul Schrodt, Paul Witt, and Paul Turman, "Reconsidering the Measurement of Teacher Power in the College Classroom," *Communication Education*, 56 (2007): 308-332.

11 Michelle L. Paulsel, Rebecca M. Chory-Asad, and Katie N. Dunleavy, "The Relationship between Student Perceptions of Instructor Power and Classroom Justice," *Communication Research Reports*, 22 (2005): 211.

12 Dugans and Komives, "Developing Leadership Capacity," 15.

13 David Luechauer and Gary Schulman, "Preparing Students for the Empowered Workplace," Paper presented at the annual Midwest Academy of Management Convention, St. Charles, IL, April 1992. Quoted in Melinda L. Costello, Penelope W. Brunner, and Karen Hasty, "Preparing students for the empowered workplace: The risks and rewards in a management classroom," *Active in Higher Education*, 3 (2002): 118.

14 Melinda L. Costello, Penelope W. Brunner and Karen Hasty, "Preparing Students for the Empowered Workplace: The Risks and Rewards in a Management Classroom," *Active Learning in Higher Education* 3 (2002), 117-127.

15 Terry Doyle, *Learner-Centered Teaching: Putting the Research on Learning into Practice* (Sterling, Virginia: Stylus Publishing, 2011), 79-87.

16 "Whole Self, Whole Life, Whole World: The Plan for Concordia College 2012-2017," Concordia College, last modified October 12, 2012, https://concordiacollege.edu/files/resources/strategicplan.pdf.

ENGAGEMENT IN A FAST-PACED WORLD

MR. RONALD TWEDT
Assistant Professor of Accounting

Time is a significant part of many processes. Sometimes, it has been a limiting factor, as we wait for the paint to dry or the plate to cool before touching it. In more recent times, however, time seems more likely to push us than to hold us back. We are pressed to decide and act as quickly as possible, perhaps even immediately. Technology allows nearly instant access to vast fields of information and enables direct interaction with almost anyone, at any time and in any location. These possibilities also present us with challenges.

How can people approach decision-making in a way that leads to outcomes of high quality while satisfying the time expectations of those who are affected? In our context, how can Concordia College approach encouraging students' development of the capacity to responsibly engage in a world that doesn't like to wait?

I. Information and Analysis

Information is an extremely valuable resource, not because of its rarity but because the right information is critical to so many ideas, decisions, and processes. In the financial accounting discipline, one of our foundational standards is to identify the qualities of financial information that are most useful to decision-makers.[1]

Information users must also develop the ability to evaluate the quality and relevance of information. This requires some sense of the type of information that might be connected to the ideas under consideration, as well as the ability to see the ideas that might grow from certain information. While sorting generally relevant information from the irrelevant, a skillful user should also be able to connect relevant information to particular questions.

Where it was once most challenging to locate information or sample an information base, current technology now makes it more important to identify or develop high-volume information bases. Data analysis, or mining, then can be used to perform comprehensive evaluation to find the information that is most relevant. It seems reasonable to expect that future developments will enhance the quality and speed of this process; however, there still remains considerable room for judgment in the art of information analysis. How do we choose the best universe of information to analyze? Can we think of information that could be important, but is currently unknown (or unknowable)? What if improved understanding changes the perceived quality of information, of the sort that converts "facts" to error or irrelevance?

Analysis of information is not independent of selecting that information, but it does require additional reasoning. Skillful analysis makes sense out of information, connecting it to existing ideas and generating new ones. It requires critical thinking that sees the depth, breadth, and impact of connections. It is also important to assess the quality of analysis that can be done in an allowable or limited time frame, to identify possible trade-offs between reliability and timeliness. Analysis may be undertaken in order to reach a single conclusion, but often it may result in multiple possible courses of action. These alternatives may be ranked or classified based on relevant variables, such as preconditions (e.g. the outcome of another event or process), timing, or cost. It may also be important to evaluate confidence levels in expected outcomes.

We are unlikely to have extensive understanding of all relevant factors in a decision or process, so we should acknowledge and deal with our levels of ignorance. If we are aware of relevant knowledge that we do not understand (e.g. agricultural practices in an unfamiliar country), or if we are concerned about "unknown unknowns," we may do well to collaborate with someone with better understanding. Fresh perspectives can help with the "what are we missing" questions, as partners share their perspectives from a variety of experiences.

Analysis and understanding should enable us to act with both confidence and humility. We should develop earned confidence that we are capable to identify and understand the critical aspects of a decision and to evaluate alternatives. We should develop humility to recognize that it's quite possible we don't understand relevant ideas as well as we'd like, and that we may not have identified all relevant information. This allows us to seek solutions that are flexible to change as we carry them out, and to consider possible unintended consequences.

II. Communication

To participate with others, it is important that we consider how people's perspectives affect the way they participate in communication. It is difficult to engage with people if we don't understand the ways they may be inclined to express respect, consideration, and enthusiasm. Listening well helps us to consider how a wider range of information and ideas may improve the outcome, and to integrate those contributions into a process.

To contribute, we must also express our ideas and understandings effectively. This will probably require skill in engaging in a wide range of forums (e.g. social media, virtual meetings, face-to-face) and a wide range of communication modes (e.g. informal or formal, brief bursts or fully developed arguments). It will also require an ability to communicate clear reasoning with brevity and precision, connecting foundation information and ideas to new ideas and proposals that lead to expected results. We also must consider how our expressions will be received by the primary audience for which it is intended and also by other audiences that may be interested. The more diverse the audience, the more important it will be to simplify language and to limit the use of idioms and cultural references.

III. Balancing Reflection with Decisiveness

While good leaders need qualities of decisiveness and reflection to be effective, the two qualities are often in tension.[2] Reflection often requires time to consider information, processes, and alternatives, and should lead to thoughtful plans, and clear communication to people involved; however, the time required could lead to missed opportunities or a decision reached too late for its benefits to be fully realized. People engaged with leaders who are reflective might perceive them as slow to understand, afraid to act, or unable to reach a conclusion.

Decisiveness often puts a premium on speed and action, and it should lead to seized opportunities, and a chance to take the lead in competitive environments; however, hasty action could lead to botched opportunities or decisions that don't consider all relevant information and alternatives. People engaged with leaders who are decisive might perceive them as rash, unconcerned with input or impact on others, or unable to think through complex situations.

The balance between reflection and decisiveness is not a new challenge; however, it has become increasingly significant as the implementation speed and impact of actions and decisions has accelerated. Our ability to connect with others quickly can be negative, as when a new disease morphs and spreads quickly, or positive, as when people collaborate to develop a vaccination or cure and spread it quickly in response. If we have a new idea or process, it might be important to complete and share it quickly with others to provide its desired benefits as soon as possible. In competitive settings, it can increase the pressure on everyone, since any moment's delay might be the moment in which someone else jumps in ahead of us. Unfortunately, bad ideas, bad processes, or bad information can be also spread widely and take root before they can be retracted or rebutted, and cause damage that requires much time and effort to repair.

Given this tension between reflection and decisiveness, how do we help students develop their capacity to act both responsibly and quickly? Reflection is generally prized in academia. Indeed, many "outsiders" are bewildered by our lengthy deliberations for some decisions that don't seem terribly important. In our scholarship, few things are as embarrassing as having our colleagues point out flaws in our research or our arguments that we know we should have caught before presenting them. We seek excellence and value quality more than speed.

Since our students are often moving on to environments where time is a more significant limiting factor, it is more likely that the need for timely action will supersede the desire to fine-tune or to bounce it off a colleague first. How should we help our students prepare to engage a world that requires these difficult trade-offs? This will require more than just asking everyone to do the same things, only faster. Rather, we should seek an approach that sees the value of both reflection and decisiveness, and intentionally consider both.

One element of this approach is to develop understanding, as best we can, of the implications of our work. How likely are negative consequences, and how bad might they be? Could we do significant damage if things go wrong with this new food packaging process? How important and likely are potential positive consequences? Would this new system allow faster communication of tsunami warnings that saves lives? How can we continue to embrace the critical learning opportunities from mistakes and failure, while limiting the possible damage? How do we deal with regret of errors while sustaining the courage to engage difficult issues?

Another element is to understand the complexity of our work, and the number of "moving parts" that might be involved. I still value and share an important lesson I learned from a mentor from my previous career in public accounting. He told me that, when working on a complex project, "the slower you work, the sooner you get done." I've seen this lived out in too many of my efforts that have stalled because of my haste, and I would hope it is a lesson long learned by any surgeon I may need.

Yet another element is the challenge of dealing with a situation where it seems that a decision must be made now, but relevant information is incomplete. How much information is enough to make a responsible decision? How do we structure our actions to make them as open as possible to future adjustment, as the consequences are monitored and as other information becomes available? How do we involve multiple parties in this process? How do we encourage responsible risk-taking? How do we compare the cost of missed opportunities to the cost of mistakes in decisions?

As with so many concepts, these ideas can be described accurately in the abstract, but must also be experienced to be learned. One of our challenges is to lead students through experiences that require and enable them to balance the requirements of thought and action, based on an understanding of what they do and an appreciation for the implications. How can this be a part of student experiences, whether it is through, between, or outside their class experiences?

IV. Core Values and Goals

The mission and culture of Concordia consistently advocate for meaningful lives and actions through responsible engagement in the world. This requires intentional consideration of values that matter to us, and of how we live out those values. It also requires that, in our work, we connect these core values to the information, issues, ideas, and processes with which we engage.

Our values drive our intentions, and intentions often lead to ideas and action. It is important that we see whether and how our work reflects those values, and how our intentions precipitate ideas and action. Understanding the connections between intentions and actions is necessary in evaluating the quality of our plans and in confirming that our plans reflect our values. Core values and goals should be an integral part of analysis and decision-making, and an element of both reflective and decisive qualities. This has been, and should continue to be, a central part of the Concordia experience for students. We do this through focused study in courses and by integrating ethical considerations in a wide range of experiences, both inside and outside the classroom. How will this critical process be affected by issues related to time pressure?

Conclusion

In a world of high speed and amplification, actions can have immediate and widespread impact. For those actions to have a positive impact on the world, it is certainly critical that Concordia graduates are thoughtful, informed, and ethical. To bring those good qualities to bear, they must also be prepared to engage quickly and act decisively. It will be important for us to facilitate our students' ability to live out Concordia's mission, in the opportunities and pressure of our fast-paced world.

ENDNOTES

1 Financial Accounting Standards Board, *Statement of Accounting Concepts*, No. 8, Chapter 3.

2 David E. Bell, "Regret in Decision Making Under Uncertainty," *Operations Research* 30, no. 5, (1982) 961-981.

BUILDING VOICE

Understanding Changing Perceptions of Authorship and Audience in the Digital Environment

MS. LAURA PROBST
Director of Carl B. Ylvisaker Library

> ". . . people act on the environment. They create it, preserve it, transform it, and even destroy it, rather than merely react to it as a given."[1]

In his introductory essay to this volume, Ernest Simmons touches upon some of the skills and competencies that our students will need to be global citizens and sustainability leaders. He goes further in explicitly reminding us of the traditions of the *trivium* and liberal arts education to train our students to "think clearly and critically" and to "creatively formulate viable responses."[2] These imply broad education and training for our students in their chosen disciplines but also in the critical thinking, problem-solving, and communication skills that allow them to apply their knowledge in college and as they go into the world. Indeed, we are already deeply engaged in this work through the core curriculum and integrative learning. We are nurturing our students' confidence in their own agency to "influence the affairs of the world" through their own actions, by their influencing the actions of others, and in their participation in collective actions of communities and groups.[3]

In this essay, I will suggest that we think more expansively about our students' communication skills and their attitudes and abilities to engage in discourse, particularly in the products of their "becoming responsibly engaged in the world (BREW)" and integrative learning. I think about the power of our words and ideas and how we encourage our students to exercise that power. As we engage with the integrative learning criteria to "construct meaningful interdisciplinary responses" and to "sharpen and apply skills and competencies that flow out of a liberal arts education," how do we teach them about their own agency, their audiences, and their rights and responsibilities as authors, particularly in the context of our students' expanding spheres of influence (from friends, to college, to work and the larger world)? The new information literacy standards from the Association of College and Research Libraries, the *Framework for Information Literacy in Higher Education*,[4] provides a complementary structure that may be useful. One of its frames, "Information has Value," explores multiple values including information as commodity and as a means to influence. When put into practice by our students, they "see themselves as contributors to the information marketplace rather than only consumers of it" and they are "inclined to examine their own information privilege." Another of the six frames, "Scholarship as Conversation," explores scholarship as an activity that occurs among communities and across time. Students will "recognize that systems privilege authorities and that not having a fluency in the language and process of a discipline disempowers their ability to participate and engage." As we think about reforming Lutheran higher education within our curricular frames of BREW and integrative learning as well as the ACRL standards, we must consider questions such as these: How will our students develop mastery in new and evolving avenues for communication? How can they reach audiences that are both insular and fragmented? How do they navigate a world where there are differing concepts around ownership of ideas? How do they manage their roles as creators and consumers of knowledge information?

I. Authorship

Our students and their peers have a different understanding of authorship than we teach in the academy. This difference is driven primarily by their digital nativity. They have grown up with tools that enable them to interact with, alter, and transform cultural objects. This ability to readily adapt and often reinterpret cultural objects fosters their perception of shared ownership of objects and creative relationships with both the authors and the objects. It becomes an act of community engagement. Their sharing and adapting builds communal meaning as well as altering the sense of authorship and ownership from "that's her work" to "that's our work." This "remix" culture may be perceived by some as a threat to authorship and ownership, but as Andrew Lessig argues, the culture and the technology enabling it offers the potential of returning to the "read-write" culture of our past. To summarize one of his examples, the dawn of a new technology—the phonograph—brought with it loss in the ability to appropriate culture. The cultural act of gathering on the front porch to sing, and possibly alter, popular songs (that is, "read-write") died away as we moved to passive listening to phonograph records (that is, "read-only"). We no longer created music, but we merely consumed it. With the evolution of technology, our new digital tools again enable the re-creation of music and other cultural objects, and a return to a new "read-write" culture.[5]

Thinking about the exciting potential of this shift from "read only" to "read-write," we might rethink how we represent the interplay of authors and readers that is scholarly communication and, more broadly, authorship in the world of work. We are caught between the authorship conventions of the academy and the "remix" culture that is challenging traditional conventions of ownership of ideas, copyright, and cultural norms. This evolving understanding of authorship is part of a longer history of changing conceptions of authorship, ownership, originality and imitation.[6] This time, though, the technology is perhaps the dominant driver in the cultural shift. Our opportunity as educators is to change attitudes of "because we can" to understanding of "why we should" and "how we can influence." The conversation shifts from evaluating and citing sources to harnessing the great potential for sharing information and ideas. From there we foster a collaborative environment where ideas can grow (both within and beyond a community), and where we acknowledge the value of information and ideas—that are intellectual property—and their creators. We have an opportunity—and an obligation—to explore with our students the continuum between their authorship in the remix/sharing culture of their social lives, their academic work, and their authorship in their careers and work beyond college. As we think about the intellectual products of integrative learning experiences in our classes and on campus, they can be the mechanism where students experiment with the rights and obligations of authorship that may be new to them. Their audiences will include external partners and these products may be accessible far beyond those partners.

Individual ownership of ideas and cultural objects is under threat. To some degree, all of us freely share what we find on the Web—an article, a photograph, a video clip. In doing that, the likelihood is strong that we may be violating copyright. Much Web content is under copyright, but that status is seldom clear. A copyright holder might post something with the intention that it be used by its audience (that is, sharing his or her exclusive ownership rights). A third party might post something that is under copyright, either without being aware of violating the copyright owner's rights or in spite of being aware. In either case, the onus is on the audience. In a digital corollary to *caveat emptor* (let the buyer beware), the audience now bears responsibility for determining their rights. As we prepare students to be authors in this digital environment—now something of a new "wild west"—we can take action as good citizens to shift the onus back onto ourselves. Open access tools and constructs, such as Creative Commons,[7] give us a mechanism to convey to our audiences that we as authors want to share our work with the community, to engage in communal discourse, but that we, in some fashion, claim and protect our original work. In doing so, we are building sustainability.

II. Audience

While we tend to the responsibilities of authorship, we must pay equal attention to changes in our relationships to our audiences. Technology has driven audience changes, but it is the underlying changes in our culture and community that threaten our ability to engage in effective communications. In a recent blog post, Chris Anderson, the curator of TED, described audiences as "co-authors" connected in an intimate relationship.[8] In that relationship of author/reader or speaker/listener, we explore meaning and understanding, or perhaps more frequently, our different understandings. The reality may not be so communal. As participants in multiple modes of digital communication, we are all keenly aware of the fragmentation of information on the Web, and of our social tendencies to affiliate and communicate with like-minded groups. Then there are also members of our communities who have withdrawn from groups. This individual isolation is a threat, too, as Robert Putnam has described in *Bowling Alone*.[9]

The lack of common space where differing opinions are shared and respected threatens the fabric of democratic society. We see it most clearly in the political sphere, but it pervades our social structures as well. In his analysis of political strategy and how the human brain responds to political rhetoric, Drew Westen exposed a critical reality. Sometimes it's not about crafting a logical, rational argument but about reaching out at an emotional level. As he wrote in 2008, "candidates who win the hearts and minds of the voters are the ones who can weave together emotionally compelling stories about who they are and who their opponents are and who can make people feel what they feel."[10] Ten years later in our fragmented political and social environment our culture may have fallen further into the lure of compelling stories that may stretch and interpret fact and truth.

As we prepare students to take on the responsibilities of authorship in their engagement with the world, how do we—and they—wrestle with these difficult relationships with our audiences? In the reality of audiences that are culturally and politically diverse, that are isolated, fragmented, and polarized, what tools do we need to inform or persuade them? In our writing and our speech, do we enter the relationship that Anderson describes, or is it the more insidious tendency toward manipulation of audiences? And which audiences do we care about? Of course, we have a responsibility first to our primary audience, but we should not assume that audience is uniform. Looking beyond that audience, especially as our communication becomes increasingly digital, we should think about how our message will be transformed among broader audiences. The culture is shifting to shared ownership of object and ideas where participants in those communities will share, adapt, and alter cultural objects. We must remember also, that in this culture, the audience may perceive differently an author's intent to inform or persuade. We may already be approaching the point where communication and information is routinely received with a lack of trust in accuracy, truth, and suspicion of an author's intent to mislead. If this is the reality of our culture, how do we as authors and as members of communities and audiences work to reverse this dysfunction?

III. Where Do We Go From Here?

The marketing guru Seth Godin talks about the connection economy where value is created by the relationships and networks that we build rather than by what we produce, that is, the values of the industrial economy. To be successful we should invest more in building relationships and networks. His argument, in part, hinges on changes in the marketplace: What was a bell curve with a large "mass market" in the middle is changing to a flattening bell curve where the potential for growth is not in the diminishing middle, but the increasingly diverse ends of the bell curve.[11] Chris Anderson dubbed this phenomenon the "long tail" in his 2004 article in *Wired Magazine* and then later in a book.[12] Growth is in the niche markets, that is, in the small, focused communities on the extreme ends of the bell curve. The hope for sustainability lies in acknowledging the dispersed (and sometimes fractured) nature of communities, but then seeking relationships—and their value—across those communities. The hope for that solution lies in the tools we impart to our students. We go back to the *trivium*, the "liberating arts," teaching the critical thinking and communication skills that will allow them to navigate our new world of sharing authorship, where relationships to and among audiences are complex and where individual responsibility lies in both the creation and consumption of ideas, knowledge, and culture.

ENDNOTES

1 Albert Bandura, "Toward a Psychology of Human Agency," *Perspectives on Psychological Science* 1.2 (2006): 167.

2 Ernest Simmons, "Lutheran Liberal Arts Education: Nurturing Vocation for Planetary Citizenship," in *Reformation and Resilience: Lutheran Higher Education for Planetary Citizenship*, eds. Ernest Simmons and Erin Hemme Froslie (Minneapolis: Lutheran University Press, 2017), 22.

3 Bandura, "Toward a Psychology of Human Agency," 165.

4 "Framework for Information Literacy in Higher Education," Association of College and Research Libraries, accessed April 5, 2017, http://www.ala.org/acrl/standards/ilframework.

5 See, for example, his book, *Remix: Making Art and Commerce Thrive in the Hybrid Economy* (New York: Penguin Press, 2008) or his presentation "Laws That Choke Creativity," TED Talk, March 2007, http://orthomolecular.org/library/jom/index.shtml.

6 Susan D. Blum, *My Word! Plagiarism and College Culture* (Ithaca: Cornell University Press, 2009), 32-39.

7 Creative Commons, accessed April 5, 2017, www.creativecommons.org.

8 Chris Anderson, "Have an Anonymous TED Talk? We Want to Hear It," *The Medium* (blog), August 24, 2016, https://medium.com/@TEDchris/have-an-anonymous-ted-talk-we-want-to-hear-it-3ca52d341b6e.

9 Robert D. Putnam, *Bowling Alone: The Collapse and Revival of American Community* (New York: Simon & Schuster, 2000).

10 Drew Westen, *The Political Brain: The Role of Emotion in Deciding the Fate of the Nation* (New York: Public Affairs, 2008), 423.

11 Seth Godin, "We Are All Inbound Now: The Epic Shift in Posture," *INBOUND* 2016, August 27, 2013, https://www.youtube.com/watch?v = RZ_D2BNqRzU.

12 Chris Anderson, "The Long Tail," *Wired Magazine*, October 2004, https://www.wired.com/2004/10/tail/ and *The Long Tail: Why the Future of Business is Selling Less of More* (New York: Hyperion, 2006).

CONTEXTUALIZING A WHOLE LIFE

Luther, Islam, and Mission

DR. JONATHAN CLARK
Associate Professor of
German World Languages and Culture

In response to the Syrian civil war, which has been raging since 2011, Germany opened its borders to over one million refugees. Not just displaced Syrians, however, have benefitted from Germany's largesse. In 2015 alone it is estimated that 1,091,894 refugees came across the border and were processed in Germany.[1] Refugees are from predominantly Islamic countries, especially Syria, Afghanistan, Iraq, Iran, Eritrea, Pakistan, and Nigeria. According to Judith Meyer, there are many reasons for Germany embracing Muslim refugees, most of which are a result of the Nazi persecution of minorities, especially Jews, and the memories of World War II, but also because there is a consensus that refugees actually contribute to German society.[2] I would argue that the decision to admit so many refugees is also largely the stance of Germany's chancellor, Angela Merkel. She has been lauded for her efforts to bring a semblance of hope for those in need,[3] and her mantra through this humanitarian crisis has been and still remains: "Wir schaffen es!" or "We can manage this!" in spite of criticism from inside her own party as well as the far right.[4] Merkel's position stands in stark contrast to the rising anxiety in the United States with regards to Muslim immigrants. The question of Islam and its links to terrorism has been front and center in the news and in political discourse since the attack on the World Trade Center and the Pentagon on September 11, 2001. Fears of Islamic roots in terrorism have become even more heightened since the Syrian civil war and the resulting refugee crisis, as well as the rise of ISIS. Since the 2016 presidential election, however, suspicions surrounding Islam and terrorism have become exacerbated by the rhetoric of the presidential candidates and, since the election, the president himself, his advisors and his supporters. Most recently, the two executive orders banning citizens of eight primarily Muslim countries, which have been placed on hold by federal courts, have only added fuel to the fire of anti-Islamic polemics and actions.

This paper asks a simple question: what is the obligation of a college of the church to fight against the prejudice and hatred directed towards Islam and Muslims and what are the best ways to achieve this? In order to answer this, we must also understand what guidance the theological founder of the church that bears his name provides. Thus, this paper, first, will try to understand Luther's views on Islam and the degree to which they may inform the Lutheran educational system. Second, I will suggest ways in which both faculty and students alike might respond to the unconscionable accusations and associations leveled against Muslims.

While Merkel's Lutheran upbringing in communist East Germany may have provided the moral conscience for Merkel's own action with regard to the Syrian refugee crisis,[5] it is questionable that Luther was her guiding spirit in embracing Islam. Unlike many of his contemporaries, Luther was at least familiar with Islam and the situation with the Turks. He had read the *Qur'an* in a poor Latin translation; he was familiar with the works of Nicholas of Cusa and Ricoldo de Monte Croce, two medieval sources of Islam; and "he kept abreast developments through oral reports, letters and pamphlet literature."[6] This did not mean, however, that Luther had any respect for Islam. On the contrary, he knew little about Mohammed, considered the *shahadah*—the Muslim testimony of faith to the oneness of God and the belief in Muhammed—to be the work of the devil, and the religion itself to be "works righteous." Because "of the Muslim denial of the divinity of Christ, the denial of his death, and the exaltation of Muhammed over Christ, all of Islam was deemed categorically false."[7] Luther published two early works against the Turks: "On the

War against the Turks" (1529) and "An Army Sermon against the Turks" (1530), and one later work, "Admonition to Prayer against the Turks" (1541). He also wrote the preface to Georg von Muhlback's *Concerning the Rites and Customs of the Turks*, as well as the introduction to Theodor Bibliander's Latin edition of the *Qur'an* and a medieval treatise, *Refutation of the Qur'an by Brother Richard of the Order of Preachers* (1542).[8]

Luther's views on Islam and the Turks should be seen largely in the context of both anti-Catholicism and Luther's own apocalyptic thinking. Luther's earliest acknowledgement of the Turks is found in his polemics against indulgences, which were also being sold in the fight against advancing Islam. According to Luther in his explanation of the 95 Theses,[9] the Turks were actually the instrument of God in order to punish Christianity for its abuses. Rather than go to war against the Turks, as many advocated, Luther said "that it was only necessary to fight their [Christians'] own sins but not the scourge God used for punishment."[10] Luther, who knew little about the Turks and Islam, used them to rail against the abuses of the Catholic Church in defense of his 95 Theses.

By 1528, Luther's use of the Turks in an anti-Catholic polemic was replaced by outright condemnation of the Turks who were seen as bent on overrunning Christian countries "to violate and murder women and children, but also trying to take away territorial justice, God's service, and all good order."[11] As Kaufmann explains, the Turks were to be fought because they violated all three estates established by God: the secular authorities, the clergy, and the peasantry.[12]

In "An Army Sermon against the Turks" (1530), Luther's writings against Islam take on a more apocalyptic tone. Luther understood Gog/Magog in Revelations "to be the biblical designation for the Turks."[13] Luther saw in Daniel and Revelations that "the Turks would be allowed dominion for a time, but then would be destroyed from on high. The Last Judgment would follow just after the defeat of the Turks."[14] Drawing on Ezekiel and Daniel, Luther understands the Turks' siege of Vienna to be God's wrath upon the Christian who has not lived up to God's commandments:

... the Turk will teach you when he comes into your land and does to you like what was done at Vienna .... Namely, he ... will attack your house and home, take your livestock and provisions, money and goods, stab you to death (if you are lucky), shame or strangle your wife and daughter before your eyes, hack your children to death and impale them on the fence posts. And, what is worst of all, you must suffer all this with a wicked, troubled conscience as a damned unchristian who has been disobedient to God and his government.[15]

These accusations against the Turks were also depicted in a 1530 broadsheet entitled "Türkische Grausamkeiten" [Turkish atrocities—see figure 1].[16]

FIGURE 1

Türkische Grausamkeiten (1530)

The relationship between the Turks and the end of times is found in the closing prayer of "On the War Against the Turks:" "So help us, dear Lord Jesus Christ, and come down from heaven with the Last Judgment. Strike both the Turks and the Pope to the ground together with all tyrants and the godless. Deliver us from all sin and evil, Amen."[17] According to Luther, the Turk is the "ultimate and worst rage of the devil against Christ" and, at the same time, "God's heaviest punishment on earth for the ungrateful and godless ones who contemplate and persecute Christ and his word."[18] And though the Turk at least recognizes Jesus to be a great prophet, they, like the Jews and Catholics, are too indebted to ritual and earthy works (deeds) to ever be saved by Christ.

While Luther's early writings about Judaism hold out hope that the Jews could, under the right circumstances, come to accept Jesus as the Christ,[19] this was never the case for Muslims and Islam. Toward the end of his life, however, Luther spoke out against both Judaism and Islam. *On the Jews and Their Lies* (1543), *On the Ineffable Name of God and the Generations of Christ* (1543) and *Warning Against the Jews* (1546), Luther rails against the Jews, essentially calling on Christians to deny them their livelihood and banish them from the land unless they convert and accept Christ. His later works against Islam, like his earlier works against the Turks, were similar in refuting the obscure reasoning found in the *Qur'an* and the threat that Islam posed to Christianity and the doctrine of justification by faith. Both religions were used to demonstrate the need for spiritual and worldly cleansing and the supremacy of true Christianity. Islam, however, was seen as an instrument of God to effect the Last Judgment.

There is a tendency to excuse Luther's writings against Jews and Muslims. As many point out, Luther's relationship to both Islam and Judaism is complex. Jesus was a Jew and the Old Testament is intimately linked to the New Testament. Jews were given a chance under the new faith to convert, but they did not, and Luther points to the relief found on the City Church of Wittenberg where he preached [see figure 2] in order to illustrate that the God of the Jews is found in the feces of the sow they are trying to suckle.[20]

FIGURE 2

Die Judensau (ca. 1440)[21]

Islam, associated with the Turkish threat against Christian Europe, was never given the benefit of the doubt. Less associated with the devil than the Jews, Muslims were, nonetheless, the instrument of God in punishing the Christians who have not accepted justification by faith. They are a warning that the end is near and that Christians need to change to be accepted into God's kingdom through faith in Jesus alone.

Luther is seen, according to his apologists, in the context of his age, of anti-Catholic sentiments, and of apocalyptic urgency. Just as one could understand the context in which Luther polemicized against both Turks and Jews, one could also view the Nazi appropriation of Luther's writings and recommendations in promoting racial anti-Semitism in a similar fashion: Nazis were a product of their time, Germans in search of living space and a truly German community, a racially pure *Volksgemeinschaft*. Would it be incorrect to understand anti-Islamic paranoia in the United States and elsewhere in the context of the age? Look at the images of murder, even genocide under the guise of ISIS and Al-Qaida and the many acts of "Islamic extremism." Is it any wonder that our top officials can draw upon these images, not in order to frighten citizens rather because they are convinced that Islam is fundamentally wrong? What excuse can we ascribe to them?

The simple truth is, Luther was wrong, as were the Nazis about the Jews and as are our contemporary biases, including those of our president and his ilk, against the Muslims. As educators, we need to underscore this message, first by admitting that we are imperfect, racist and prejudicial. We need to stand as an example, not just in showing students "difference" but also by engaging ourselves in acts of empathy: working with the homeless; building bridges to our neighbors of all ethnicities, religions, and cultures; participating in marches and demonstrations instead of just talking about them; preaching against prejudice in the classroom instead of skirting the issue. Take a stance.

Second, we need to underscore our commitment in our courses, our core, and the message of the mission. While there are numerous courses which deal with the politics of Islam, conflicts in the Middle East, and the Holocaust, even some dealing with Islamic art and music, few courses celebrate diversity in Islam or Judaism. The Concordia College core, though united under the rubric "Becoming Responsibly Engaged in the World," is really only a collection of courses serving the interests of various disciplines. The diversity requirement—both U.S. and World—which some courses meet is less than adequate. Even the mission is hardly understood by or welcoming to those of different faith backgrounds. Yes, it is true that being "dedicated to the Christian life" also means accepting other cultural views and religious backgrounds, but for those from other cultures and religions, the mission is the first hurdle to being part of the Concordia community. In all fairness, however, the core and the mission give as little concern to questions of sustainability, immigration, and environment, even though we ask our students to tackle the big issues. The college has done much to underscore its commitment to environmental sustainability. It is also beginning to focus some energy on questions of diversity, and the hiring of a diversity officer is a first good step. Until we find a way to unite the disciplines in addressing these issues that are ultimately linked, however, we will have little effect.

I write this as both an indictment and as a challenge. Perhaps in this year of Luther, it is not inappropriate to issue a call to debate the very foundation of the college. We advocate critical thinking and becoming responsibly engaged in the world, yet I would submit that we do neither. Assuming we even broach these issues in the core, let alone individual courses, our response seems at best contradictory: condemn such contemporary attitudes—without trying to insult the political sensitivities of our students—but excuse Luther as a man of his age. Critical thinking requires us to identify a problem and understand the context, becoming responsibly engaged to take action, hopefully for the well being of society as a whole. Luther was wrong about the Turks and the Jews. What can we learn from Luther's error in the context of religion, nation, culture and power? And how can we apply these lessons to our current cultural debates?

ENDNOTES

1 As taken from "Zahlen zu Asyl in Deutschland," *Bundeszentrale für politische Bildung,* Web. (March 14, 2017). In 2015, 890,000 immigrants were allowed to remain, whereas in 2016, only 280,000 remained.

2 For full article see Judith Meyer, "Why Is Germany Ready to Take So Many Refugees and Asylum Seekers?," *Quora*, Web. (October 17, 2015).

3 Merkel was even awarded *Time*'s Person of the Year in December 2015 for her efforts in mitigating the refugee crisis.

4 The steady stream of immigrants to Germany has not been without criticism, and it gave rise to the right-wing protest group, PEGIDA [Patriotische Europäer gegen die Islamisierung des Abendlandes or Patriotic Europeans against the Islamicisation of the West] as well as the political party, Alternative for Germany [AfD, Alternative für Deutschland].

5 Merkel's father was a Lutheran pastor in East Germany just 50 kilometers north of East Berlin. Rather than attend the traditional Jugendweihe (the coming of age ceremony for socialist youth), Merkel was confirmed in the Lutheran church.

6 Gregory Miller, "Luther on the Turks and Islam," in *Harvesting Martin Luther's Reflections on Theology, Ethics, and the Church* (Grand Rapids, MI and Cambridge, UK: William B. Erdmans Publishing Co., 2004), 186.

7 Miller, 187.

8 As cited in Miller 186. According to Miller, Luther was only interested in the publication of the Qur'an "because he considered the public knowledge of the hideousness of the Qur'an to be the greatest weapon against Islam" (189).

9 Martin Luther, *Resolutiones Disputationum de Indulgentiarum Virtute* (1518), as cited in Thomas Kaufmann, "Luther and the Turks," *Martin Luther and the Reformation, Essays,* (Dresden: Sandstein Verlag, 2016), 342.

10 Kaufmann, 342.

11 WA 26, 229, 26-27, as quoted in Kaufmann 343.

12 Cf. Kaufmann 342-343. These three estates are outlined in "instructions for Visitors," a set of standards and rules "concerning doctrine and discipline" drafted by the Wittenberg reformers in 1528.

13 Miller, 201.

14 Miller, 201.

15 As quoted in Miller 199.

16 Also known as Türkengefahr [Turkish Danger], this broadsheet depicts Turkish atrocities in the Vienna Woods. The woodcut is by Hans Weigel, Sr. (ca. 1530), as found in the Bayerisches Historisches Lexikon, Web.

17 As cited in Miller 201.

18 Luther, Army Sermon (WA 30/II, 162, 20-24), as quoted in Kaufmann, 343.

19 See Martin Luther, *Das Jhesus Christus eyn geborner Jude sey* (Wittenberg, 1523).

20 As found in *Shem ha'phoras* (1543).

21 As found in "Lutherstadt Wittenberg—*Judensau (um 1440) an der Stadtkirche St. Marien*," Web, March 2014.

WHOLE WORLD

INTRODUCTION

Extending to the entire world Roy Hammerling's spirited call in his introductory essay to this volume, to open new doors of educational and social reform, quakes the mind while trembling the soul. The complex of impediments that block a more sustainable future threatens to stop us in our tracks before we have taken a single step forward. Indeed, there are so many doors that must be faced—to adopt Hammerling's metaphor taken from Luther's life—it is hard to know which one to approach first. The essays collected in this section make clear that a multitude of doors must be approached, unlocked, and opened simultaneously if reforms looking towards global sustainability stand a chance of making a real difference. They also convey instructive paradoxes, an appropriate concept perhaps for a theological tradition steeped in them.

Looking out, first, from the academy to the world with sustainability in view, we must set to the side our religious and intellectual heritage long enough to grasp alternative wisdom and illuminating ways of being in the world beyond the West. Here the focus shifts: not how can we save the world, but how can we learn from the world that we might be saved?

Essays by Anne Mocko and Abhijit Gosh insist in their own ways that we consider this question long and hard. Both examine the promise of traditions from South Asia for approaching the intractable challenges of climate change and ecological crisis. Mocko, adopting the perspective of comparative religion, shows how insights, beliefs, and practices of Jainism may fill in significant gaps in conventional Lutheran theology when it comes to how human beings understand and live out their fundamental relationship with other living things.

Readers be warned that Jainism's appreciation of what constitutes the living will surprise and rebuke. Taking a practical philosophical direction, Gosh interprets pivotal Gandhian concepts to outline a radically different way of thinking about community, economy, and ecology. He conjures a unified conception of reality that collides with Western constructs of economic materialism and the good life, both Marxian utopian and developmental capitalist, which have domineered the natural world and externalized its damage over time.

A second paradox comes into view in these essays: in order to become active efficaciously in a world of increasing ecological dangers, the college must honestly look inwards to take stock of its own relationships and practices. The global in this sense must originate at home. Timothy Hiller's essay examines a troublesome pattern—the exploitation of adjunct academic labor—that has become a permanent feature of higher education around the country, no less true at Concordia. He argues forcefully that the presence of adjuncts are fundamentally inconsistent with the college's mission and identity; moreover, the practice is ultimately unsustainable for the college, its students, and for adjuncts themselves. Similarly, Richard Chapman, taking his cue from African-American history, calls the college to greater responsibility for being a learning community that models racial and cultural inclusion. He reminds readers that cultural, social, and economic sharing and fair play, often flagrantly violated and abused in the history of the United States, must not be sacrificed on the altar of a vision of sustainability for the privileged and well-heeled—at home or abroad.

The final essay by Leila Zachirova, a specialist of energy policy, considers the imperative question of how and when the world might transition to a more sustainable energy regime. Her analysis posits the global influence and economic power of that society which leads the way in harnessing sources and technologies of clean energy. Leadership is crucial at all levels—state, corporate, local, and individual—and as she maintains, now more so than ever. The notion of energy conversion cycles back to a central drama of Luther's own life, his liberation through disciplined investigation and pivotal spiritual conversion. Much as in Luther's own day the world desperately wants for conversion—for the transformations needed to enhance resiliency and to restore equipoise in the relationship of humans and the natural order. Considering that monumental task, these essays announce another vital message: that the rediscovery of a profound humanism that enabled the reformations of the sixteenth century will prove no less essential to the conversion we are now seeking, and to fling wide the doors that detain us.

—Dr. Richard Chapman, Professor of History

LEARNING FROM OTHER RELIGIONS

What Jains Might Teach Lutherans About Sustainability and the Forgiveness of Sins

DR. ANNE MOCKO
Assistant Professor of Religion

There are seven hundred thousand earth-embodied beings,
seven hundred thousand water-embodied,
seven hundred thousand fire-embodied,
seven hundred thousand air-embodied,

There are a million plants that host a single living being,
one million four hundred thousand
hosting collections of beings;

There are two hundred thousand two-sensed beings,
two hundred thousand three-sensed beings,
two hundred thousand four-sensed beings,

There are four hundred thousand heavenly beings,
four hundred thousand infernal beings,
four hundred thousand five-sensed animals,
fourteen hundred thousand humans:
in this way, there are 8,400,000 forms of existence.

Whatever harm against all of them
that I have done,

or caused to be done,
        or approved of,
by mind, speech, or body,
may I be forgiven.

—Saat Laakh Sutra[1]

One of the central themes of Luther's writings is the forgiveness of sins. But when Luther discusses the forgiveness of sins, what he normally means is forgiveness for misconduct either in the behavior of humans toward other humans, or in the behavior of humans toward God. Thus, Luther (and his followers) might be concerned about idolatry, adultery, pride, theft, and doubt, but not air pollution or hunting or the wanton destruction of forests. Action toward the non-human world generally becomes sin only indirectly in Christian traditions. Non-human life might be identified as "created by God" or "entrusted to humans," and thereby enter into human relationships with divinity, but violence toward animals or plants or natural ecosystems cannot, in most Christian formulations, be "sin" in its own right, because Christian thinkers and practices rarely frame non-human life as an independent object of human moral obligation.

Moreover, the notion of sin has been flattened in much contemporary American Protestantism, to the point that sin is nearly inextricable from sexuality.[2] For most Americans (Christians, as well as non-Christians trying to understand Christians), considering sin means considering whose genitals give pleasure to whose, and inquiring whether the possessors of those genitals are bound to one another in marriage. As a result, many churches (especially those from more socially liberal perspectives) have moved away from thinking and talking explicitly about sin, in an effort to promote a more gender/sexuality-inclusive Christianity. These trends mean that modern American Christianity is particularly impoverished when it comes to analyzing and lamenting the many complex damages that human actions can cause in the world.

If we were to take a "whole world" approach to learning, however, we might find that there are constructive approaches and practices in other religions and cultures that might enrich our thinking about human action, and inspire us to return in new ways to the languages of sin, repentance, reconciliation, and forgiveness.[3] In particular, I would draw attention to the religion of Jainism, and the ways that Jains conceive of moral responsibility toward non-human life forms. I would particularly wish to introduce readers to Jain liturgies that ask the reciter to articulate the different ways her/his actions have damaged various forms of life, and to express regret for harms done. I would like to suggest that by examining this Jain practice of formal repentance, we might find a useful counterpoint to Christian resources for thinking about human responsibility—to suggest, in other words, that Jain traditions could inspire Lutherans toward a more environmentally attentive orientation toward the world, and that Jains might reframe for Lutherans a life of repentance and reform.

I. Radical Non-violence and the Jain Notion of Sin

Jainism is one of the three ancient religions of India, together with Hinduism and Buddhism. Established in its institutionalized forms in approximately 500 B.C.E., at almost exactly the same time and place as Buddhism, it shares with the more famous religion several basic tenets and practices, particularly an insistence that the religious life best lived must involve detachment from conventional life in societies and households. Unlike Buddhism, however, Jainism never spread widely; while today there are millions of Buddhists spread all across South, Southeast, and East Asia, Jains are largely restricted to a few provinces in western and central India, comprising less than 1 percent of the nation's population. The influence of Jains far outweighs their negligible numbers, however, insofar as they have been respected for millennia in Indian society for the rigor of their principles and the vigor of their practices—especially the strictness of their monks and nuns, who refuse to live in permanent monasteries, refuse to eat food cooked uniquely for them, refuse to travel in vehicles, and in some instances refuse to wear clothes.[4]

According to all three of the ancient Indic religions (Hinduism, Buddhism, and Jainism), all living beings are caught in an eternal cycle of birth, death, and rebirth, a system known as *samsara*. As each being travels through *samsara*, they must act in the world—and each action will inevitably result in consequences. This is *karma*-theory: the conviction that positive actions will always yield positive fruits (*punya*, usually translated as "merit"), while negative actions will always yield negative fruits (*paap*, often translated as "sin"). Each living being's *karma* will come to fruition sooner or later, though the fruits of many actions will take multiple lifetimes to mature.

Within this overall worldview, Jains are distinct from Hindus and Buddhists in two ways. First, whereas Hindus generally emphasize the centrality of correct ritual practice, and Buddhists emphasize the importance of rejecting mental failings like ignorance and attachment, Jains insist on the religious centrality of *ahimsa*: the active practice of non-violence toward all living beings.[5] Second, Jains classify far more types of beings as participants in *samsara*, and therefore presume that a far greater number of beings are subject to moral consideration. Whereas Hindus and Buddhists include among the denizens of *samsara* only "sentient" beings capable of motion and some degree of cognition (humans, animals, insects, hell beings), Jains also presume *samsara* to include anything that is alive, including plants, microbes, and some elementals (ice-bodied beings, water-bodied beings, fire-bodied beings).

Because Jains assume the world is teeming with life forms, they also presume that acting in the world almost inevitably leads us to commit violence—to cause death or bodily suffering—to other living beings in the world, and that this endemic violence (*himsa*) causes every living being in the world to carry a heavy burden of *paap*, or "sin," which will produce inevitable negative consequences in this lifetime or the next. The religious life, then, demands that the practitioner actively guard against harming living beings around them, increase their meritorious actions, and undertake austerities (*tapasya*) such as fasting, which can scrub away past sins.

This sensibility holds some important parallels to ancient and medieval Christian views of human life—including the idea of balancing sins with merits and the insistence that bodily austerities can overcome sin—but it diverges from Christian perspectives in a few crucial ways. First, *paap* is generated first and foremost when one acts negatively or negligently against other life-forms in the world: when one eats meat, when one squashes a spider, when one has plenty of food but lets people or cows in the community go hungry, when one rides in an airplane that crushes a bird, when one uses a cosmetic made from fish scales. While Jains also worry about theft and lying and sexual misconduct, they primarily focus on protecting vulnerable non-human life-forms from the impacts of human actions and appetites.

Jain sensibilities also diverge from Christianity in that *paap* is generated and resolved without reference to any divine figure. While Jains believe in the existence of gods and goddesses, and while the majority of Jains venerate statues of enlightened beings (*Jinas*), *paap* is created by negative actions toward other embodied beings, and not through violating any kind of agreement with a divine being. Moreover, no divine being ever "judges" someone's *paap*: instead, the consequences of sinning are part of the natural justice of the universe, an almost Newtonian law whereby actions will always and inevitably "bounce back" at the actor. *Paap* is thus comparatively impersonal, and it plays out across lifetimes until it has been exhausted (rather than accumulating for a single lifetime before a judge determines one's eternal fate).

II. Repenting Jain Sins

Jains are deeply attentive to the impacts of their actions on the world around them: they are constantly reminded by monks and nuns of the importance of reducing the *paap* they commit, and they engage in an array of daily practices to try to reduce or avoid *himsa* (violence). Thus, they eat strictly vegetarian, they assiduously filter their water, and they avoid leather products, among other practices. They also routinely repent of the death and suffering that they continue to cause despite all their precautions to the contrary. This repentance is particularly encapsulated in the Prakrit-language phrase "*micchami dukkadam*" ("may the evil that has been done be fruitless," or "may I be forgiven"), which Jains variously say to each other, to the enlightened *Jinas*, and to all the living beings in the world.

The phrase *michhami dukkadam* is deeply embedded in Jain liturgical practice. It is a repeated phrase in the relatively brief *aalochan paat* recitation performed by many Digambar Jains on a daily or weekly basis, and it is a similar refrain in the longer *pratikraman* liturgy recited by Shwetambar lay Jains on an annual basis (and by Shwetambar monks and nuns on a daily basis). The *Saat Laakh Sutra*, which is provided in full as an epigraph to this essay, forms part of both the *aalochan paat* and the *pratikraman*: this particular text lists all the different kinds of living beings toward whom the reciter has moral obligation, and then concludes, "Whatever harm against all of them that I have done, or caused to be done, or approved of, by mind, speech, or body, *michhami dukkadam* (may I be forgiven)."

The formal, liturgical repentance of violence is particularly enshrined in Jain life through the annual eight-day observance of Paryushan, an opportunity for fasting and reflection observed by both Digambar and Shwetambar Jains in late summer or early fall. All Jains observe particularly rigorous dietary restrictions at this time, and many will undertake dramatic fasts to protect the non-human world temporarily from the impacts of their consumption. Many Jains are more stringent than usual in the clothing or cosmetics they permit, the medicines they will accept, and so forth, all in the effort to observe and limit the damages one's daily lifestyle tend to have on the non-human world at large. They will also typically undertake far more elaborate devotional activities than usual, often spending several hours per day at temple praying and reflecting. Many Jains also take this time to search out people they have wronged in the past year to ask for forgiveness with the same phrase: "*michhami dukkadam*."[6]

It is thus a central feature of Jain life to reflect on and repent of the harms one causes toward the world—to identify sins and regret them, and to commit oneself to better efforts in the future. It thus performs some self-formative work parallel to Christian traditions of repenting sins, though with some important differences. Chief among these would seem to be an absence of individualized shame. Whereas many Christians experience repentance as a shame-inducing experience (and indeed Luther himself spent many years in acute agony over the state of his soul and his inability to reduce his sin), Jains experience their traditions in a far more matter-of-fact way. While Jains concur with many Christian thinkers that sin is an inevitable part of being a person, they don't see *paap* as evidence of shame-worthy weakness or brokenness, but rather as a natural fact of having a body. While a Christian might theoretically become perfectly humble and chaste and charitable, no Jain expects that they could possess a body without at some point drinking water or stepping on an ant or eating an apple (and thereby incurring *paap*). As James Laidlaw points out,

> The penitent [Jain] is not required, as a result of introspection, to report on the sins he or she is aware of having committed. This "confession" does not require a review of the things one has done that day, an examination of one's conscience, or an account of how one has spent one's time. Indeed, the opportunity for such imaginative or evaluative thinking is systematically excluded.
>
> The ethics and the psychology of both shame and guilt are bypassed as an exhaustive enumeration is attempted of all the possible sins there are. After each list everyone declares that they 'cast off' the self which committed them.[7]

In other words, because all Jains recite the same lists of possible violences against other embodied beings, they simultaneously both claim their own *paap* and reject their own uniqueness in incurring *paap*. There is no individual blame about needing to drink water or walk around, and this seems to free Jains to repent their sin matter-of-factly, without suffering shame or self-hatred, in ways that Christians rarely if ever achieve. This appears to provide Jains the resources to develop a rich and complex ethical consciousness of others, without risking individual moral paralysis.

III. Toward a More Environmental Lutheranism

I hope this essay has already made available some ways that Lutherans interested in sustainability could learn from a Jain view of *paap*, but let me close the essay by trying to collect and make more explicit two main lessons or challenges:

1. Jains might invite Lutherans to expand their notion of sin.

If Christians have trouble doing environmental ethics and sustainability in part because their notion of sin is very human-centric, Jains might inspire them to reimagine sin as also encompassing negative acts toward non-human life forms. What would it mean to theorize not just sins against God or human neighbor, but also sins against chicken and algae and rain forest and ocean? What biblical, theological, and liturgical traditions might be adapted to this broader notion, and how might a more environmentally sensitive notion of sin help move Christian conversations away from sexuality and toward sustainability?

2. **Jains might inspire Lutherans to expand their rituals of repentance, to help people recommit regularly to living more environmentally attentive lives.**

   At present, most Lutherans only formally repent their sins through group prayers during worship, but what kinds of ritual or prayer practices might Lutherans be able to rework or invent, to help people to reflect more regularly and more deeply on how their actions affect the world around them? How might Lutherans answer or borrow from the annual practices of Paryushan, the long form of *pratikraman*, or the short daily *aalochan paat*?

The task, I think, is not to ask Lutherans to become Jains, but rather to ask Lutherans to listen more deeply to the whole world, and to invite them to open themselves to strategies from other religions for attending to the natural world and its needs.

ENDNOTES

1 Translation adapted from the English version provided by John E. Cort in "Green Jainism? Notes and Queries toward a Possible Jain Environmental Ethic," in Christopher Key Chapple, ed. *Jainism and Ecology: Nonviolence in the Web of Life* (Cambridge, MA: Harvard University Press, 2002), 75.

Please note that, in order to maximize the essay's readability for non-experts, none of the discussion here will utilize diacriticals and some of the discussion will not utilize fully standardized transliterations when reproducing Indic terms. Instead, all non-English words will be rendered in English letters in combinations judged to be maximally effective at producing appropriate non-specialist pronunciation.

In addition, the essay employs a mix of vernacular versions of Jain terms with more classical Sanskrit iterations. (Hence, *tapasya* instead of *tap* or *tapashariya*, but *paap* instead of *pāpa*.) I appreciate any patience and flexibility from specialist readers who might stumble on this distinctly non-specialist essay.

2 There is an extensive evangelical literature on sex and its dangers. See for example Robert Daniels, *The War Within: Gaining Victory in the Battle for Sexual Purity* (Wheaton, IL: Crossway Books, 2005).

3 See for one start Phyllis Granoff and Koichi Shinohara, editors *Sins and Sinners: Perspectives from Asian Religions* (Boston: Brill, 2012).

4 For more robust introductions to Jain history and practice, see Jeffrey Long, *Jainism: An Introduction* (New York: I.B. Taurus, 2009); John Cort, *Jains in the World: Religious Values and Ideology in India* (New York: Oxford University Press, 2001); Paul Dundas, *The Jains* (New York: Routledge, 1992); James Laidlaw, *Riches and Renunciation: Religion, Economy, and Society Among the Jains* (New York: Oxford University Press, 1995).

5 Michael Tobias, *Life Force: The World of Jainism* (Berkeley, CA: Asian Humanities Press, 1991).

6 For more on Paryushan, see Laidlaw, *Riches and Renunciation*, 275-286, and Cort, *Jains in the World*, 144-162.

7 Laidlaw, *Riches and Renuciation*, 213.

EXPLICATING GANDHIAN PRINCIPLES FOR WORLD REFORMATION

Satya, Swadeshi, and *Sarvodaya*

DR. ABHIJIT GHOSH
Assistant Professor of Strategic Management

> If we could change ourselves, the tendencies in the world would also change.[1]
>
> —M.K. Gandhi

This essay explores the connections between three fundamental concepts that form the bedrock of Gandhi's worldview and explicates how these concepts might be appropriated to engage and transform the transient world that we live in and enact through our day to day actions. These concepts are *Satya* (Truth), *Swadeshi* (Self-Sufficiency), and *Sarvodaya* (Welfare of All). The world we live in, as Gandhi once said, has enough for every person's need, but not enough for a single person's greed. Increasingly we find ourselves in a planet which, fueled by greed, seems to be at the precipice of a cataclysm. Yet for a few concerned human beings, it also represents an opportunity—a potential tipping point—to make a difference today so that we may leave a better world for posterity. These indomitable optimists envisage a world of hope, compassion and courage, of social justice and communal harmony, a world where the word "development" connotes not shallow material growth, but signifies a range of substantive freedoms that allow us all to progressively self-realize to our fullest potential.

This essay, by exploring the connections between *Satya*, *Swadeshi* and *Sarvodaya*, directs attention to our sacred responsibility of transforming this world by pursuing truth (realizing oneself) through recognizing the essential oneness of all creation. As this essay will make clear, a profound understanding of interdependence of the whole universe presumes non-violent means and rests on a humble appreciation of the duty of human beings to assume stewardship of God's creation. As Gandhi stated in the spirit of *ahimsa* (nonviolence), "To see the universal and all-pervading spirit of truth face to face, one must be able to love the meanest of creation as oneself."[2] Thus recognition of oneness makes it increasingly difficult to justify *himsa* (violence) emanating from unjust and inequitable socio-economic structures as well as violence toward nature's precious resources that have been abused on account of greed and anthropocentrism. The pursuit of Truth through non-violence fosters courage and humility—the former required to speak truth to power to shift inequitable structures of domination and accumulation, and the latter required to remind ourselves that we must exercise restraint in our "wants" in a spirit of "self-abnegation" while honoring our moral obligation of stewardship to God's wonderful creation.

I. *Satya* (Truth) and Its Salience in Gandhian Philosophy

The Sanskrit word for Truth, *Satya*, is derived from *Sat*, which literally means "that which exists." Nothing is or exists in *reality* except Truth. Nothing is or exists in reality except God. Gandhi repeatedly affirmed that Truth is God and that devotion to Truth is and should be the sole purpose of human existence.[3] In Gandhi's words, "to find Truth completely is to *realize oneself* and one's destiny, that is, to become perfect."[4] Truth was to Gandhi the supreme moral law—the source of all moral principles including *Ahimsa* (Nonviolence/Love). For Gandhi, actions based on Truth are judged to be morally good.[5] An action carried out in adherence to truth (*Satyagraha*) could not be immoral as it would necessarily be infused with virtues of honesty, humility, sincerity of purpose, and other moral principles deriving from truth.[6] It was not merely a concept of theoretical import, but one that needed to be *practiced*. Gandhi affirmed that "There should be Truth in thought, Truth in speech, and Truth in action."[7] Thus

Gandhi underscores the value of being "authentic" in all our engagements within all realms of life, not only to others, but to ourselves. As truth-seekers, we must all speak what we think and do what we say.

II. Humility and Courage in the Pursuit of *Satya*

The pursuit of Truth involves tremendous sacrifice and there is no place for even an iota of self-interest or cowardice.[8] A seeker of truth (*Satyagrahi*) has to go through severe disciplined practice (*abhyasa*) and renunciation of material pleasures (*vairagya*) in order to come anywhere close to Truth.[9] Gandhi affirmed that "the seeker after Truth should be humbler than the dust . . . Only then, and not till then, will he have a glimpse of Truth."[10] This meant that the *Satyagrahi* must demonstrate the willingness to unlearn and the humility to discard knowledge which, after repeated experiments and deep contemplation, is proven to be untrue. The true possessor of humility is unaware of its existence. In Gandhi's own words, "To feel that we are something is to set up a barrier between God and ourselves . . . a drop in the ocean partakes of the greatness of its parent, although, it is unconscious of it."[11]

The honest pursuit of truth requires us to speak from our heart unto others, bringing our *authentic selves* to bear, even when this may result in consequences apparently inimical to one's self-interest. Speaking truth to power, upon seeing injustice, requires potent courage and is often times the last choice because people dread the consequences of doing so. But unveiling the truth requires shedding appearances and standing up to the fear that sustains untruth. Fear and anxiety disappear when we recognize that this body is perishable, the spirit is not. A person who holds to the truth is unlikely to have many friends. A Satyagrahi must therefore summon the *courage to walk alone*. In Gandhi's words, "Truth alone will endure, all the rest will be swept away before the tide of time. I must, therefore, continue to bear testimony to Truth even if I am forsaken by all."[12]

III. Gandhi's Swadeshi, Non-violence and Social Justice

According to Galtung, Gandhi was the only author and politician who "fought against both the sudden, deliberate direct violence engaged in by actors, and the continuous, not necessarily intended, violence built into social structures.[13] Gandhi, in his sharp critique of modern Western civilization, pointed out that "modern industrialism" was based on the violent displacement of human beings and animals from their natural habitat and their substitution by heavy machinery. The ideal underlying this shift from a human-centered economy to one based on machinery was "material progress" and an unreasonable profit motive fueled by greed. This starkly contrasted with Gandhian spiritual ideals of *aparigraha* (non-possession), *ahimsa* (nonviolence/love) and *sarvodaya* (welfare of all) which pervaded his views on what "true economics"[14] should look like.

Greed accompanying industrialism was so great that industrialists were willing to deprive human beings of their dignity and relegate them to the status of a cog in the wheel[15]—a mere dispensable means subservient to the end of profit. In so doing, industrialists were enacting a system without conscience. Capitalism in this form was not an economic system meant to serve human beings, but a system that made slaves out of human beings. This dehumanization is violence, as Gandhi made clear when he spoke of exploitation in economic terms.[16] Gandhi, who openly advocated self-abnegation, said "our civilization, our culture . . . depend not upon multiplying our wants—self-indulgence, but upon restricting our wants—self-denial."[17] Gandhi considered social and economic inequalities violence in and of themselves because these structural inequalities prevented a vast majority from accessing basic needs like food, shelter and clothing. Those who helped sustain these structured patterns of interaction committed theft and violence.

Gandhi's critique of industrialism makes sense when seen within the context of the colonial subjugation of India that thrived on systematic exploitation of India's abundant natural resources[18] and human labor to fuel the industrial revolution. This subjugation culminated with the British colonial regime decimating India's age-old hand-woven industry of fine cotton textiles,[19] putting millions of weavers out of work and forcing farmers to switch to raising cash crops (chiefly cotton and indigo) needed for the British machines, thus playing havoc with India's agricultural pattern, all the while using the huge

Indian market as a dumping ground for expensive British textiles.[20] Ian Jack of the *The Guardian* writes, "For at least two centuries the handloom weavers of Bengal produced some of the world's most desirable fabrics, especially the fine muslins, light as "woven air," that were in such demand for dressmaking and so cheap that Britain's own cloth manufacturers conspired to cut off the fingers of Bengali weavers and break their looms."[21] Gandhi's age-old critique also resonates with numerous contemporary movements across the world trying to fight back the rapacious excesses of another form of colonization through multi-nationals, often referred to as globalization and thrust upon the third world in the name of "free-trade"—a doctrine invented at the height of British colonialism.[22]

Why is all this relevant and how does Gandhi's *Swadeshi* campaign, if at all, provide a solution to the ever-widening disparity between the haves and the have-nots in the contemporary world? Gandhi defined *Swadeshi* as "that spirit in us which requires us to serve our immediate neighbors before others, and to use things produced in our neighborhood in preference to those more remote. We cannot serve humanity by neglecting our neighbors."[23] Gandhi noted the apparently exclusive nature of this doctrine:

> I buy from every part of the world what is needed for my growth. I refuse to buy . . . if it injures those whom Nature has made my first care. I buy useful healthy literature from every part of the world . . . But I will not buy an inch of the finest cotton fabric from England . . . because it has injured and increasingly injures the million of the inhabitants of India.[24]

Continuing to patronize foreign produce over local was a grave sin in as much as it contributed to millions of weavers being put out of work and to the systematic impoverishment of one's country to satisfy a distant country's extravagant wants. Gandhi wanted Indians to choose truth over untruth by refusing to partake in the systematic structural violence of modern industrialism through self-denial and the *Swadeshi* spirit (self-sufficiency through local production). For Gandhi, *Swadeshi* was a calling to serve one's immediate neighbor in the spirit of humility and love. In the economic realm, this meant taking full responsibility for how one consumed and produced. Gandhi's critique of excessive consumerism promoted by industrialism's shallow notion of "material progress" was combined with a critique of bureaucratic, centralized production that threatened to destroy morally both consumers and producers. The pursuit of truth through non-violence meant that the entire set of consumption and production choices had to be reimagined so that these were non-violent acts of love. Gandhi argued, "If we follow the *Swadeshi* doctrine, it would be your duty and mine to find out neighbors who can supply our wants and to teach them to supply them where they do not know how to proceed, assuming that there are neighbors who are in want of healthy occupation."[25]

Schumacher, inspired by Gandhian economics, saw the difference between "production by the masses" and "mass production." The former provided "dignity and meaningful contact with others . . . while the latter is violent, ecologically damaging, self-destructive in its consumption of non-renewable resources and dehumanizing for the individuals involved."[26] By propagating this doctrine, Gandhi, in one fell swoop, tackled the evils of excessive wants and dehumanization of labor and proposed localized, decentralized and humane solutions that promoted self-sufficiency of the community, dignity and autonomy of the worker and one that allowed for renewal and resuscitation of the lost arts and traditions of the world (in this case hand-weaving).

IV. *Sarvodaya*, *Ahimsa* and Their Relevance for Ecological Citizenship

Gandhi realized that "modern industrialism" was also responsible for environmental degradation through pollution and over-utilization of non-renewable resources. According to Bhikhu Parekh, Gandhi "challenged the anthropocentric view that man enjoys absolute ontological superiority to and the consequent right of unrestrained domination over the non-human world."[27] Gandhi championed the philosophy of *Sarvodaya*[28] which literally means the "welfare of all." He argued that "man's ultimate aim is the realization of God . . . the only way to find God is to see Him in His creation and be one with it. This can only be done by service of all."[29] Gandhi wrote, "I believe in the essential unity of man and for that matter, of all that lives."[30]

Gandhi's philosophy of *ahimsa* was framed on a profound understanding of interdependence of the whole universe and on a humble appreciation of the duty of human beings to assume stewardship of God's creation. For Gandhi, "nonviolence meant not only non-injury of human life, but of all living things."[31] Given these views, the ecological scope of Gandhian nonviolence is boundless.

Thomas Weber[32] points out that what is less well known is Gandhi's enormous influence on three significant bodies of knowledge—deep ecology, peace research and Buddhist economics—that have gained wide popularity and spawned important social movements in the West. Gandhi's faith in nonviolence and vegetarianism made him a "votary of conservation of all diversity" including all forms of life.[33] His respect for nature is evident in his thoughts about cow protection: "Cow protection to me is one of the most wonderful phenomena in human evolution. It takes the human being beyond his species . . . Man through the cow is enjoined to realize his identity with all that lives."[34]

Arne Naess, the father of "deep ecology," argues that ecological preservation is "non-violent at its very core." He admits his debt to Gandhi's writings on Sarvodaya and nonviolence, and its influence on his crafting of some of the basic precepts of deep ecology.[35] Gandhi made manifest the internal relation between self-realization, non-violence and what sometimes has been called "biospherical egalitarianism." Starting with Gandhi's ultimate goal of achieving "self-realization,"[36] Naess lays out the fundamental link between self-realization and non-violence reproduced in:

1. Self-realization presupposes a search for Truth
2. In the last analysis all living beings are one
3. *Himsa* (violence) against oneself makes complete self-realization impossible.
4. *Himsa* against a living being is *himsa* against oneself.
5. *Himsa* against a living being makes complete self-realization impossible.[37]

At a more practical level, what does all this mean for the Cobbers who have pledged to "responsibly influence the affairs of the world?"

A whole lot! First and foremost, this means moving from a narrow conception of a self (*egoistic*) to an ever-widening and all-embracing perception of a universal self (*atman*). This means consciously deepening one's identification with all of God's creation. This realization enjoins us to choose the path of renunciation of violence in order to achieve complete self-realization. Such renunciation of violence is not passive, but an active attempt to redefine our relation with the world we inhabit. This means rejection of "shallow ecology" (fighting pollution or resource depletion primarily because of the effect this will have on human health or affluence), which is anthropocentric in approach, and replacing it with "deep ecological attitudes" which operate out of a "deep-seated respect and even veneration for ways and forms of life, and accords them an equal right to live and blossom."[38] For this generation, it means openly challenging taken-for-granted assumptions about what constitutes "development" (often defined by mainstream economists in terms of "growth") and institutional policies that sustain such unenlightened conceptions that promise more universal harm than good. This also means learning to reframe and indeed reconstitute our identity from one defined in terms of material possessions that provide transitory pleasure and enhance our standard of living—to one described in terms of spiritual treasures made possible through the pursuit of passions, callings and relationships which provide unadulterated joy and enhance the "quality of lives."

The discussion above brings us to an important actionable argument that Godrej[39] makes about two salient ingredients of Gandhian ecological citizenship. Gandhi's *ahimsa* has for the most part been appropriated by environmentalists to focus on the *ascetic*—self-abnegating, self-scrutiny of thoughtful consumption—component of ahimsa. This however, Godrej argues, is a very limited and politically passive conception of the Gandhian concept of *ahimsa*. Nonviolence in action (*Satyagraha*) is much more active and warrior-like. It goes way beyond the passive denial of material wants and enjoins us to seek deep transformation of institutional arrangements that make for a just society even if that means undergoing untold suffering. His notion of duty obliges individuals to "seek truth as a matter of internal spiritual transformation, but also to actively engage in the world of political and social justice, thereby transforming society in accordance with truth."[40] Gandhian nonviolence would "require ascetic self-scrutiny, but it would also ask activists to fast unto death, go on strike, place their bodies at the frontlines of breaking unjust laws or defying unjust phenomenon, and pay the price in terms of embodied pain: police action, arrests, incarceration or even harsher violence."[41] This "interweaving of the ascetic and the warrior" is imperative for us to become responsibly engaged ecological citizens if we are to rejuvenate and renew our fragile planet.

ENDNOTES

1 M. K. Gandhi, *The Collected Works of Mahatma Gandhi*, Vol. 13 (Delhi: Publications Division, Ministry of Information and Broadcasting, 1969), 241.

2 Gandhi, 1925

3 Gandhi, from *Yeravda Mandir*, (Ahmedabad: Navjivan Press, 1957), ch. 1, 4.

4 Gandhi, *The Collected Works of Mahatma Gandhi*, Vol. 25 (Delhi: Publications Division, Ministry of Information and Broadcasting, 1969), 120.

5 R.C. Pradhan, "Making Sense of Gandhi's Idea of Truth," *Social Scientist* 34, no. 5/6 (2006): 36-49.

6 Ibid.

7 From *Yeravada Mandir*, ch. 1.

8 Ibid.

9 Ibid.

10 Gandhi, *The Story of My Experiments with Truth* (1925), introduction.

11 From *Yeravda Mandir*, ch. 12, 29.

12 *Harijan*, (1946), 284.

13 T. Weber, "Gandhi, Deep Ecology and Buddhist Economics," *Journal of Peace Research* 36, no. 3 (1999): 349-361.

14 True economics stands for social justice; it promotes the good of all equally, including the weakest and is indispensable for decent life (*Harijan*, October 9, 1937).

15 S. Kumar, "Gandhi's Swadeshi: The Economics of Permanence" in *The Case Against the Global Economy*, eds. Jerry Mander and Edward Goldsmith, (San Francisco: Sierra Club Books, 1996).

16 Weber, "Gandhi, Deep Ecology," 355.

17 *Young India*, 1921, 59.

18 India was known as the "jewel in the British crown" and for a reason.

19 India, till the late eighteenth century was a producer nation; its textiles were in great demand in Europe and its agricultural produce was enough to feed its population, with a surplus to sell abroad (Khushwant Singh, 2010)

20 Khushwant Singh, 2010.

21 Ian Jack, "Britain Took More Out of India Than it Put In," *The Guardian*, June 20, 2014. https://www.theguardian.com/commentisfree/2014/jun/20/britain-took-more-out-of-india

22 Sheppard, et. al, *A World of Difference: Encountering and Contesting Development*, (New York: Guilford Press, 2009).

23 *Young India*, April 20, 1919.

24 *Young India*, 1925, 88.

25 *Young India*, May 12, 1927, accessed from http://www.gandhiashramsevagram.org/swadeshi/definition-of-swadeshi.php

26 Weber, *Journal of Peace Research*, 357.

27 Quoted in Moolakkattu, J.S., "Gandhi as a Human Ecologist," published online by Satyahgraha Foundation for Nonviolence Studies, September 6, 2012.

28 The concept of Sarvodaya was inspired by John Ruskin's work *Unto This Last*.

29 Gandhi, *Socialism of My Conception*, 1966.

30 *Young India*, 1924, 398.

31 Weber, *Journal of Peace Research*.

32 Ibid.

33 T.N. Khoshoo, *Mahatma Gandhi, an Apostle of Applied Human Ecology*, (New Delhi: Tata Energy Research Institute, 1996).

34 *Young India*, October 1921, 318.

35 Arne Naess, "Self-Realization: An Ecological Approach to Being in the World," *The Trumpeter Journal of Ecosophy* 4, no. 3 (August 1987): 35-41.

36 The "self" for Gandhi, as Naess makes clear is the supreme or universal Self —the *atman*—that is to be realized. This involves identification with all living creatures and ultimately the whole universe.

37 Weber, *Journal of Peace Research*.

38 Arne Naess, "The Shallow and the Deep, Long-range Ecology Movement: A Summary," *Inquiry* 16, no. 1-4 (1973): 95-100.

39 Farah Godrej, "Ascetics, Warriors, and a Gandhian Ecological Citizenship," *Political Theory* 40, no. 4 (2012): 437-465.

40 Ibid.

41 Ibid.

SUSTAINING THE MISSION OF CONCORDIA

Student Moral Formation in the Age of Adjuncts

DR. TIMOTHY HILLER
Instructor in Religion

In a Religion 200 (Introduction to Christianity and Religious Diversity) course I taught at Concordia College, I had a very bright exchange student. He struggled with the course and his grades were far below his expectations. The Western theological tradition was fundamentally foreign to him: he did not have the background knowledge of the biblical narrative, of basic concepts, or of important figures in order to be able to master the material. Nevertheless, a persistent student wanting to do well, he asked if we could meet outside of class to go over the material he did not understand. He thought a weekly meeting would help improve his comprehension. I told him when my office hours were and invited him to meet then. He had a class conflict and asked if we could meet at another time. Unfortunately, as an adjunct, I did not have other time available in my schedule: in addition to teaching a 2-2 load as an adjunct at Concordia, I worked around 20 hours a week at another job and, at all other times, was a full-time father to my three young children. Beyond my office hours and time in the classroom, my schedule left no room to meet with him. I had to decline. We never met and his grade suffered as a result.

I am deeply troubled by this incident. At a fundamental level, I failed this student as a teacher. He came to Concordia College wanting to learn and took reasonable steps to aid his learning, yet I was unable to do anything to help him. Had he enrolled in a course with a full-time faculty member, he certainly would have received the assistance he needed. Enrolling in a course with an adjunct meant a direct loss of educational value.

This incident displays one set of problems with the new reality of adjunct and contingent labor. While the use of adjunct labor to teach courses is not entirely new, the ubiquity as the chosen model for employment is. The rise of contingent faculty labor has quadrupled over the past 40 years; by 2011, 70 percent of college faculty were contingent faculty, a classification that includes all non-tenure track faculty.[1] Colleges save an enormous amount of money through adjunct labor, and, in this regard at least, adjuncting is an economic good for colleges. Yet, the use of adjuncts poses deep ethical and moral questions, particularly for institutions like Concordia that seek to be responsibly engaged in the world. Is the use of adjunct labor a just mode of employment for Concordia?

This essay explores that question. In most ways, there is not a real question here: the use of adjunct labor contravenes the values and mission espoused by Concordia College. Adjunct labor is an unjust practice that exploits faculty, takes advantage of students, and betrays the espoused mission of the college. Concordia is failing to educate students for global citizenship by using adjuncts. Perhaps a better question is for what?

******

> No form of learning can better cultivate the habit of asking searching questions about human being and purpose than ours–if we will (in our freedom) push against our frantic lives and build the room in which to do it. If we want the examined life for our students, we will need to live it ourselves. And no form of learning can better encourage students to take on difficult tasks, fall short, and regroup to try again than a residential community

> of scholars, where students work shoulder to shoulder in apprenticeship with faculty who practice the same intellectual risk taking and invention.
>
> —President William Craft, Inaugural Address[2]

Walmart employees are often cited as the paradigmatic instance of unjust labor relations. Despite its massive profits, Walmart employees depend upon government subsidies to meet their basic needs such as housing and healthcare, somewhere in the range of $7.8 billion a year.[3] Nevertheless, Walmart employees receive more compensation than adjunct Concordia faculty members: a Walmart cashier in the Fargo area can plan on making $21,994 a year,[4] while an adjunct who teaches four courses to 100 students at Concordia will makes $20,304.[5] Factoring in educational expenses and student loans necessary for teaching, full-time Walmart employees far outearn Concordia professors who teach a 2-2 load (16 credit hours), the maximum an adjunct can teach.

This compensation package is particularly glaring as the brunt of the low pay and labor without benefit is carried by those who seem to be most central to Concordia's educational mission—professors. Compared to departmental secretaries, teaching a 2-2 load pays around $6,000 less and comes without benefits; compared to assistant cooks at the college (who are .75 FTE compared to .67 FTE), the compensation is similar, but the cooks receive benefits while adjuncts do not.[6] Most telling, comparing Concordia's compensation package to the U.S. poverty guidelines, adjunct professors are paid far below. For someone with three children, the U.S. poverty guideline is $28,440— teaching at Concordia pays $8,136 below the poverty level![7] The decision to use adjunct labor is the decision to have a portion of Concordia's teaching faculty be poor.

Because of low compensation, adjunct professors have no choice but to work a second job. On the one hand, this is necessary because Concordia does not provide medical insurance to its adjuncts, which, if a professor chooses to purchase insurance, will cost around $320/individual per month. Additional income is also necessary due to the significant costs of graduate education. The New America Foundation reported in 2014 that the median loan debt for those with advanced degrees in the humanities is $58,539. One in five graduate students now carry debt over $100,000 and one in ten owe more than $153,000. If we take the median loan payment for an adjunct as our example, that individual will owe $494 a month for student debt. [8] So, if an adjunct pays taxes, purchases health insurance, and repays their student loans, they will earn a little less than $7,500 for their entire year of adjuncting or $625/month. This means that an average adjunct at Concordia will not earn enough to pay rent, let alone pay rent and eat.[9] If an adjunct has a family, this compensation makes childcare impossible, as is maintaining currency in the field, much less pursuing independent scholarship. Adjuncts are thus compelled to find additional employment, entailing less time and attention to the classroom and to the education of Concordia students. The decision to rely upon adjunct labor is therefore the decision to have teachers who are able to devote significantly less time to teaching.

Finally, perhaps less directly, the use of adjuncts is detrimental to full-time faculty. As adjunct positions grow, more of the administrative burdens, committee work, and institutional labor will fall upon tenured and tenure-track faculty. As their workload increases, however, they will have also less grounds for negotiating higher salaries. If Concordia can cover more and more courses for less cost with adjuncts, why increase compensation for the full-time faculty? Relatedly, as more teachers are without voice in college decisions, faculty governance will likely diminish or, at the very least, become unrepresentative of all the teachers of the institution.

The decision to have adjuncts is the decision to have a portion of the faculty live in poverty, devote less attention to teaching, and forgo research. It means a higher burden of work for those who are tenured and on the tenure-track, even as it decreases faculty governance. While economically beneficial, it is not immediately obvious why choosing to keep a portion of the teaching faculty poor, having them spend less time on teaching, and not doing research is the best solution for Concordia's budgetary worries. Money is saved in the short run, but at what cost?

******

> That grad was right that faculty (and staff) are where all the ladders start, and the subtext of his declaration was right too: that it is the relationships of students with those faculty and staff that transform young lives. But the plans that faculty, staff, regents, and friends of the college make together matter too: they matter because the lives of those young people are at stake.
>
> —President William Craft, 2013 State of the College[10]

What about the impact of adjunct teachers on student learning? I myself was unaware of the detrimental effects on students until I became an adjunct. As it may not be immediately obvious, it bears comment and reflection, particularly as Concordia faces budgetary woes and may be tempted to opt for more and more adjuncts in the future.

Currently, Concordia employs as many as 35 adjunct instructors.[11] When students enter class with an adjunct, there are tangible inequalities compared to students who have a full-time faculty member. Since adjuncts work multiple jobs and take on other responsibilities, adjuncts are unable to devote themselves fully to teaching. In my own situation, I teach 50 students a term in a writing-intensive course. This means I am unable to mentor them through the writing of their long essays; likewise, their essays come back far slower than they should, and they do not have the comments they deserve. This has direct effect on my student's learning. A significant amount of research shows that students learn best from their writing if there is a quick turn-around on grading.[12] Likewise, it is well-known that personal contact with faculty helps students engage in learning; as I said at the beginning, though, adjuncts find it largely impossible to meet with students.

The system of adjuncts creates a two-tiered educational experience for students and poses a serious ethical problem. Some students receive the benefits of full-time faculty; others the diminished attention of adjuncts. But if students are paying the same amount, they should expect the same services and level of attention; at the very least, they should expect that their money is going to their own education in the same proportion as other students. However, this is not the case. The students are paying the same, but they are receiving less goods for their money.

Students enter the classroom expecting their faculty to be devoted to the class and to their Concordia education as a whole. The decision to use adjuncts impedes the ideal student-faculty relationship that students seek when they choose Concordia. While they think they are investing in an education where instructors care about them as individuals and will do all they can to educate them, Concordia cannot deliver this ideal insofar as it uses adjuncts. The adjunct faculty may be doing his or her best, but this is severely curtailed by administrative decisions. This is a heavy cost. If Concordia is purposefully choosing arrangements that prevent educational mentorship and student development, and, if the lives of young people are at stake in the maintenance of these relationships, Concordia is failing these young people.

******

> Throughout those conversations, I began to see and hear something I never forget: your relationship with the college is not casual, nor simply instrumental; it is missional. You are here because you love something: you love the work and life of Concordia, and you love it enough to long for its highest expression and fulfillment.
>
> —President Craft, 2015 State of the College[13]

Often in discussions of adjuncting, administrators are caricatured as penny-pinchers, who ruthlessly look to cut costs by exploiting teaching faculty. While this picture has power to mobilize activists, it mischaracterizes most administrations. College deans and presidents face enormous pressures to maintain budgets, manage institutions, promote the college's welfare, and handle internal politics; adjuncts are not the central concern of most administrations. Moreover, the growth of the use of adjuncts is a far more complicated story that depends on the decentralized structures of higher education, the lack of coordination between graduate school admissions and available positions, and the restructuring of higher education that favors the creation of administrators over faculty.[14]

While the activists' picture is too crude, and the roots of the rise of adjuncts in higher education are far more complicated, nevertheless, the administration is ultimately responsible for the decisions of the college. Even if they inherited the system and are merely one instance in a larger shift in higher education, the administration is responsible for the situation at Concordia. The key point here is that there is nothing necessary about the situation. Budgets are always the products of human decisions and reflect the priorities of those in power. How Concordia chooses to spend its money is the product of the administrators' decisions. While budgets have been tight with lower enrollments, the decision to employ adjuncts was not necessitated by the situation; it was an option among many others.

The idea of adjuncting would perhaps be reasonable if there were only a few courses that needed to be filled. The pay, without question, could be more just, but hiring part-time positions makes sense if there are only a few courses that need to be filled. This, however, is not the case. There have been instances in which departments requested adding additional courses due to student demand and these courses were rejected on the sole basis that adding a course would have converted an adjunct into a benefited position. Similarly, a number of departments rely on multiple adjuncts to fill courses. In most every case, a full-time position could have been created which would have paid a living wage, granted benefits, and allowed far more attention to students and research.[15] At the very least, the administration demonstrates its priorities in relation to contingent labor: given the option, adjuncts are the *preferred* form of employment and will be used, not merely as a last resort, but wherever the opportunity arises.

There is a deeply troubling maxim operative here. Recall that an assistant cook at the college who works .75 FTE receives benefits while adjuncts who work .67 FTE do not. If we sit with this for a minute, two things are obvious: first, the faculty member with a Ph.D. will have received more education and will have invested significantly more time and money into their work than the assistant chef. The pay and benefit differential is not based on higher qualifications. Second, teaching is more tightly tied to the mission of the college than the food services of the college. Yes, it is nice that Concordia's food service is so good; yes, it is the right thing to do to provide benefits to chefs; but no student chooses to come to Concordia only for the food. They come to receive a first-class education, which the Ph.D. holder supplies.

So, why the substantial difference in pay and benefits? The short answer is as ugly as it is obvious. Someone who has a Ph.D. will have invested far more time, money, and effort in preparation than someone who is an assistant chef. This means that the Ph.D. holder will be far more wed to his or her identity as a scholar, and, in the eyes of the institution, this means that they will therefore be easier to exploit. Someone who will work as an assistant chef, because they do not have such specialization, will be far more flexible in regards to their professional identity and will need more incentive to take a position at Concordia. While they work an almost equivalent FTE, the chef will receive benefits while the professor will not.

At root, when Concordia hires adjuncts, it operates on this principle that if someone has a deeply established love and loyalty to an academic pursuit, that love can be easily exploited. Adjunct faculty members do not need to receive benefits, a living wage, or other financial incentives, precisely because the college knows that they have a deep loyalty to their discipline and are unlikely to leave it; they are therefore easy to exploit. The operative moral here appears to be: if you can find a way to exploit an employee, do it. This principle stands at the core of Concordia's relationship to adjuncts—precisely because a Ph.D. holder invested so much of their life into their academic work and are willing to sacrifice their lives for their study, the college can and does exploit them.

Sometimes members of the Concordia community will say, "Concordia doesn't use that many adjuncts in comparison to other institutions." True enough. But, morals do not work on averages—treating 99 people as ends in themselves is morally irrelevant, if this depends on using one as a mere means. The moral law is to treat everyone as an end in themselves; treating one person as a means is still gravely immoral. Simply because you can exploit faculty does not mean that you should.

******

> We must, on the contrary, think and want the best for our students and our colleagues; we must want, in the fullest sense, their happiness, lives well lived. If we imagine less of the other, we diminish ourselves, and we, as Robinson writes, "diminish the worth of institutions of society [like college] . . . when we forget respect and love for the imagined other . . . who will take the good from these institutions that we invest in them, or who will be harmed or disheartened because our institutions are warped by meagerness and cynicism.
>
> —President William Craft, 2015 State of the College[16]

At the outset I had hoped to conclude by outlining the goals and purposes of a liberal arts education and how the system of adjuncts fails to achieve them. Instead, the inclusion of several quotes by President Craft beautifully articulate the purposes of Concordia and its liberal arts mission. His vision of an inclusive community shaped by love, interested in the moral formation of students, and deeply vested in practices of attention, respect, and mutual affirmation is as attractive as it is necessary in these times. If we take these claims to be correct, the best way to educate students for a global world is a residential community of scholars devoted to the twin pursuits of scholarship and education, normed by visions of love and justice.

Concordia's use of adjuncts, however, represents a profound failure to live out her mission and purpose; if anything, it achieves the precise opposite of President Craft's vision for the college. My hope is that he has not paid sufficient attention to these effects of adjuncting on faculty and students alike, particularly to the ways failing to pay a living wage devalues Concordia's educational mission.

Bringing these issues to the fore, I sincerely hope a conversation can be had about ways that the high moral vision of the college can translate into the material practices of education. Recognizing that reliance on adjuncts is no longer a stop-gap measure, but a permanent practice, President Craft should, at the very least, form a working group focused on treating adjuncts humanely.

Finally, adjuncting is an extension of late capitalism into the hallowed halls of academia. If Concordia hopes to send thoughtful and engaged students into the world dedicated to the Christian life, it needs to show that institutions can be run by something other than the logic of the marketplace. Before we can fix the world, Concordia needs to address its own systemic economic abuses. Let's hope that the moral claims of justice and truth are not simply ideology, but have some power to shape Concordia for a sustainable future.

ENDNOTES

1 Dan Edmonds, "More Than Half of College Faculty Are Adjuncts: Should You Care?," *Forbes* (May 28, 2015), https://www.forbes.com/sites/noodleeducation/2015/05/28/more-than-half-of-college-faculty-are-adjuncts-should-you-care/#50b10e201600.

2 William Craft, "Inaugural Address," Concordia College, Moorhead, MN, April 28, 2012, accessed at https://www.concordiacollege.edu/about/president/speeches-presentations/inaugural-address/.

3 Ned Resnikoff, "Walmart Benefits from Billions in Government Subsidies: Study," MSNBC, April 14, 2014, http://www.msnbc.com/msnbc/walmart-government-subsidies-study.

4 "Walmart Cashier Salaries: Fargo," *Glassdoor.com*, accessed April 23, 2017, https://www.glassdoor.com/Salaries/wal-mart-cashier-salary-SRCH_KO0,16.htm.

5 There is an obvious difference here: Concordia's adjuncts are part-time, while Walmart employees are full-time. Even so, it is impossible to believe that anyone who invested their lives into getting a Ph.D. desires to work a decent part-time job.

6 "Assistant Cook," Human Resources, Concordia College, Moorhead, MN, website, accessed November 3, 2016, https://hr.cord.edu/postings/2547.

7 "U.S. Federal Poverty Guidelines," U.S. Department of Health and Human Services, accessed April 3, 2017, https://aspe.hhs.gov/poverty-guidelines.

8 Jason Delisle, Owen Phillips, and Ross Van Der Linde, "The Graduate Student Debt Review: The State of Graduate Student Borrowing," *New America Education Policy Program*, March 2014, https://na-production.s3.amazonaws.com/documents/the-graduate-student-debt-review. Because they are not full-time employees, adjuncts are not privy to Public Service Loan Forgiveness.

9 This is assuming around 15% going to taxes; $200/month in student loans; and medical insurance around $300/month out of pocket for a single coverage.

10 William Craft, "2013 State of the College," Concordia College, August 22, 2013, https://www.concordiacollege.edu/about/president/speeches-presentations/imagine-concordia/.

11 The exact numbers are difficult to pin down exactly, as Concordia has not adopted official nomenclature on its website to describe the positions. At the very least, there are currently 23 adjuncts.

12 See, for example, Barbara Walvoord and Virginian Johnson Anderson, *Effective Grading: A Tool for Learning and Assessment*, 2nd Edition (San Francisco: Josey Bass, 2013).

13 William Craft, "2015 State of the College," Concordia College, Moorhead, MN, August 22, 2013, https://www.concordiacollege.edu/about/president/speeches-presentations/2015-state-of-the-college/.

14 John C. Cross and Edie Goldenberg, *Off-Track Profs: Nontenured Teachers in Higher Education* (Cambridge: MIT Press, 2009).

15 Some of these adjuncts, like those in business and music, may have other full-time work and not experience the same stress of adjuncting. Adjuncts in the business school, many of whom have outside jobs, make significantly more per course (c. $8,000) than those in the humanities.

16 William Craft, "2013 State of the College," Concordia College, August 22, 2013, https://www.concordiacollege.edu/about/president/speeches-presentations/imagine-concordia/

LEARNING TO RENOVATE THE DREAM

A Trinity of Resilience

DR. RICHARD CHAPMAN
Professor of History

Near the close of his award-winning essay, "Between the World and Me," writer Ta-Nehisi Coates decries the destructive consequences of the (white) American Dream in a chilling passage.

> Once, the Dream's parameters were caged by technology and by the limits of horsepower and wind. But the Dreamers have improved themselves, and the damming of seas for voltage, the extraction of coal, the transmuting of oil into food, have enabled an expansion in plunder with no known precedent. And this revolution has freed the Dreamers to plunder not just the bodies of humans but the body of the Earth itself. *The Earth is not our creation.* It has no respect for us. And its vengeance is not the fire in the cities but the fire in the sky. Something more fierce than Marcus Garvey is riding on the whirlwind. Something more awful than all our African ancestors is rising with the seas. The two phenomena are known to each other. It was the cotton that passed through our chained hands that inaugurated this age. It is the flight from us that sent them sprawling into the subdivided woods. And the method of transport through these new subdivisions,

> across the sprawl, is the automobile, the noose around the neck of the earth, and ultimately, the Dreamers themselves.[1]

We are inheritors of the Dream along with the scientific and imaginative revolutions that propelled it. They tug persistently at our daily lives and occupy our very souls—inexorable forces of materialism, technological advance, and private satisfaction; gods of profit and pleasure; of endless progress and insatiable consumption, avalanche of things plundered and possessed.

More a nightmare to the many it excluded and exploited, so also the Dream increasingly appears at present to those it has perennially favored—its logic flawed, its fruits unsustainable, its religion a false hope. Coates finds us on an express train to perdition. Slowing down the locomotive is difficult for us to imagine, much less reversing its course. The vehicle hurtles onwards into night with no hope of redemption in sight.

The Dream's siren of success and salvation has long been at the core of our collective identity as a people. It comes to us shrinkwrapped in the sacred and secular mainstays of the national myth of ineluctable advance: Christianity and capitalism. For colleges and universities like Concordia, attuned to the Dream, Coates's message poses a stark challenge.[2] Overwhelmingly white, Western, and Christian, our institutions, practices, and constituencies disclose our participation in the economic values and social patterns underlying gaping inequality, societal division, and planetary exhaustion. We own a proud and rich heritage, a braiding of divine calling to influence the world, a mission to improve it through our good work, and a religious-inflected certainty of civic virtue. But a sacred inheritance can easily make us inattentive to the many ways we inhabit the world's problems rather than its solutions. Where does this leave us as an institution of higher education, boasting a mission to repair a world in sore disrepair through students ostensibly readied for responsible engagement in its affairs?

If we accept the basic sense of Coates's indictment—and I think we must—then the educational task at hand requires nothing less than a full-scale renovation of the American Dream. Dreams die hard, but Coates's judgment of a whole way of life thankfully comes packed with hidden insights and clues that may nudge us in the right direction. The full content of a truly new, and worthier, Dream for this moment has yet to come into view—if ever it does—but it must announce a new collectivity and a new commons: that privilege and power are rightfully gifts of the whole for the whole; that all lives matter, the weak and dispossessed, people of color, as much as the exalted and mighty; that we must sit with the planet and listen to it as never before; that "We are caught in an inescapable network of mutuality, tied in a single garment of destiny."[3] The grand task before us is to challenge our students to work out nobler dreams—and to guide them in the process. To that end our educational efforts going forward must somehow foster fresh discovery—a re-formation—of radical historical honesty before the past; hard-edged humility seasoned with hearty humor to live in the present; and hopeful humanity to act courageously in the face of an unknown future. Together they might compose a trinity of resilience as we accompany our students into uncharted territory.

Coming to the close of a semester course on African-American history recently, several students enthusiastically chortled, "Everyone should take this course." I happily agreed. Students were transformed by knowledge that "the half has never been told,"[4] as a recent study of slavery is provocatively titled. My training and deepest conviction as a historian persuade me that we cannot begin to face the present, much less prepare for the future, without a sober grounding in the past, deep knowledge of how we arrived to the present stage of global ecological and social impasse. We need more history, not less. But it must be thoroughly critical, honest to a fault, eyes wide open.

Supportive student voices reflected hard-edged readings and bitter films that exposed our racial history and deep societal divisions. I like to tell students that *Black history is American history*. Keeping it real is the safest path to awakening, pot-holed and scarred though the road be. The country's enormous economic achievements were built on dusky backs; our democratic liberties purchased through repeated exclusion of black folk—and others. It cannot be said that Ferguson, Missouri, is an aberration; it represents who we are. Students must recognize how a social hierarchy distributing both great reward and damning disadvantage partakes of a racial legacy in which they also dwell, the remnants of social sins committed through many past generations—and committed still. They must be led to inquire, where am I in the story?

Race is a powerful antidote to a triumphalist, progressive national narrative. But what of the history of the land itself, of the soil, water, and air; epochs past of plants, forests, mountains, and animals that populated the earth? Coates reminds us of a harsh truth and an on-going tragedy. Those who objectified human bodies to enact progress and to achieve profit paused even less at the thought of doing similarly to nature's. The environment has vital stories to share that must likewise be rescued from oblivion. Students will never develop resilience from ideal and mythic renderings of the past. Such readings intoxicate them in worlds of easy comfort that never were, and leave them utterly incapable of apprehending our present challenges.

Radical historical honesty extends to the beliefs, values, and ideologies that justified the subjugation of people of color the world over along with devil-may-care pillaging of the planet's resources. When the American Dream is unclothed to expose the Dreamers who erected its lineaments—and all of us who dream it still—questions of responsibility implore. Denial or celebration must recede to embrace a posture of hard-edged humility, learning that works an intellectual, spiritual, and social conversion.

Coates's words strike close to the soul of our own hallowed institution. As much as we might wish to identify with Martin Luther's heroic struggle against the principalities and powers of a sixteenth-century order, nowadays we more closely reside in places of social, political, and economic advantage. To claim Luther's mantle is at best misleading, at worst deceitful. We are impostors unless and until we squarely confront our responsibility in the face of Coates's intertwined challenges of human inequality and environmental devastation. Hard humility entails unqualified recognition that the Dream has proved horrendously destructive to the world's majorities, we the beneficiaries. The Dreamers have despoiled the land and its inhabitants—and they are us. "We are agents of extinction," as Paul

Kingsnorth puts it.[5] "But this isn't what we meant!" we protest. And yet, here we are. The college's memorable mission to influence the world is not wrong, but must be better calibrated to its woes; and we who do its work made fearfully mindful of our privileged status.

Hard humility demands a cultural *kenosis* of sorts,[6] emptying ourselves of the American Dream's worst features, its swill of control, its bitter draft of superiority, its poisoned dram of king-of-the-hill competition. The Dream seduces us to believe that we are masters of our own destiny. We are not. "The Earth is not our creation," Coates chides the powerful and prideful. Kingsnorth similarly warns that we are but a part of the natural world, which has changed many times over. He explains that "The brief period of climatic stability in which human civilizations have evolved is just that: a brief period. . . . Why should the state of the planet to which we have adapted survive forever? Nothing does."[7] Seeing more clearly our individual and collective responsibility for asserting control, unrightfully, over fellow humans and nature, we might adapt to our global situation in new and creative ways.

Resilience, explains political scientist Leslie Paul Thiele, is "[adaptive] change in the service of stability."[8] Hard-edged humility promises to be a handmaid of creative adaptation, opening a portal to the discovery and development of resilience. It may give us fresh eyes to see the promise and possibility of communal, contemplative, collective, and cooperative ways of living, especially those available in non-western spiritual traditions. Are there not better dreams than the ones we have dreamed so long?

There is great tragedy in our current predicament. We must take it seriously and yet we must also learn to laugh with it and about ourselves at the same time. I do not for a moment think that we should make light of the horrors visited upon societies and cultures in the name of human betterment, nor the holocaust that destroys the natural habitat in the name of progress. But the Dream we have dreamed is replete with ironies and absurdities and ought to be recognized as such with a healthy dose of humor. How laughable it seems, after all, that we murder the planet and each other in order to save them both. Humor may be the surest sign of a hard humility's discipline, laughter its best tonic. How else are we to move on knowing what we have wrought; knowing the harm we are capable of doing to achieve goodness, knowing how powerless we stand before nature's grandeur and vast complexity?

Learning to renovate the Dream must finally imbue students with new purpose and meaning—hope that liberates the seemingly impossible. But if the Dream has often animated their strivings and disciplined their choices and values in the past, what's to replace it? As much as globalization has changed the world we inhabit, students continue to chase individual success, financial independence, private comforts, and technological convenience, if only as a default. St. Louis native and community artist-activist Damon Davis speaks directly to the tension.

> [Humanity] may be in a time where collectivism has to happen because individualism and capitalism is eating itself. . . . For humanity to survive, a lot of this shit we been talking about for generations, for centuries, gotta be dealt with now. How we gonna get to the point where we talking about save the planet that we live on when we still talking about race, sexism, fighting about homophobia, fighting about this shit that's purely constructs of humanity and society?[9]

Davis reads from the same script as Coates—we have to do things differently, way differently. Perhaps at the end of the day real and lasting change is impossible, perhaps it is far too late in the day—certainly we cannot even venture a start without realization of a hopeful humanity.

Hopeful humanity can sink roots only in the fertilized soil of radical historical honesty and hard-edged humility. It recognizes the damage done to human and natural ecologies, admitting our own participation in these ruptures. We have "othered" both people and the natural environment for our own aggrandizement, treating as instrumental ends relationships that should be held sacred and inviolable. Coates's dire warning of "fire in the sky" echoes his prophetic mentor, James Baldwin, "God gave Noah the rainbow sign, no more water, *the fire next time*."[10] Now we see cataclysms of *fire and wa-*

ter—and far worse beyond the near horizon. Coates, I am convinced, would have us heed such warning, believing against the full weight of history and the awesome freight of the present that it is still possible to do so.

A hopeful humanity maintains that we might yet discover the capacity to come together across the fearsome divisions we have fashioned. Its pathway follows a course of reparative justice to narrow the chasms of alienation between our fellows and between ourselves and the environment. The latter is inconceivable without the former. Davis is surely correct—how can we even begin to address planetary environmental change if we cannot get our act together and figure out how to get along cooperatively across our manifold differences? Diversity amongst ourselves, as in the natural order, should fortify us—we need all the help we can get. It ought to tender hope, not sunder and destroy us.

So long as differences divide us, hatred and tribalism will win the day, and the resources of our common life will continue to be hoarded, monopolized, privatized, and commercialized in a frenzied race to the bottom that will leave us all, finally, losers. Thus is sustainability pillared not on *ecology* alone but upon the pylons of *society* and *economy* as well—to which Thiele sagely adds a fourth supporting column, that of *cultural creativity*.[11] A hopeful humanity is the bedrock for creative adaptation, flexibility, compromise, empathy, sharing, and trust—thickening out the heart and soul of resilience—when the going becomes treacherous and disappointments set in.

How might our students grow a robust sense of hopeful humanity? Our institutions will need, first, to become more representative of the societies in which we live. Otherwise we simply replicate the social privileges and economic imbalances that currently impede us, along with the implicit "us" and "them" attitudes such inequities engender. There is no better place to begin reparative work than at home with real and lasting investments in the diversification of students and faculty alike. How else will our campuses embody the hopeful humanity we wish to foster? We must value this most of all, beyond imperatives of demography, institutional diversity, numbers, and the budget's bottom line.

Looking out at an uncertain future, Damon Davis predicts matter-of-factly, "We a cold, the environment will fight back and get rid of whatever is making it sick."[12] He is surely right. Do we have the resilience to fight back first? Will our students? Only time will tell. But they have slim chance of dreaming truly redemptive dreams without first developing radical historical honesty, hard-edged humility tempered with hilarity, and a hopeful humanity. Little else matters. Even if, after all, we have sealed our collective fate, wouldn't it be nice to go down together? Better yet, what if we learned to summon the collective resources of our communities the world over to heal our social and ecological wounds? That is a syllabus we'd all love to see.

ENDNOTES

1 Ta-Nehisi Coates, *Between the World and Me* (New York, 2015), 150-151, emphasis added.

2 Since the (American) Dream is, for Coates, a belief in the reality of Whiteness, a racialized construct designed to promote the privileged of color and demote those of another color, it is not at all innocent, nor an accidental or well-intentioned meme, but is directly complicit in manifold pernicious processes of racism and racial domination at the core of United States history.

3 Martin Luther King Jr., "Letter from a Birmingham Jail," excerpt in *Voices of Freedom, A Documentary History*, Volume 2, 4th edition, ed. Eric Foner (New York: Norton, 2014), 269.

4 Edward E. Baptist, *The Half Has Never Been Told: Slavery and the Making of American Capitalism* (New York: Basic Books, 2014).

5 Paul Kingsnorth, "The Witness, Opening our eyes to the nature of the earth," *Utne Reader* 188 (Fall 2015), 62; originally published in *Tricycle: The Buddhist Review* (Spring 2015).

6 *Kenosis* from the Greek verb, to empty, recalls the passage in the epistle to the Philippians (see 2.7) where the writer explains how Jesus "emptied himself" of the privileges and powers of divinity to become human.

7 Kingsnorth, 63.

8 Leslie Paul Thiele, *Sustainability* (Cambridge, UK, and Malden, MA: Polity Press, 2013), 36.

9 Damon Davis interview with Mike Herr, "The Definition of an Artist," *Eleven Magazine: The Liner Notes of St. Louis* 12, No. 4 (May 2016), 12.

10 James Baldwin, *The Fire Next Time* (New York: Dial Press, 1963).

11 Thiele, 5.

12 Davis, 12.

THE WHOLE WORLD IS IN TROUBLE, SO WHAT CAN WE DO ABOUT IT?

DR. LEILA ZAKHIROVA
Assistant Professor of Political Science

> "We do not inherit the earth from our ancestors, we borrow it from our children."
>
> —Native American Proverb

The industrialization that broke the constraints of the agrarian age has clearly come at a price. The increased power associated with adapting carbon fuels to numerous economic applications has increased the risk of human damage to the environment and possibly even human survival. Carbon dioxide emissions appear to be the major culprit. As they accumulate in the atmosphere, they lead to changes in temperature. More carbon dioxide emissions means warmer temperatures. Human activities are releasing millions of tons of carbon dioxide into the atmosphere each year, about 80 percent of which is due to the use of fossil fuels. We have already seen some temperature increase (1.5 degree Celsius from pre-industrial level) and can anticipate more increases—perhaps in the range of 2 to 6 degrees Celsius—depending in part on how much more carbon dioxide is emitted. The 2 degree Celsius increase that so many of the early proposals aimed at ameliorating seems pretty much guaranteed. Now the question is how much higher will the temperature rise—3 degrees? 4 degrees? 6 degrees? If one chooses to allow less developed countries (LDCs) to proceed with economic development and relatively high CO_2 emissions, developed countries would have to cut their emissions to one-fourth of their current rate just to meet the 2 degree Celsius target. Therein lies two of the major roadblocks to taking effective action. Minor adjustments are not going to make much difference. Major adjustments are anathema to LDCs if it means freezing their opportunities to develop economically. After all, they reason, the developed economies made the problem; let them fix it at their own expense. Developed countries are no more eager to sacrifice their economic growth prospects than anyone else.

Therefore, the problem has multiple facets. Developed countries are not cutting back on their carbon habits very rapidly. Less developed countries are increasing their carbon consumption in hopes of achieving developed status. The question is just how acute the symptoms of global warming must become before something concrete in terms of a serious response can be accomplished? Whatever else they may have achieved, none of the multilateral, Kyoto-like agreements on responding to climate change problems have managed to cut back on CO_2 emissions so far. The Paris 2015 meeting was more positive than earlier meetings in Copenhagen or Kyoto; however, how and when the specific measures will be carried out remains uncertain under a Trump administration.

So what can we do about the deteriorating state of our global climate? We know that states must cut their reliance on carbon fuels. But how do we force states to do that in the absence of a world government? More importantly, how can a Lutheran liberal arts education prepare our students for a world in which a fairly benign environment can no longer be taken for granted? Concordia's Strategic Plan for the "whole world" gives us one answer in inviting us to "open the world to our students so that they understand and embrace the call to national and global citizenship."[1] For another answer, we must look to the history of global energy transitions. The following sections take up, in turn, the historical record of energy transition and the question of global citizenship. The history of energy transitions provides critical context to our current dilemma and establishes the imperative of civic engagement on a global scale.

First, if we look at historical patterns of global energy transitions—major shifts from one fuel source to another—these energy transitions have been driven primarily by leading economies in the world.[2] That is because to go beyond agrarian economies, leading economies needed cheap and abundant sources of energy to fuel their economic leads. While wind and peat were important parts of the rise to systemic leadership in the past, it took coal for the British and petroleum for the Americans to become predominant powers in the international system. The technology that they pioneered changed the type of energy that was most critical to operating at the production frontier. Assuming the new technology of the twenty-first century will be information technology based, that means whatever is useful for generating electricity at the least cost. Thus, a prime candidate for the next developmental breakthroughs involves substitutions for the coal and petroleum-driven innovations of the past several centuries. Presumably, this next cluster of technological innovation would then revolve around reducing CO_2 emissions in a significant way. In turn, reducing CO_2 emissions most practically involves systematically raising world energy efficiency, electrifying its transport systems and shifting from fossil fuels to the earth's wealth of renewable energy sources.

As the world approaches exhaustion of carbon fuels coupled with the high cost of consuming these resources for the environment and human health, we must ask whether the United States and China—the world's two leading economies as well as its biggest carbon emitters—are leading the world in replacing fossil fuels with alternative energy sources. More importantly, is their pace to the next carbon free energy regime fast enough to address adequately the threat of fundamental climate change? One thing is abundantly clear: coal and oil, which have fueled the global economy for the last two centuries, cannot be the power source of the twenty-first century. Making the transition away from carbon fuels will not, however, be easy nor will it come soon. One major reason is that the world has a high dependence on carbon fuels. In 2014, for instance, carbon fuels generated over 86 percent of the world's energy and the demand for energy is only expected to grow in the coming decades. Our collective appetite for energy is so great that some energy analysts claim that if oil did not exist we would have to invent it. As long as fossil fuels remain attractively priced thanks to ample supply, and continue to enjoy subsidies that far outweigh those given to renewables, they are likely to dominate the global energy mix for some time to come. New U.S. leads in petroleum and natural gas production, thanks to the fracking boom, are also difficult to suppress or ignore, even if the gains are unlikely to be long-term in nature. Most of the world is in a similar position. Consequently, even as late as 2015, renewables accounted for only about 9 percent of the U.S. energy supply—not much different from the share it had in 1980. These trends are more than sobering and suggest that the renewable age may well not emerge before the dawn of the next century—that is, if we wait for the lead economies to show the way to the next global energy regime as they have done in the past several centuries.

The leading economies to date have been moving at a snail's pace toward a clean energy based global economy. But, to address the threat of fundamental climate change we must act "at wartime speed to move the world onto an economic path that can sustain [our] civilization."[3] Even the most complex and sophisticated past civilizations, including the Mayan, the Mesopotamian, and the Sumerian, have collapsed due to mismanagement of natural resources and inability to adapt to climate variability. Despite geographic and temporal separation in each case, pretty much the same thing happened: governments collapsed, urbanization ceased, trade stopped, population growth ended—all forcing "a great simplification in human societies."[4] Our modern civilization is not immune to a similar fate. The collapse of ancient civilizations illustrate how fragile human societies can be. But more importantly, they indicate how resistant they can be to changing established patterns of behavior and action. Ironically, unlike ancient civilizations, the most astounding fact about our civilization is that we know what is happening to the climate and why. It is even more astounding how little we act upon what we know. As one American environmentalist puts it: "We are in a race between natural and political tipping points, but we do not know exactly where nature's tipping points are. Nature determines these. Nature is the timekeeper, but we cannot see the clock."[5] Thus, the challenge for the whole world in the twenty-first century is to transition away from fossil fuels before the clock runs out.

So to do something meaningful about global warming, we must galvanize our colleges by opening "the world to our students so that they understand and embrace the call to national and global citizenship."[6] It is our call, as educators, to nurture in our classrooms a generation of avid global citizens, which brings me to my second point. To be a global citizen means to be an active participant in addressing the challenges facing our highly integrated and interdependent world. A global citizen is "someone who identifies with being part of an emerging world community and whose actions contribute to building this community's values and practices."[7] Education for the sake of the whole world, then, is about redefining the meaning of citizenship from one based on legal rights and duties within the confines of a sovereign nation-state to one based on belonging to the wider world community and taking actions toward creating a just and sustainable world. It is our duty as educators to help our students understand that their daily existence is dependent on a global community and the health of the environment. In the twenty-first century we are connected in inextricable ways to people and events around the world through social media, transportation, technology, and communication such that every choice we make may have repercussions for people and communities around the world. Perhaps the most important understanding students can gain from Concordia is to ask themselves such critical questions as: What is my role in the world? How can I acquire the skills and experiences that will prepare me for the twenty-first century? Our role as educators is to direct our students to effective ways to ask and answer these hard questions and to prepare what some call "a global game plan" that includes language training, opportunities to study away, and internships that will develop their cross-cultural and global competencies."[8]

Global citizenship is a sticky concept that lacks a definitive meaning on which everyone agrees. At a very minimum, a global citizen, according to some, must be aware of the world's complexity and interdependence, appreciate differences, and be able to communicate across cultures.[9] To be a global citizen in this century particularly entails what Concordia's Strategic Plan calls practicing "thoughtful and informed stewardship of natural resources and to conserve earth's vitality and beauty."[10] Conserving earth's natural resources will not come from the developing world nor should we place that burden on the countries that are struggling to meet the basic needs of their people. Conservation must emanate from the developed countries that use a disproportionate share of the world's finite resources. What would most benefit the planet as a whole would be an intensive race between China and the United States to see which economy could become greener faster, they are not leading fast enough to make a difference. Businesses have a natural inclination to continue exploiting natural resources as long as they remain profitable, and the fossil fuels remain immensely profitable despite the falling prices. Thus, the responsibility of reversing the clock falls on the citizens of developed countries that must demand their governments save the planet from further deterioration. Global citizens who are truly concerned with the plight of the whole world can place normative constraints on their governments against undermining our very ability to live on this planet. Martin Luther did something similar by challenging the prevailing worldview of his age, questioning conventions he found offensive. Time is ripe for us to ask our own hard questions starting with "Is the industrial model of development based on fossil fuels sustainable and just?" We owe our students, at the very minimum, an exposure to alternative models of development that do not use up the global commons (such as clean air, fresh water, oceans, forests, etc.). Sustainable development, after all, is about meeting our needs without compromising the ability of our children to fashion societies that make their life worth living. That is difficult enough in good times and is likely to become even more difficult if the environment continues to deteriorate.

ENDNOTES

1 "Whole Self, Whole Life, Whole World: The Plan for Concordia College 2012-2017," Concordia College, last modified October 12, 2012, https://concordiacollege.edu/files/resources/strategicplan.pdf.

2 The argument on energy transitions and systemic leadership is based on the author's forthcoming book with William Thompson in *Racing to the Top: How Energy Fuels System Leadership in World Politics* (Oxford University Press).

3 Lester Brown, *The World on the Edge: How to Prevent Environmental and Economic Collapse* (New York: W.W. Norton & Company, 2011), 18.

4 T. Prugh, R. Constanza, and H. Daly, *The Local Politics of Global Sustainability* (Washington DC: Island Press, 2000), 8.

5 Brown, *The World on the Edge*, 15.

6 "Whole Self, Whole Life, Whole World," Concordia College.

7 Ronald Israel, "What Does it Mean to be a Global Citizen?" *Kosmos: Journal for Global Transformation*, (2012), available at http://www.kosmosjournal.org/article/what-does-it-mean-to-be-a-global-citizen/.

8 Heide Hobbs, Harry Chernotsky, and Darin Van Tassell, "International Studies and the Global Community: Transforming the Agenda," *International Studies and the Global Community*, (2010), 4606.

9 Heidi Hobbs and Harry Chernotsky, "Preparing Students for Global Citizenship," paper given at APSA, Charlotte, NC, 2007.

10 "Whole Self, Whole Life, Whole World," Concordia College.

WHOLE COLLEGE

INTRODUCTION

In my discipline of social work, students are drawn to and sometimes overwhelmed by the challenge of complex human and social problems. For over 100 years, the social work profession has been addressing poverty, marginalization, and oppression and striving to provide conditions of hope and models of change. According to the National Association of Social Workers, a "historic and defining feature of social work is the profession's focus on individual well-being in a social context and the well-being of society. Fundamental to social work is attention to the environmental forces that create, contribute to, and address problems in living."[1] In recent decades, social work scholars and practitioners have paid increasing attention to the disproportional effect of climate change on under-resourced populations of lower economic privilege or social status. Social work is concerned with the impact of climate change for all, but pays special attention to vulnerable populations when it comes to the climate change consequences of natural disasters, prolonged droughts, urban pollution, food insecurity, disrupted employment, displacement, and destabilized assets. In response, social work seeks to work alongside and empower vulnerable populations and others to affect meaningful change. It has identified strengthening "social responses to environmental change" as one of the twelve "Grand Challenges for Social Work" and has developed strategies to respond to the environmental inequities of the Anthropocene epoch.[2]

When faced with such large scale environmental and human rights challenges, how does one avoid becoming overwhelmed to a point of inaction? How does a person maintain hope in the capacity of human agency for change? My experiences in teaching and in social work practice have taught me that strategies that target social problems only through the macro sphere of policy and systems change, without involving people in community, are less effective and contribute to feelings of helplessness. Certainly policy and systems change need to be part of the response to the climate crisis and other human rights concerns. But for social work and others, these strategies need to include a *person-in-environment perspective*, or focus on the *interaction* between people and their environments in order to create the most meaningful change. Establishing human relationships and involving people who experience and care about the problem on the community level is essential to the process of change and to planetary citizenship. This perspective can inform how we prepare students at Concordia College. As Eleanor Roosevelt famously reminds us, we have the greatest potential to impact change in the world by first harnessing the influence and opportunities we have in our daily lives and local contexts. She states,

> Where, after all, do universal human rights begin? In small places, close to home—so close and so small that they cannot be seen on any maps of the world. Yet they are the world of the individual person; the neighborhood he lives in; the school or college he attends; the factory, farm, or office where he works. Such are the places where every man, woman, and child seeks equal justice, equal opportunity, equal dignity without discrimination. Unless these rights have meaning there, they have little meaning anywhere. Without concerted citizen action to uphold them close to home, we shall look in vain for progress in the larger world.[3]

At Concordia, how do we take a Whole College approach to prepare students for planetary citizenship "close to home"? How do we instill knowledge, skill, and hope among students so that they can be resilient and know that their actions (small or large) do matter, even in the face of enormous global challenges. The collection of essays in this section of *Reformation and Resilience* propose how Concordia College *is* and *can* harness opportunities in a Whole College context to prepare students as liberally educated leaders, informed about the world, and ready to make a difference as they engage in community problem-solving and service. In the tradition of the Lutheran reformation and the Lutheran notion of vocation, it is the examined self, the examined experience, and the collective action of individuals that create change. This will be the process needed to address the challenges of climate change. In his opening essay, Dr. Ernest Simmons asks, *what could be the role of Lutheran higher education in the current global context and what resources do we have to prepare our students to be effective sustainability leaders?*[4]

The following essays provide examples or proposals of how the student experience and program offerings at Concordia is, or can be, the resource and path by which students develop key knowledge about themselves, their vocation, and their environment. The essays also provides examples of how students can, and do, develop essential skills to interact with others and impact change. These are the building blocks of planetary citizenship.

Readers will learn how music at Concordia promotes discovery and builds compassionate connection, and how participation in music leads to engaged citizenship. In other essays, readers are invited to imagine how the college may be able to better blend curricular and co-curricular activities to enhance holistic learning for students as well as meet aspirations of the college's strategic plan and the newly formed integrated learning initiative. An innovative and brave proposal for residence life is presented that paves a way for transformational student learning and leadership development. Finally, readers will review the history of the college's commitment to student vocational development though both the liberal arts and professional programs and explore potential synergies as the College prepares students as leaders for planetary citizenship. These essays contain themes of reformation, student growth and development, and appreciation and hope of what is possible at the college as it sends forth leaders to meet the challenges of the twenty-first century.

The essays presented comprise just a few examples of college activity that prepares students for the demands of planetary citizenship. Numerous other examples can be found in athletic programs, theater, campus ministry, student organizations, student affairs, and academic programs. Essays included in other sections of *Reformation and Resilience* have likely revealed the many rich learning experiences at the college.

While presented as distinct examples, these and all college activities are bound together by their service to the Concordia's mission[5] and to its current strategic plan which aims "*to offer an education of the whole self, for the whole of life, for the sake of the whole world*".[6] Certainly, this is the work of the whole college. And it is the great privilege of the faculty and staff to undertake it, in the small place, close to home, that we call Concordia.

—Dr. Kristi Loberg, Associate Professor and Director of Social Work Program

ENDNOTES

1 National Association of Social Workers (NASW) Code of Ethics, Preamble, accessed at http://www.naswdc.org/pubs/code/code.asp

2 Susan Kemp and Lawrence Palinkas, "Strengthening the Social Response to the Human Impacts of Environmental Change," *Grand Challenges for Social Work Imitative Working Paper* No. 5 (Cleveland: American Academy of Social Work and Social Welfare, 2015), 3-4.

3 See United Nations Foundation website, "10 Inspiring Eleanor Roosevelt Quotes" at http://unfoundationblog.org/10-inspiring-eleanor-roosevelt-quotes/

4 Ernest Simmons, "Lutheran Liberal Arts Education: Nurturing Vocation for Planetary Citizenship," in *Reformation and Resilience: Lutheran Higher Education for Planetary Citizenship*, eds. Ernest Simmons and Erin Hemme Froslie, (Minneapolis: Lutheran University Press, 2017), 19.

5 "The mission of Concordia College is to influence the affairs of the world by sending into society thoughtful and informed men and women dedicated to the Christian life," accessed at Concordia College, Moorhead, MN, website at https://www.concordiacollege.edu/about/our-mission/

6 "Whole Self, Whole Life, Whole World: The Plan for Concordia College 2012-2017," Concordia College, last modified October 12, 2012, https://concordiacollege.edu/files/resources/strategicplan.pdf.

TOWARDS A HOLISTIC LEARNING EXPERIENCE

Embracing the Full Scope of a Residential Liberal Arts Education

DR. KENNETH FOSTER
Associate Professor of Political Science and Program Director of Global Studies

Residential colleges have long struggled to understand the relationship between the faculty-led academic work that students do and the wide variety of other activities students engage in on campus. Traditionally a hard distinction was made between the academic curriculum and what was termed the *extra-curricular* side of the college experience. The understanding was that the real and important learning occurred in the academic courses. Extra-curricular activities were fun and extraneous things that could be pursued, but certainly not at the expense of time spent on academic work. Over the years, at places such as Concordia, this understanding shifted somewhat with the new term *co-curricular activities* suggesting that these other parts of the college experience work alongside the academic curriculum to help students develop as whole individuals. Now, in 2017, the drive to broaden and deepen our commitment to integrative learning offers an unparalleled opportunity to move further in the direction of integrating the traditional academic curriculum with the co-curricular activities and learning experiences that students find to be so meaningful. The sustainability and diversity initiatives likewise call faculty, staff, and students to think in new ways about where and how learning happens and to develop a new model for education in a residential liberal arts college.

If Concordia College and other residential liberal arts institutions are to maximize their potential as places of transformative learning and student development, we need to dismantle the barriers between the traditional academic and co-curricular sides of the campus in order to create a holistic learning experience for our students. This will entail taking the outstanding pieces we already have and fashioning a new system in which there is *one curriculum* that spans the entire life of the college. In this holistic curriculum that demonstrates the unique power inherent in a residential liberal arts college, the various pieces of the student's college experience will be integrated, enabling each student to achieve personal development as a whole person committed to planetary citizenship and equipped to forge a meaningful career path. Webs of connections between the former curricular and co-curricular parts of the campus will facilitate the emergence of new ways of organizing learning that prepare students more effectively for the lives and careers they will pursue after college. Students will no longer see a basic distinction between academic classes and their other activities—instead, they will achieve learning goals and outcomes through an integrated program that transcends the traditional credit-hour model and includes the entire campus and surrounding community.

To be sure, the vision set out in the preceding paragraph is highly abstract and incomplete, raising all sorts of difficult (but exciting) questions. One way to start exploring this is through an examination of how activities on campus (not only those labeled as co-curricular) are already helping students to engage in learning that ties directly into academic learning goals. My involvement with campus sustainability work at Concordia has opened my own eyes to the learning value of co-curricular activities and to the many ways in which students learn while in residence. In the rest of this chapter, I explore some of what I have seen, from a faculty perspective.

One of the most exciting things I have encountered here is students taking the initiative to develop and bring to completion projects aimed at benefiting the college. Early on in my involvement in sustainability work, a couple of students from the Student Environmental Alliance (SEA) came to me for advice on how to convince the administration to create a Concordia EcoHouse. Through working on this, the students learned a great deal about how to do research, how to write proposals, how organizations work, and how to make change happen. They were also able to practice their public speaking skills. In subsequent years, I had opportunities to work with SEA students on other projects, such as one to create a bikeshare program for the campus and one to gain approval to have chickens at the EcoHouse. Even though the latter was not successful, through all of these and others, students acquired both what we might call academic knowledge and concrete practical skills. Unfortunately, these students struggled to make time to pursue their projects and were unclear about how this work related to what they were accomplishing in their academic programs. Yet they will always remember and draw lessons from their experiences working through SEA to make change happen even as they forget many of the courses they took. But what if their involvement in SEA and participation in pushing a project forward was formally recognized by the college as a vital part of the education they received at Concordia? What if their academic major rewarded them for this work and enabled them to integrate it into their academic studies?

Involvement in student organizations gives students the opportunity to develop valuable skills. At first glance, the typical skills that come to mind here—interpersonal communication, holding meetings, planning events, etc.—may seem one step removed from the more lofty intellectual aims of the academic side of the campus. Yet, in fact, students in most organizations are routinely engaging in critical thinking, exploring new perspectives, and acquiring new knowledge. Members of the Student Government Association (SGA) grapple with complex issues as they seek to pursue priorities and simply to manage existing SGA commitments. The turn at Concordia to embrace sustainability more fully was partly driven by the efforts of a particular SGA leadership team, which created the SGA Sustainability Fund. Since then, because of the existence of this fund, each SGA team has had to learn about sustainability and to decide how best to incorporate attention to sustainability into its structure and programs. Another example is how members of the SEA have struggled to define their organization's purpose as they have sought to combine traditional environmental concerns with newer justice-centered perspectives on sustainability. At the same time, they constantly face the question of how to attract members and influence the campus. As the leadership changes every year, new students are given a chance to learn through doing. The learning that goes on in student organizations is profound, with connections to many fields of study over on the academic side of the campus. What if involvement in any student organization was part of the college curriculum and recognized as such on the transcript? What if faculty across campus told students how valuable these organizations are and invited students to bring their experiences in them into their academic program?

Student residence halls provide another site for a rich array of learning opportunities. Liberal arts colleges are committed to the residential model of education not just because it provides convenience for students, revenue for the college, and peace of mind for parents. We insist on it because we know how much students gain from learning to live in community as a community of learners and of diverse people. A tremendous amount of time and energy is put into creating a rich residential experience for students, and students engage in all kinds of learning as a result. Residence life programs explicitly seek to promote learning that goes beyond simply learning to get along with a roommate. As an example, the eco-reps program at Concordia supports a group of students who work to promote environmentally friendly living in the residence halls. This theme, and the activities that could emerge from it, links to a wide variety of academic disciplines on campus, and those who serve as eco-reps become immersed in a powerful interdisciplinary learning experience. What if living in a residence hall was explicitly conceived as a core feature of the Concordia curriculum, an essential part of the learning experience? What if a partnership between the faculty and residence life staff enabled the joint pursuit of learning goals and new forms of academic learning that fully tap into the potentials inherent in the residential college model?

Lastly, the experience of being involved in the campus organic garden has further demonstrated to me the problematic nature of the distinction between the academic curriculum and other student activities at Concordia. From the beginning, students have driven the campus garden project forward with help from faculty and staff. The excitement and energy students have shown when it comes to the garden pales in comparison to how they feel about most of their academic courses. Yet they have already learned so much through their involvement with the garden, including a great deal of what we would call academic knowledge. One of the most interesting aspects of this experience working with the garden is how apparent it became that the staff of facilities management has a great deal to teach our students. What if the staff of the Office of Student Affairs, Facilities Management, and other non-academic units of the college were formally recognized as teachers and mentors? What if faculty and staff worked together with students to bridge the divide (sometimes real, sometimes only perceived) between academics and the real world?

Few would disagree with the proposition that, while at a residential liberal arts college, students learn a great deal outside of their academic coursework. One merely needs to think for a moment about music ensembles and athletics, two areas not touched on above, to realize how much learning goes on outside of academic courses. By keeping the academic curriculum separate and distinct from all those things we call co-curricular, we are missing the opportunity to harness the full power of a residential liberal arts education. In various subtle and not so subtle ways, we continue to send the message—always problematic but especially damaging these days—that the academic study of subjects is separate and distinct from the real life that goes on across campus and out in the world in between class sessions. In fact, the co-curricular and other activities in which students engage clearly help students to achieve the college's Goals for Liberal Learning. Yet these goals seem to be applied only to the academic side of the college. What would it take to fashion *one curriculum* that would fully unleash the power of an education at a residential liberal arts college? Structural change, to be sure, plus a willingness on the part of faculty and staff to understand and learn from one another while entertaining radically new notions of what a college education should look like. Concordia has begun this process through the adoption of integrative learning as a core feature of a Concordia education and the new PEAK (Pivotal Experience in Applied Knowledge) requirement. Rigorous and forward-thinking implementation of the integrative learning initiative, and some additional bold steps along the way, are needed to enable the college to thrive in a future in which preparing students for planetary citizenship amidst a world of complex problems is of paramount importance.

I joined the faculty of Concordia College in the fall of 2012, and I have encouraged the singers in the choirs I conduct to engage in numerous and meaningful texts that celebrate God's creation. During my second year, I enjoyed teaching the Chapel Choir Aaron Copland's "In the Beginning," a large work for mixed choir and a woman soloist. (We were honored to collaborate with one of our voice professors, Dr. Holly Janz, on a regional tour that included this score in the spring of 2014.) This particular work uses the text from Genesis 1 that describes the moments of God's creation of the world. Many singers stated throughout the year that they enjoyed revisiting this text that, though familiar to most, was made new to them with Copland's genius touch.

In the fall of 2016, the choir prepared music that focused specifically on the natural world, and the choir enjoyed dialogue and discussions on themes of sustainability and what it means to be a member of a global community. We sang a score by Argentinian composer Alberto Grau titled "*Kasar mie la gaji*," which translates to "the earth is tired." The score uses only those four words and alternates between a sense of mourning and a sense of urgency. We paired that score with Australian composer Stephen Leek's work titled "*Ngana*," which is a choral meditation on the aboriginal words for shark, fish, and the blue water. This set included Dan Forrest's "Hymn of Creation," which uses Isaac Watts' text "I Sing the Mighty Power of God" as a reminder that the world is not ours, though we are charged with its protection. I intentionally selected works by composers who span the globe to emphasize the worldly importance of increased awareness of sustainability issues and practices.

Described above are examples from the choral corners found within Hvidsten Hall of Music, but it is important to note that the celebration of creation is happening in all our ensembles at any moment. The orchestras and bands on campus program music through which the composers may be taking us on a trip along the Danube River, or through Arabian deserts. In private studios, students can be singing solo songs with similarly descriptive texts, or working through piano pieces that call to mind images of nature. Connections between music and nature are tangible, and our students are both the providers

THE LIBERAL ARTS AND PROFESSIONAL PROGRAMS

Moving from Dissonance Danger Zone to Opportunities for Synergy

DR. CYNTHIA CARVER
Chair of Division of Professional Programs and Communication Studies, and Professor of CSTA

The current Concordia College Strategic Plan is built around a framework that calls for a Concordia education that will offer an education of the whole self, for the whole life, for the sake of the whole world.[1] While "Whole College" is not a designated area in the current strategic plan, Concordia has long thought about the education it offers in terms of the educational experience delivered by the "whole college." For a number of years Concordia captured this philosophy in an approach that was known as "The Concordia Equation,"[2] arguing that a Concordia education did not come from just classroom experiences, but also from co-curricular and extra-curricular activities, from residential life experiences, and from the religious life of the college. Publicity materials at that time, however, described a whole college experience that included a liberal arts education and career preparation, the two being described as separate parts of the whole rather than intersecting or overlapping parts.

So for years despite embracing a broad view of an educational experience Concordia College, like many liberal arts colleges, struggled with articulating, understanding, and at times accepting the role of professional programs given our liberal arts educational mission. Hence the question, do professional programs at a liberal arts institution lead to a dissonance danger zone or an opportunity for synergy?

I. The Early Years

The early years of the college clearly displayed what might be termed a dissonance danger zone. Carroll Engelhardt, in his history of the first century of the college, notes that practical instruction was a defining element of the early years of the school with programs in business, teaching, domestic science, and physical education.[3] However, when the second principal of the school, H.H. Aaker, began to push for more of a business college model, dissonance on campus reached the point that Aaker eventually resigned. He established a new business college while Concordia moved to embed itself more firmly in the liberal arts tradition, creating questions about professional programs and laying the seeds for an assumption that traditional liberal arts disciplines and professional program are in opposition to each other, engendering a sense of dissonance, or at best ambivalence at the college.

Given the Lutheran heritage of Concordia, it is perhaps surprising that the college was not more successful at integrating professional programs and the traditional liberal arts. Several Lutheran principles might have served to engender synergy including Luther's beliefs about the importance of vocation in occupations, the importance of holistic understanding, or the existence of paradoxes.

II. The 1990s to the Present

The author of this essay joined the faculty of Concordia College in 1989 as a member of an academic department that straddled the divide between traditional liberal arts disciplines (rhetoric) and professional programs (public relations, organizational communication, speech-theatre education). By this point in time, professional programs on Concordia's campus had expanded to include: nutrition and dietetics, nursing, journalism and other broadcast media, social work, exercise science, additional business tracks, etc. Almost from the start, however, it was apparent to this new faculty member that questions remained about the appropriateness, role, and desirability of professional programs at the college. It was also apparent that even some faculty members in the professional programs saw their programs as falling outside the bounds of Concordia's liberal arts mission.

A turning point may have come in 2006 as the college began the implementation of a new core curriculum. This was a change that involved not only a complete revision of the college's core requirements, but also the development of a new set of Liberal Learning Goals for the college. The new Liberal Learning Goals included:

- Instill a love of learning.
- Develop foundational skills and transferrable intellectual capacities.
- Develop an understanding of disciplinary, interdisciplinary, and intercultural perspectives and their connections.
- Cultivate an examined cultural, ethical, physical, and spiritual self-understanding.
- Encourage responsible participation in the world.

The adoption of the new Liberal Learning Goals contributed to redefining the role of professional programs within Concordia's liberal arts mission. First, the new liberal learning goals defined the liberal arts in terms of the learning outcomes a liberal arts education should achieve, as opposed to whether a program was one of the traditional liberal arts disciplines. Second, with the new liberal learning goals it was easier for professional programs to see themselves as centrally located within the liberal arts. Developing a love of learning, honing transferrable intellectual capacities, encouraging responsible engagement, etc. were all in alignment with goals and outcomes that Concordia's professional programs were already working toward. Finally, the Liberal Learning Goals assisted faculty members in professional programs with articulating to prospective students and parents, faculty colleagues, and even themselves, ways in which their programs were so much more than just "training" for a job or career. Today, there are multiple ways in which Concordia's professional programs contribute to our student's liberal arts education. Just a few examples include: providing an emphasis on discerning and developing a strong sense of vocation; giving extended attention to the development of intellectual capacities such as oral and written communication, critical thinking, problem solving, perspective taking, etc.; and providing an appreciation for and attention to the interdisciplinary nature of areas of study. Examples of several mission statements for Concordia's professional programs capture the synergy that is possible when professional programs are a grounded part of a liberal arts education.

> Education: The mission of the department is to prepare caring, competent, and qualified teachers who act in the best interests of the students they serve in working to become professional educators.
>
> Nursing: The mission of the nursing program is to influence the health of the world by sending into society compassionate, thoughtful, and informed baccalaureate-prepared professionals dedicated to the vocation of nursing.
>
> Joint Mission Statement for Concordia Professional Programs: The mission of programs in the Division of Professional Programs and Communication Studies is to provide students with knowledge and experience to develop competencies that integrate the goals for liberal learning, develop a sense of vocation, and foster a commitment to service and leadership in their chosen professions.[4]

In the past several years Concordia College has moved to make integrative learning the hallmark of a Concordia liberal arts education. In 2015 Concordia's Faculty Senate approved a conceptual framework for integrative learning that included five criteria:

1. Venture beyond the classroom.
2. Encounter and work alongside persons or groups wrestling with complex situations, problems, questions, or challenges.

3. Construct meaningful interdisciplinary responses to these encounters, taking seriously multiple perspectives.
4. Discover questions, perspectives, and problems not necessarily scripted in a course syllabus and work through ambiguity, frustration, and disequilibrium.
5. Sharpen and apply skills and competencies that flow out of a liberal arts education and are relevant to future employment.[5]

As the framework for intensive integrative learning experiences (PEAK Experiences) was developed, synergy between the liberal arts and Concordia's professional programs was again demonstrated as professional programs at the college were used by integrative learning working groups as exemplars, both in conceptualizing the five criteria that would define integrative learning and in operationalizing those criteria. Student teaching experiences, semester-long social work practicums, nursing clinical experiences, and exercise science internships are some examples.

While some may still question the continued growth of professional programs on Concordia's campus, this author would argue that today the Concordia Equation is well-positioned to argue that the strong liberal arts education Concordia College provides comes from the "Whole College," our traditional liberal arts disciplines, our core curriculum and our professional programs that are deeply grounded in Concordia's Liberal Learning Goals.

III. The Future

Carroll Engelhardt argues in his history of the first 100 years of Concordia College that while the college has clearly changed over the years, continuity has usually characterized those changes.[6] The changing nature of professional programs and the liberal arts on Concordia's campus, is but one example of that. In so many ways the college has moved from viewing professional programs as a source of dissonance, to an opportunity for synergy. The question that remains is what types of changes we will see in the future that will continue to strengthen a "whole college" approach to our delivery of a liberal arts education.

While this essay has concentrated primarily on the evolving nature of Concordia's professional programs, the author also sees opportunities for the evolution of Concordia's traditional liberal arts disciplines. Professional programs on our campus would be strengthened by additional opportunities for interaction with traditional liberal arts disciplines. While larger college majors may have decreased the potential for double major combinations between professional programs and traditional liberal arts disciplines, other areas of synergy are possible. Examples might include: interdisciplinary minors, certificates, or cognates developed from courses in traditional liberal arts disciplines that would be taken by majors in professional programs. The development of a medical humanities program would be one example. Courses developed by traditional liberal arts disciplines and customized for professional programs could extend the impact of traditional liberal arts disciplines. Examples might include an English course on writing for business or the sciences or a religion course on death and dying for nursing or social work students. Or in keeping with the Concordia Strategic Plan initiative of moving beyond traditional credit bearing classes, professional programs and traditional liberal arts disciplines could join together for intensive case study experiences that would bring together students from diverse disciplinary perspectives, an approach that is currently being used by a group of professional programs on our campus.

Conclusion

As the introductory essays in this book make clear, the problems and challenges our world will face going forward will continue to increase in complexity and severity, with effective responses being key to our survival. Our world today needs a "Whole College" approach to a liberal arts education. Our world needs the synergy that comes from professional programs that are solidly grounded in the liberal arts and our world needs the synergy that can come from traditional liberal arts disciplines embracing creative partnerships with professional programs.

ENDNOTES

1 "Whole Self, Whole Life, Whole World: The Plan for Concordia College 2012-2017," Concordia College, last modified October 12, 2012, https://concordiacollege.edu/files/resources/strategicplan.pdf.

2 *The Concordia Equation: A Complete Person*, marketing materials for Concordia College, Moorhead, MN.

3 Carroll Engelhardt, *On Firm Foundation Grounded* (Moorhead, MN: Concordia College, 1991).

4 *Concordia College Catalog*, Volume 114, 24.

5 "Integrative Learning Task Force Report" prepared for Concordia College, Moorhead, MN, 2015.

6 Engelhardt, op.cit.

MUSIC AT CONCORDIA COLLEGE

Sustaining the Garden

DR. LEIGH WAKEFIELD
Associate Professor of Music

Concordia's culture of learning is a rich blend of shared experiences. A vibrant faculty, supportive administrators, sound leadership, and a caring support staff are all dedicated to a common goal. Each strives to create a place where heart, mind, and spirit become one. As a colleague of mine likes to say, "Concordia is all about liberating the arts rather than simply studying the liberal arts." Building connections and relationships are key elements of the Concordia education: *whole* self, *whole* life, *whole* world. Our students are encouraged to embrace the wonder in the world as they build the foundation for a lifetime of learning. What an incredibly fertile environment this is!

As a community of learners we are all stewards of our shared intellectual and spiritual resources. This responsibility is not taken lightly. Historically, Concordia has been intentional about its programming, staffing, and planning. Short-term goals and long-term planning are remarkably cohesive and embody the college's commitment to creating a sustainable spirit of inquiry. What defines the Concordia experience? It is a place where the liberal arts have taken root in a faith-based environment that is rich in tradition and steeped in an eloquent mission. *The purpose of Concordia College is to influence the affairs of the world by sending into society thoughtful and informed men and women dedicated to the Christian life.* Anything is possible in such an environment. In today's world, where the value and purpose of a college education is increasingly questioned, examining and identifying those qualities unique to Concordia's four-year experience are critical to the future of the college. We are a community that shares its passions, seeks truth, explores the world, embraces faith, and welcomes all into the active process of discovery—life together, through each other, tethered to faith and bound by a profound sense of vocation. Hard to define, but easy to sense, these are the qualities that define Concordia. It is within this rich environment that music is taught, experienced, and created at Concordia. It is an art form that has come to embody the spirit of the college and a medium through which experiential learning takes root.

Studying music at Concordia College is much more than acquiring an advanced skill set. Creating music is the art of communication—between composer and musician, musician and audience, musician and musician, and between conductor and ensemble. It is experiential in nature, cross-disciplinary in scope, and exists in all cultures. In this context music is the study of relationships and systems of interaction. It is fluid, interconnected, and codependent. It doesn't exist apart from other disciplines; rather, it reflects the world around it. While the courses are music specific, universal concepts such as listening skills, flexibility, creativity, organization, problem solving, and verbal communication are intentional outcomes of each course. This is what makes teaching music so exciting at Concordia! It is as varied as every student. I recently received an email from a student of mine, Brandon Salden '15, who spent the past year teaching in an inner city school in Minneapolis, Minnesota. He is about to leave for the Santa Cruz Cooperative School in Santa Cruz, Bolivia, where he'll be teaching grades 5-12 band. He writes:

> I find myself nervous for the new position: new curriculum, new students, new school, new town, etc. But not once was I worried about the fact that it is in another country. Of course I have the nerves of moving so far away from family and friends, but I'd feel the same way moving to another state. I believe I have to thank Concordia for a large part of that. Through my experiences and education at Concordia, I have learned to be flexible,

> adaptable, open-minded, curious, critical, and tolerant of different cultures and ideas. Through my studies as a Spanish minor I am able to speak the language of this new country and will be able to communicate to the people of Bolivia. I am familiar with Hispanic culture and while I will most definitely experience culture shock, I will not run away from it. I will embrace the differences and soak up as much as possible. In the end, I can break all this down into a few short words: I love you Concordia. You have given me everything I need to be successful; not only in my field, but also as a human being. You have made me inquisitive of all, critical of information, and a lifelong scholar. Soli Deo Gloria.

Time and time again I find our graduates, whether a music major or not, transformed by the process of discovery they experience through their engagement with music. Nearly one-third of the student body is involved in music because opportunities to participate are numerous and varied. As such, music is at the core of Concordia and, in many ways, shapes the collective pursuit of discovery across the college. Furthermore, music's pedagogical paradigm allows for interaction with the student at every level. Imagine if every subject area had one-on-one instruction (lessons), small group discussion (chamber music), large group interaction (orchestra, bands, choirs), core classes (music theory/music history), career-specific courses (conducting, diction, music education, etc.) and creative presentations and collaborations (performances). Just think of the possibilities this structure affords. It is the hope that all students become co-inquirers, independent thinkers, and active learners and that these skills are transferred to their learning in other areas. Music is an active agent for intellectual and personal growth and opens portals to co-inquiry and self-actualization. However, no matter how confident an institution is in its mission, what we think is being taught and what a student learns may not be the same. Missy VonItter, a student of mine who graduated in 2013 (after having spent two years teaching music in Palestine) provided this perspective on her education. It is reassuring when a student shares thoughts such as these:

> Within the music department, I did not just learn about performing and practicing music. I developed a lot as an individual, a leader, and a thinker. My studies in music incorporated many things. I learned that conducting is more than standing in front of a group of people—it demands confidence and leadership; developing a teaching methodology; thinking about the mind and human practices; creating theories for good teaching and defending those theories. Teaching music itself requires patience and understanding. Within music there exists all external subjects and life skills.

What remarkable testimonies these are. While by no means can it be assumed that every student who studies music at Concordia shares the same depth of experience, I am confident that most find their musical experiences invaluable in shaping their college experience and beyond. One needs only to attend the annual Christmas concert, homecoming concert or numerous performances throughout the year (both large and small) to witness the breadth of commitment and engagement. Why is this? What is it about studying music at Concordia that is unique? I believe it is in large part due to the college's Lutheran tradition, the college's mission and campus culture. While trends in education come and go, the underpinnings of a Concordia education continue to be influenced by its Lutheran roots, the emphasis on service to our neighbor (local and global), and the cultivation of a community of learners. Music at Concordia is about building relationships. It is a multi-dimensional human endeavor in which the tangible is transformed by the intangible and the concrete (notes, rhythms, dynamics, text, etc.) are infused with the abstract (balance, phrase, harmony, timbre, etc.) In this way, music's impact lies less on what one hears at the moment and more on what one experiences between the notes and over time. It taps into the spiritualty of existence and places trust in the unseen. In doing so, participants build deeper and lasting connections that extend beyond themselves. When music is made in community (ensembles) this depth of the experience grows exponentially. Harmony and the good for the whole supersede the needs of the individual. Empathy towards others, care for all, cooperation and communication are core values of music at Concordia.

While much of this conversation has focused on the musician, I would be remiss if I did not mention another and perhaps the most important component of music—the audience. Music has the potential to touch us in ways that transcend our everyday existence. Performance art is a dialogue between performer and listener. It is through this act of giving and receiving that students are transformed by the world within themselves and the world that surrounds them. The beauty of music is discovered through communion with others, in the sharing of gifts and the nurturing of mind, heart and soul. This is Concordia. This is music.

Because it is both curricular and co-curricular, music at Concordia cultivates an organic process where inquiry, reflection, and faith meet to form connections that infuse learning with new meaning. Music becomes the portal through which students explore issues of faith, passion, compassion, justice, and curiosity, while Concordia provides the context. Wonder, curiosity, passion, and humility take root as students embark in a transformative four-year journey. Emphasis on active engagement, integrated disciplines, and experiential learning prepare students for the rapidly changing world in which they live. A college is a fluid and active ecosystem. It is a garden of education: seeds of discovery are sown into soil that is rich in fertile thought and tended by those who deeply care about the health of the harvest. Concordia is fortunate to have this vibrant legacy. By bringing together such a vibrant mix of perspectives where each is in pursuit of a shared common goal, music has the potential to create an end product that is greater than the individual. Whether in the classroom or rehearsal hall, the study of music encourages the development of the whole person. Students are co-creators and partners in the process of discovery. The synergy this creates is palpable.

We are entering an exciting time at Concordia and higher education in general. Are the liberal arts relevant in today's world and, if so, what changes are required to reflect the changed social, environmental, and global context in which we live? I believe Concordia is uniquely equipped to meet these challenges and thrive for years to come. The college's foundation is strong and its vision is timeless. The gift of community, inquiry, and faith has created an environment capable of change and sustainability. Music will play an integral role in shaping the future of Concordia. It has helped to create a culture of harmony that resonates across disciplines and fosters the creative spirit necessary to adapt and embrace the challenges that lie ahead.

MUSIC, NATURE, AND THE DEVELOPMENT OF COMPASSIONATE CITIZENSHIP

DR. MICHAEL CULLOTON
Assistant Professor of Music

Concordia College students who participate in the choral program here often meet at an intersection of two of Martin Luther's passions: music and nature. The *music* part of this equation is quite simple to understand. These singers gather in community each afternoon following what has been a day of rigorous academic pursuits to seek similar enriching rewards in their musical activities. The *nature* part of this equation is found in texts that offer praise to God and to all of God's creation, and such texts are regular inclusions on concert programs both on campus and as part of national and international choir tours. Furthermore, these texts offer the students an opportunity to reflect on the world around them and the important role we all must assume as the protectors and sustainers of our natural world.

If the students who participate in music at Concordia can graduate with a greater appreciation of God's creation, they will be likely to transfer this appreciation into works of service within the communities that they settle into after commencement. This is one of the motivating factors for our faculty as we work to find a musical home for each and every student that desires to participate! Research examining the positive impact that choral singers have within their communities will be discussed below and may provide ample inspiration for Concordia and colleges like ours to encourage its students to participate in choirs for the betterment of the campus and community life.

I. Music and Nature at Concordia College

For many years, nature has been a strong theme in the music performed by choirs at Concordia College. Paul J. Christiansen, the conductor of The Concordia Choir from 1937 to 1986, often programmed works that included texts that spoke to the beauty of God's creation. Examples include his arrangement of "Vidi Aquam (See the Water)," his original composition, "Four Travel Pictures (Mountains, Trees, Rolling Plains, and The Ocean)," and his father's arrangements of "O Day Full of Grace," and "Beautiful Savior."

In 1986, René Clausen was hired to replace Christiansen and brought a new musical style to the choral program and especially to The Concordia Choir. These differences notwithstanding, his programs are rooted in the sacred tradition and also include many scores that offer singers and listeners alike the chance to reflect on themes related to the natural world. Such examples include his own composition "Canticle of Praise" along with Aaron Copland's "The Promise of Living," "i thank You God for most this amazing day" by Eric Whitacre, movements from F. Melius Christiansen's "Celestial Spring," and even "What a Wonderful World," made famous by jazz great Louis Armstrong.

Besides music sung by The Concordia Choir under Clausen's leadership, there is also a prevalent theme of nature and creation woven into the fabric of our annual Christmas Concerts. It is quite common to see and hear these themes appear in the opening sequence of the concert, thus providing an outlet for all singers in the program to experience these types of inspiring texts firsthand. Examples include the use of the hymn tunes "All Creatures of Our God and King" and "This is My Father's World," as well as "The Heavens are Telling the Glory of God" by Marty Haugen, "Jesus Christ the Apple Tree" by Elizabeth Poston, and the American folk song "Now is the Cool of the Day," to name but a few.

and the recipients of these wonderful messages of hope, renewal, and awe as we stand in the presence of all that God has created.

II. A Musical Move Toward Compassionate Citizenship

In 2009, Chorus America undertook a major survey and research project that examined the lives and habits of singers. The final report from this study is titled *The Chorus Impact Study: How Children, Adults, and Communities Benefit from Choruses*[1] and shows that there are many connections made between those who participate as singers in a choir and the ways that they live their lives with regard to choices they make to positively affect the communities in which they live. For example, the report finds that "adults who sing in choruses are remarkably good citizens."[2] Among other attributes, the research shows that adult chorus members serve as volunteers "significantly more frequently than the general public . . . and are significantly more likely to attend a church, mosque or synagogue than general public members." The research also indicates "choral singers contribute much more financially to philanthropic organizations than the average American." Additionally, "chorus members exhibit greater civic leadership than their fellow Americans as they are significantly more likely to report voting regularly, reading books and newspapers regularly, serving as officers of civic organizations, and working for political parties."[3]

In their foreword to the final report, Todd Estabrook and Ann Meier Baker, chairman of the board and President/CEO of Chorus America respectively, state the following: "Simply put, if you're searching for a group of talented, engaged, and generous community members, you would do well to start with a chorus . . . In a society that seeks civic engagement and student achievement, the data in this report suggests that it would be a mistake not to leverage the benefits that choruses bring to children, adults, and the communities they serve."[4]

Such findings motivate me to encourage our collegiate singers to continue their choral adventures after they graduate from Concordia. By participating in church choirs or community-based ensembles, our graduates will surround themselves with many other community members who share their ideals and concerns with regard to local and global citizenship. They will contribute greatly to the life of their community while having their own musical cup filled to overflowing at the same time.

In the winter of 2015, a move toward compassionate citizenship was demonstrated in our music building when students in the Concordia Chapel Choir created a new sustainability council that was open to any singer who wanted to participate. Caleb Heaton served as the first chair of the council and states that "the mission of the sustainability council is to produce the least amount of waste possible and to create an exemplary department in this respect."[5] This committee considered several ways that we can be more thoughtful in our actions including the recycling of concert programs, the use of less paper used for reproducing music and other announcements or information, electronic distribution as the sole option for syllabi, and the use of refillable plastic water bottles on tours. The sustainability committee will continue their work into the foreseeable future and desires to expand to include students from all major ensembles as well as faculty and staff members as we consider ways to limit and reduce our use of natural resources throughout the whole department.

Concordia's students are well equipped to drive progress, inspire action, and positively influence the affairs of the world in whatever ways they choose. It is my hope and, perhaps more importantly, my belief that we can reawaken them to the beauty of creation and the ubiquitous presence of God within and around it through the sharing of their musical gifts. Creating awareness of this beauty can help to increase their desire to become more aware of their role as the guardians of the natural world through important work toward sustainability and the protection of natural resources.

ENDNOTES

1 Todd Estabrook and Ann Meier Baker, *The Chorus Impact Study: How Children, Adults, and Communities Benefit from Choruses* (Washington, D.C.: Chorus America, 2009).

2 Ibid., 5.

3 Ibid., 5.

4 Ibid., 3.

5 Caleb Heaton, in discussion with the author, July 11, 2016.

THE RESIDENCE HALL AS LABORATORY FOR PLANETARY CITIZENSHIP

MS. MIKAL KENFIELD
Director of Residence Life

A liberal arts education was, at one time, provided solely by an institution's formal academic curriculum. With the rise of a more comprehensive and professional field of Student Affairs in the twentieth century, this traditional formula of education began to change. Through this natural evolution of higher education, there is now an increased emphasis on the co-curricular experience of the college experience. Once viewed as extra-curricular, involvement such as residential living, participation in student organizations and campus leadership opportunities are now viewed as an integral part of a student's liberal arts education. The benefits of this rich, collaborative partnership between Academic and Student Affairs are described in *Learning Reconsidered* as providing a transformative education. Specifically, "[a] transformative education [that] repeatedly exposes students to multiple opportunities for intentional learning through the formal academic curriculum, student life, collaborative co-curricular programming, community-based, and global experiences."[1] If we desire to send forth graduates who are prepared to be planetary citizens, it is vital that these co-curricular opportunities be utilized to their fullest—and no greater opportunity exists for transformative education than that of the residential experience.

Incoming students may be apprehensive about many parts of their transition to college, but living in residence is often the part of this transition that generates the *most* anxiety. For the majority of students, this is the first time they have had to share a bedroom (or even a bathroom) with another person—and it is likely to be with a complete stranger. However, as is often the case, discomfort and engagement with "the other" creates a rich environment for growth. It is this environment that makes the residential experience a perfect laboratory for planetary citizenship—and one that, with appropriate resources and structure, has the potential to positively impact the behaviors and actions of a generation of students.

New students face the challenges of academic rigor within the classroom, but back in their residence hall room they grapple with equally weighty issues. Thrust into a novel living environment, this new community of peers may include individuals whose values, cultures, and beliefs are unknown or misunderstood. Increased independence, while often exciting, may feel disorienting or unstable. Interactions with peers from diverse backgrounds may cause students to question their own beliefs and values—even their own identity.

Indeed, this residential experience is rife with paradox and ambiguity—an ideal context for students to put into practice their liberal arts education. This first (for many students) foray into independent living means an increased focus on personal decision making, and many of these decisions will not have clear right or wrong answers. Similarly, students will likely encounter group norms that conflict with their personal ethics.

The typical Student Affairs approach to assisting students with this ambiguity is by using the Sanford's theory of challenge and support[2] in conjunction with frameworks for moral, ethical and identity development.[3] [4] In general, students are challenged by purposeful creation of environments (like residence halls) that are rich with ambiguity and pluralism. Student Affairs practitioners then appropriately support students by equipping them with skills to navigate, and even flourish, in this uncertainty.

I. Looking Forward

This philosophy of challenge and support is alive and thriving at Concordia, and in countless other institutions of higher education. And yet, much more can (and should) be done to harness the potential of the residential experience as a part of a transformative education. Although the official era of *in loco parentis* is over, much of the traditional framework of the residence hall environment harkens back to this belief that students need an adult caretaker. This can be seen not only in the long list of housing policies and procedures that exist, but also in the power structure put in place to adjudicate those who violate policy or standards. Additionally, the increased focus on student as customers means residents are unlikely to be involved in the upkeep of their physical environment, as well as perhaps sheltered (or rescued) from uncomfortable peer interactions.

The residential environment has the potential to deeply influence students' understanding of their impact on their surroundings and their neighbors—if an institution is willing to deviate from the concept of housing as purely customer-service driven. This change in philosophy would set Concordia apart in an increasingly competitive enrollment landscape, as well as allow the college to find greater alignment with our founders' initial vision and mission.

Much of the current community nature of the residential experience is closely controlled. Administrators of the college set and enforce policy, create the community standards, and hold students accountable using prescribed methods. While the intentions are well-meaning, this sets up the residents to be passive members of their own community. How can we expect our students to be active in the pursuit of social justice or understanding of multiple perspectives if they have never had practice engaging in challenging dialogue with their neighbor? Or in setting a common vision for their environment—a vision that respects the rights of all members, not just those who are in the majority?

To truly prepare our students to be planetary citizens, we would do well to view the residents and staff as co-inquirers, working together to create standards of behavior and conduct. This would allow residents to take ownership of their living experience, and to consider how their own behaviors may impact their peers. Conflicts with roommates could be utilized to grapple with the reality of differing values and beliefs, rather caving to the pressure from parents to quickly "fix" the problem for students. Approaching conflicts through this lens of a transformative educational experience could help students (and parents) understand why the quick fix—and desire to avoid uncomfortable conversations—is not ideal. By allowing students to gain skills in successfully navigating conflict with peers, we would more fully prepare them to be responsibly engaged in their communities.

Just as policies and procedures are currently established *for* the residents, the conduct system seldom allows for students—as members of the impacted community—to be involved in the adjudication of cases. Instead, an administrator handles the investigation and adjudication of all conduct cases. Moving to a system of peer conduct boards, or even a system based wholly on the concept of restorative justice, would allow students to fully engage in the challenge of balancing the ideals of community with the realities of human behavior. Students whose behavior infringed on the rights of others would have to engage in honest dialogue with their peers, finding ways to repair any damage to the community they caused. Conversely, the victims of the actions would have the opportunity to see the humanity of the perpetrator—not a one-dimensional villain, but a flawed and complex human, worthy of grace. Seeing peers in such vulnerable and raw circumstances would allow students to put into practice radical love of neighbor.

In the same way that community standards are currently generated and monitored by administrators, so is the physical environment of the residence hall. Students have little control (or involvement) in energy or water use, waste disposal or other environmental needs. They are, in many cases, passive consumers with little incentive to change their behaviors.

Shifting the philosophy away from "student as consumer" to "student as partner" would allow for a much deeper, more meaningful and engaged living experience. To incentivize more sustainable practices students could have their housing fees pegged to actual energy use: they might be charged a flat initial housing fee, and then weekly or monthly charges based on their floor or building's average energy use. Of course, this would require students to be educated on what kinds of behaviors are the most costly, in terms of energy, as well as a willingness to work collectively for the benefit of all.

Similarly, students are not involved in the physical upkeep of their residence hall. Building services staff clean common areas, remove garbage and recycling, and attend to other maintenance issues. By shifting to a model where students are responsible—or even partially responsible—for cleaning or waste removal, there would be a real and compelling incentive to reduce the amount of waste generated. Students could research methods such as composting, choosing items with less packaging, recycling or reusing, and then set goals for the building regarding waste reduction.

Finally, the residence hall environment can be rife with consumerism. Even before first arriving to campus, students are inundated with messages that they should buy all-new bedding, accessories and decorations. In fact, some of these mailings are even generated by the college. Moving to a more sustainable, minimalist philosophy would send a powerful message to incoming students and families. Suggestions such as utilizing thrift stores or providing in-hall "free-stores" or "lending libraries" of seldom used items could change the consumer patterns of students—patterns that would last long after graduation.

II. Making Change Possible

This shift in philosophy (from *in loco parentis* toward student and administrator as co-inquirers) would provide students with a truly transformative educational experience—but it would require significant dedication and resources. Administrators and hall staff would need the appropriate development, education, and support to successfully engage students with these issues. It is likely that staffing levels would need to be increased, or job descriptions reimagined. Most importantly, significant work would need to be done in providing a rationale to students and families about why residents are expected to be so engaged and involved in their residence hall communities. With many institutions now providing luxurious amenities to draw in prospective students, it would be critical to articulate why the college is choosing to focus on meaningful engagement in care of community, rather than marble countertops or climbing walls.

To be sure, there would be real and numerous challenges to creating this kind of transformative residential experience. But now, more than ever, we have an obligation to face these challenges and must pledge to do the necessary hard work. We must rededicate ourselves to sending out into society thoughtful and informed planetary citizens—citizens who are committed to tending to their neighbors, their communities, and their earth.

ENDNOTES

1 Richard Keeling, ed., "Learning Reconsidered: A Campus-wide Focus on the Student Experience," National Association of Student Personnel Administrators and American College Personnel Association (2004), accessed January 15, 2017, https://www.naspa.org/images/uploads/main/Learning_Reconsidered_Report.pdf.

2 Nevitt Sanford, *Self and Society: Social Change and Individual Development* (New York: Atherton, 1966).

3 William Perry, *Forms of Intellectual and Ethical Development in the College Years: A Scheme* (New York: Holt, Rinehart, and Winston, 1970).

4 James Marcia, "Development and Validation of Ego Identity Status," *Journal of Personality and Social Psychology* 3 (1966): 551-558.

CASE STUDIES

INTRODUCTION

As a Christian institution, we have been called to address the challenges of the twenty-first century and consider our role in addressing them. This book has helped us think about who we are, why we are here, where we have come from, and where we are going. These reflections prompt questions about application: How can we live lives of purpose? What is our sense of neighbor? How can we empower students to take responsibility?

This book has addressed sections of the strategic plan including Whole Self, Whole Life, for the sake of the Whole World, and addressed by the Whole College. The following section is intended to provide examples of best practices in preparing students for twenty-first century problems at Concordia College. With a guiding purpose of education, each case study provides a perspective that addresses the nature of today's educational environments with careful consideration to the diverse ways that this happens. Programmatic and specific applications invite readers to imagine how they can implement practices that address the changing nature of education.

The following case studies address diverse aspects of our campus including Academic and Student Affairs with science, social science, and humanities represented. The case studies include the incorporation of Community-Based Research in a communication capstone course, the examination of food waste use and campus change in an English classroom, changes made for a more sustainable science student education, the creation of a High Impact Leadership Training (HILT) trip model that connects Academic Affairs and Student Affairs for student-led sustainability experiences, and a model for teachers to engage their students in discussions about climate change.

—Dr. Stephanie Ahlfeldt, Associate Dean of the College
and Professor of Communication Studies

TECHNOLOGY WASTE AND SUSTAINABILITY

Community-Based Research in the Computer-Mediated Communication Capstone

DR. STEPHANIE AHLFELDT
Associate Dean of the College and Professor of Communication Studies

Our communities are abundant with people working to create better lives for those around them. When we are able to connect our passion and gifts with the needs of the world, we are able to experience the gift of vocation. The mission of Concordia College is to prepare students to address the needs of the world using their gifts. In order for students to realize and develop these gifts, they need opportunities. Opportunities for self-discovery and development can be found in every corner of this campus, but experiences that push us further than we previously thought possible are unique. As the needs of the world evolve and challenges grow, we are faced with an even greater demand to develop core competencies in our students.

Content matters, but process allows for problem solving regardless of content area. Further, scholarly research skills are fundamental to social progress. If we aim to make the world a better place, we must use the skills we have to ask the challenging questions, draw on the knowledge of others, and find answers to pressing problems.

Community-Based Research (CBR) is one approach to fostering these skills in students. In addition to high-level academic rigor, CBR develops mutually beneficial relationships between community partners and faculty-student scholars.[1]This case study provides a description of CBR and how it connects to Concordia College, an example from our institution, and considerations for the future.

I. Community-Based Research

Community-Based Research (CBR) is collaborative, change-oriented research that engages faculty members, students, and community members in projects that address community-identified needs.[2] There are many ways to integrate CBR into the curriculum. The assignment must have a clear question to be answered. It also must be important to the community, and of significant interest to an academic discipline.[3]

Trisha Thorme, CBR Director at Princeton University, shared examples of projects with our campus in a recent workshop. Examples included: program evaluation, data compilation, needs assessment, asset mapping, oral history, policy research, risk assessment, promising practices, business planning, website construction, public relation campaigns, grant writing, literature reviews, curriculum development, archival research, and case studies. The course could be a CBR course or it could be a non-CBR course with an optional or required CBR project. Other models include independent CBR projects or research with faculty members, CBR internships or practicums, theses or capstones, and dissertations.[4]

In the academy, we have other community-based examples to draw from. Service learning and internships are two examples of community learning. In these examples, students are able to offer their time and talents to help organizations meet their goals while being very intentional about applying their learning to the experience. Ideally, the process is beneficial to the organization and student. These models are cornerstones of our institutions and certainly need to continue, but they are distinctly different from a CBR project.

At Concordia College, our curriculum is built around responsible engagement with the world.[5] If we are to act responsibly, we must first consider the needs of our neighbors. As many organizations are limited by time, money, and personnel resources, college students have a unique opportunity to meet the needs of our community organizations. They are highly educated, looking for challenges to develop their skills, and have the time to devote to such work. As academics, we know that knowledge comes from careful, systematic research designed to answer important questions. As the world becomes increasingly more complex and resources for organizations decrease, we are seeing an increase in student competency and interest in research work.

Many colleges across the country are building strong undergraduate research programs on their campuses. Students are entering their undergraduate studies looking for and expecting to have research opportunities. Further, students are taking the courses that prepare them to take on the research projects previously reserved for graduate-level studies. As colleges continue to build strong research programs, the opportunities for students to apply their skills must be parallel.

Our institutional mission calls us to influence the world by sending into society thoughtful and informed men and women dedicated to the Christian life.[6] CBR does exactly that. It sends thoughtful and educated men and women out to help their neighbors and friends with the gifts they have been given. Further, Concordia has recently adopted an integrative learning model for our curriculum. This model challenges us to prepare students for high-level problem solving by presenting them with complex dilemmas and empowering them to discover answers. The CBR model aligns with integrative learning in that it requires students and faculty to venture beyond the classroom, encounter, and work alongside people dealing with complex challenges, and respond using unscripted processes. These experiences provide important information for organizations, but they also help students better understand themselves and their potential in the world.

II. Case Study Application

The capstone course I teach, Computer-Mediated Communication, challenges students to use communication theories related to technology to research the impacts of our changing modes of interaction. Here, students connect with local organizations for CBR projects.

As a class, we initially worked with the United Way of Cass-Clay to find organizations that were newer to the community and looking for more support. In groups, students met with each organization to clarify their research question(s). Groups had the semester to dive into the literature, collect and analyze data, and present their findings to the class and the organization. This model worked well and has led to continued relationships with several of the organizations.

As the world continues to evolve, the "real life" application of our research also evolves. It has become clearer to me over the years that we cannot study technology without discussing the impact it has on people and places. The CBR project that I had been doing was more diverse as students worked with different organizations on different topics. This fall, I integrated sustainability into the course, and we worked with one local organization to better understand technology waste.

To prepare for the project, we read and discussed the global complexities of technology and sustainability issues. We examined the relationship between technology and the environment by inviting local leaders into our class and also visiting them in their organization. Students asked the community leaders more about the problems they face and what questions they wanted to work on right away. The students returned to the classroom, split up into groups, and clarified their research questions. The conversations with the organization continued throughout the semester as students tested their perceptions and assumptions before moving ahead with their work. In the end, the groups explored knowledge and barriers to technology recycling, and best practices and recommendations for recycling campaigns. The organizational leaders joined us in class for the final presentations. Students wrote research reports for the course requirements and provided their presentation slides with executive summaries for the community partners.

III. Limitation Considerations

A successful community research program takes resources. Faculty and students must be willing and capable of accomplishing the tasks. With already stretched schedules, there must be a way to compensate faculty for the important and time-consuming work of mentoring students. Students also have limitations to their time and are better able to fully contribute to the project with credits that can be factored into their full time load. By using existing courses for these experiences, we are meeting the goals of our mission without unreasonably challenging our resources.

The abilities of undergraduate students are limited. Most have few, if any, professional research experiences. The level of expertise that would be ideal is typically found among graduate students, but those students are at a point in their careers where the focus of their research must be more field-related, which may or may not align well with community research. Undergraduates are in a position to be more open to diverse projects, but will have more limited skills. This is where the faculty become an even more significant factor in the model. The advising of the faculty member or faculty instructor is critical to the success of these projects.

Even with strong faculty mentoring, projects may be limited in their success. It is possible that organizations will have limited use for the results of the research. Further, the scope of the projects will be limited as good research takes significant amounts of time and the semester is short.

There are potential costs to the organizations. Partnering will require some time to work with the faculty and students throughout the semester. Organizations will also be letting someone into their organization and the results may not produce the desired outcome. Projects can be designed to address questions that have limited costs based on outcome. As these relationships develop in coming years, there may be room for more vulnerable analyses. Better yet, students may find themselves as employees for these organizations where they can continue their work as an organization insider.

Conclusion

The opportunities for CBR far outweigh the challenges. With careful planning, organization, and attention to relationships, our undergraduate students can have a meaningful impact and incredible learning experiences in our community. Community and policy research programs are designed to match student skill with community need. In a growing community like Fargo-Moorhead, there is plenty of community need.

ENDNOTES

1 Greg Halseth, et. al, *Doing Community-Based Research: Perspectives from the Field* (Montreal: McGill-Queen's University Press, 2016).

2 Kerry Strand, et. al., *Community-Based Research and Higher Education: Principles and Practices* (San Francisco: Jossey-Bass, 2003).

3 Tricia Thorme, *Introduction to Community-Based Research*, workshop at Concordia College, Moorhead, MN, on August 11, 2016.

4 Deanna Cooke, and Trisha Thorme, *A Practical Handbook for Supporting Community-Based Research with Undergraduate Students* (Washington DC: Council on Undergraduate Research, 2011).

5 "Academics" page on Concordia College, Moorhead, MN, website, accessed in 2016 at www.concordiacollege.edu/academics.

6 "Mission Statement" on website of Concordia College, Moorhead, MN, accessed at www.concordiacollege.edu/about/our-mission/

SUPPORTING STUDENT INGENUITY FOR SUSTAINABILITY IMMERSION

MS. NATHALIE RINEHARDT
Director of Student Engagement

Alternative break trips (ABs) are a form of hands-on learning that colleges and universities have utilized in order to engage students in critical thinking, service, and the outside world. Often these trips have strong student input and student leadership, seeking student voice and opinion when it comes to what the itinerary should include and what learning outcomes students are seeking. Melody Porter's research found that ABs help students better understand the complexity of social issues, make connections to their academics and future plans, and become active citizens.[1] Concordia College is no stranger to the alternative break program, having sent students on immersion and service trips locally, nationally, and globally through established programs such as Habitat for Humanity, Justice Journeys (faith-based service trips), Campus Service Commission and Lead-Now to name a few.

The first Concordia Habitat for Humanity spring break trip went out in 1991 after the campus chapter was established.[2] It was in 1992 that the chapter had expanded enough to send multiple trips over spring break. About 55 members total spent an entire week in one of four states: Georgia, Texas, Mississippi, and South Carolina.[3] Since then, the tradition of student-led ABs at Concordia has been strong and intentional, supported by faculty and staff for almost 25 years. I also know that with each successful AB have come incredible resources dedicated to managing logistics, securing partnerships, establishing fundraising ventures, writing learning outcomes, developing reflection tools, recruiting students and trip advisers, and building student leader capacity. Because of the time-intensive nature of ABs and Concordia's already strong programs, I was not immediately supportive of a new AB brought to my attention in fall 2011 when a student walked in to my office and said "I have an idea."

"I have an idea" is a common statement from student leaders that I've heard in my time working as a student affairs professional. It's a sign that students are excited and committed to learning, but it also is a sign that more work is coming my way, and perhaps a tough conversation about how their idea is certainly valued, but it just isn't possible for the college to support it. When presented with new ideas, questions I commonly consider include: Will this idea live on longer than the student leader who initiates it? What value will this new idea bring to campus, specifically student life? How will the idea be implemented, who will need to help, and are there resources available? The questions come from my concern for sustainability, a term explained by Leslie Paul Thiele: something is sustainable if it endures, persists, or holds up over time.[4]

Ironic then, that the new idea brought to me in the fall of 2011 was in regards to a sustainability AB trip: a student-planned, student-led alternative spring break trip that would allow students to research, study, and propose solutions to a sustainability issue in the United States. Fast forward six years, and this spring break trip program is still occurring with a commitment to student leadership and learning. After its first year, the program was so impactful on students, that student leaders gave it the formal name of HILT: High Impact Leadership Trips. Wanting to ensure that it didn't end after they graduated, two seniors further developed the principles of the program, wrote a HILT handbook to guide future student trip leaders, and petitioned campus administrators for support. Although HILT isn't a recognized student organization or housed within one campus department or office, the program has proven sustainable and popular among students.

The HILT model incorporates five core principles set forth by the student founders:[5]

1. Organic student leadership—The HILT trips are student-designed and student-led. The leader(s), themselves, receive invaluable experience as they take on the full responsibilities of planning and executing their ideas while also gaining the satisfaction and excitement that comes with successfully turning a dream into a reality.
2. A focus on important issues with both local and global dimensions—When trying to understand social, cultural, political, environmental, or any other issues that exist in our world today, it can often be difficult to connect the localized impact these issues have with their globalized impact and vice versa. However, as Concordia seeks to positively influence the world through the education of its students, it is vital that students be able to appreciate a "big picture" view while also appreciating the importance of local action and grassroots efforts.
3. Purposeful yet fun immersion—HILTs allow the natural inquisitiveness, passions, and enthusiasm of the students to shine by bringing students out of the classroom setting and into a new, exciting, and freeing environment. Each student is encouraged to pursue the questions and ideas that most interest him or her, so that the trip is individually meaningful. To add to the fun, students are given free time to build relationships with the other students on the trip and to explore the place which they have traveled to.
4. Centered on developing leaders and activists—The HILT leader(s) are likely to gain the most leadership experience. However, one main purpose of having student leaders rather than faculty leaders is to support the group's functioning as a cohesive, co-

operative decision-making student team, with each person contributing to the experience in his or her own way. The HILT focus on activism enters through the meetings and conversations that students have with individuals who have taken outstanding action to positively impact the issue of the trip. By learning from the examples of activists who have made a difference, students can determine ways that they could also lead and advocate.

5. Impacting campus—Whenever possible, students who participate in HILTs engage with other students who are active in the issue at hand. This gives Concordia students a very beneficial view of what other colleges around the nation are doing and what Concordia could do as well. It is the goal of HILTs to foster individual enthusiasm, passion, and know-how so that students can choose to take greater action not for credit, not because they are told to do so, but by their own initiative, and from their own drive and passion.

The first HILT was to Berea, Kentucky, in February 2012. Two student leaders, a faculty adviser, and 13 student trip participants embarked on a week-long immersive experience to study the environmental and social impacts of mountain-top removal for coal mining.[6] Since the inaugural trip, subsequent trips have occurred:

2013: Portland, Oregon—focused on studying Portland's progressive city infrastructure.

2013: Bemidji, Minnesota—focused on local and organic food movements, as well as community movements surrounding sustainability.[7]

2014: Everglades National Park, Florida—students experienced and studied the Everglades while discussing the social and environmental concerns of Florida's shrinking wetlands.[8]

2015: Sacramento, California—students studied sustainable agriculture and organic farming methods.

2016: Yellowstone and Zion National Park, Utah—students learned about conservation efforts within the national park system.

2017: Portland, Oregon—students studied mindfulness and minimalism, visiting a Tiny House Project and considered how they could live with less.

2017: Detroit, Michigan—students studied environmental justice and learned how a city's laws and policies can impact its citizens.

Challenges have certainly presented themselves with this type of model. To have students plan basically every element of a trip means that details go missed, hard lessons are learned (lessons that could have been avoided), and last minute surprises are common. But the learning from these challenges is also invaluable. To give students a sandbox in which they are challenged to think on their feet, to make do with what they have, and to understand the consequences of poor planning is just as important as the knowledge they've gained through analyzing data, understanding policy, or conducting research around a sustainability issue.

One student HILT trip leader explained the difference between this leadership experience and other experiences she's had at Concordia: "Planning a HILT has been a lot more rigorous than I initially thought. Since I chose to lead the trip by myself, I have had to set aside large chunks of time where I can organize my thoughts, call people, and get things planned out. In other leadership roles, I can usually delegate tasks so that there is a team of people working on completing a task, which is much easier to do than bearing the workload alone."[9]

One of the unintended benefits of this new program has been the connectivity between academic affairs and student affairs. The roles of student trip leaders, the Office of Student Engagement, the faculty trip adviser, and the Sustainability Office have all differed from trip to trip, but one constant commitment has remained: supporting student ingenuity is the business of all and is a key factor in engaging student leaders to think critically and globally. For a community to thrive, connections are critical. Often we might work in our silos, relying on those closest to us to weigh in on decisions and offer up partnership. However, the approach with the HILT program has been to look across campus and form uncommon partnerships between offices and programs that don't necessarily work together. These connections have led to richer conversations, greater understanding of each office's role on campus, and an enhanced experience for students when it comes to their out-of-the-classroom education. The collaborative approach is one that students embrace as well, as one HILT trip leader articulates: "By building student led trips specifically targeted with sending a message in a way students want to receive it, collaborative opportunities become present."[10]

An important lesson I've learned from the HILT program has been to embrace the "I have an idea" statements and encourage more of them from aspiring student leaders. These ideas can spark far better results than what staff and faculty may be able to conjure in a meeting room or classroom setting, and it gives students an active role in their learning. It is active learning that I see played out time and time again, as students are given the responsibility for the HILT trips from start to finish. Norleen Pomertanz articulated the importance of the individual in the learning process with "to learn is to act; a learner must do something in order to learn."[11] When presented with this opportunity for active learning, I had no idea if it would be sustainable and what the future would hold. A HILT trip participant saw the possibility and said, "Hopefully, this trip will start a sustainability chain reaction."[12]

ENDNOTES

1 Melody Porter, "Assessing Alternative Breaks: Moving Beyond Sleeping on Floors and Pass-the Candle Reflection," *About Campus* (November/ December 2011): 21-24.

2 Jeanne Grommes, "Habitat for Humanity Fighting Homelessness by Building Homes," *The Concordian* (Concordia College, Moorhead, MN), Nov. 2, 1990.

3 Patricia Blum, "First Habitat House Dedicated, Spring Break Plans Underway," *The Concordian* (Concordia College, Moorhead, MN), January 24, 1992.

4 Leslie Paul Thiele, *Sustainability* (Cambridge: UK Polity, 2013), 7.

5 "High Impact Leadership Trips (HILTs)," Concordia College, Moorhead, MN, website, accessed 2016 at https://www.concordiacollege.edu/about/sustainability/student-leadership-and-learning/co-curricular-involvement/hilt/.

6 Stephanie Barnhart, "Sustainability Trip to Appalachians Planned," *The Concordian* (Concordia College, Moorhead, MN), February 3, 2012.

7 Mark Melby, "Biking for Sustainability," *The Concordian* (Concordia College, Moorhead, MN), October 20, 2013.

8 Hans Peter, "An Enlightening Souvenir: The HILT Brings the Everglades Back to Concordia," *The Concordian* (Concordia College, Moorhead, MN), March 12, 2014.

9 Samantha Ferguson, email message to author, February 17, 2017.

10 Brett Drevlow, email message to author, February 17, 2017.

11 Norleen K. Pomerantz, "Student Engagement: A New Paradigm for Student Affairs." *College Student Affairs Journal* 25, no. 2 (Spring 2006): 176-185.

12 Andrew Carlson, "Living the Green Life," *The Concordian* (Concordia College, Moorhead, MN), March 7, 2013.

TEACHING CLIMATE CHANGE IN FULFILLMENT OF THE CALL TO LOVE ONE'S NEIGHBOR

DR. DARRELL STOLLE
Chair and Professor of Education

There has never been a more exciting time to be or become a teacher! This statement often elicits surprise from those who hear it, as stories of discontented teachers, parents, and students abound. Some of these stories are grounded in frustration at the narrowing of curriculum over the last decade, largely due to increased politicization of education and the corresponding accountability movement. Others are grounded in a sense of inadequacy teachers feel when faced with increasingly complex psycho-social-emotional developmental needs of today's children—and greater expectations that those needs be met in the classroom. But from my perspective as a department chair of a teacher education program in a Lutheran liberal arts college, this is exactly *why* it's such an exciting time to be a teacher. Because given the current state of affairs, there has never been a *greater need* for teachers who can not only respond to these contextual realities, but who are also willing and able to go to the source of these realities and actively engage and challenge the social structures that support them. This new teacher will be a specially prepared teacher; one that is not only knowledgeable and competent, but who is also sensitive to a "call" to teach in the Lutheran sense of vocation. This is one who is aware of the broad spectrum of community needs, and of their responsibility to love and serve others, and who has considered the full measure of their own gifts and talents in light of that responsibility.

In this case study, I will examine the professional development of teachers within a Lutheran college where the imperative to love and serve one's neighbor is extended to include love and care for creation. It is self-evident that the well-being of our students is dependent on a healthy environment. And it seems obvious that a teacher who is called to love and serve their neighbors should be actively involved in efforts to protect that environment for their students' sake. It's also plausible that teachers could consider the environment itself as their neighbor, so that efforts to protect the environment are a direct act of love towards one's neighbor. Either way, teachers are obligated to teaching clear and accurate information in service to those efforts.

But the question of how environmental issues should be taught remains to be explored, especially given the politically charged atmosphere that surrounds this issue. According to a recent survey of U.S. science teachers, 30 percent of middle and high school science teachers know that the scientific consensus on human-caused global warming is around 80 percent.[1] The same survey found that around 47 percent of those science teachers teach that climate change is human caused, but also teach that it is naturally occurring. This pedagogical approach is known as "teach the controversy," and allows a teacher to frame the issue as an active debate. It is popular among teachers who reserve skepticism concerning prevailing scientific thought and, on the surface, seems reasonable given science's normal reference to the null. But when there is resounding consensus within the scientific community, one has to ask where the real controversy is? As John Cook writes, "The problem with 'teach the controversy' when it comes to human-caused global warming or evolution is that there is no controversy—not a scientific one at least. Teaching that scientists have major disagreements where they do not, is simply to spread misinformation."[2]

The suggestion that the real controversy surrounding climate change is of a social, rather than scientific nature raises significant opportunities for teachers who are responding to a call to teach in the Lutheran sense. On the one hand they are called to love and serve their neighbor by ensuring that their students are able to act responsibly with accurate information with regards to their interactions with the environment, also to act directly on behalf of the environment. On the other there is the radical imperative to love others unconditionally—even those who perpetuate beliefs and misconceptions that stand in direct opposition to those efforts. The teacher trained within a Lutheran perspective must look beyond the political debate and see this issue as one where the well-being of their students is the central organizing feature of their work, *and* work in a loving way to challenge the misconceptions of those who perpetuate information that stands in the way of that work.

The good news is that more than 20 years of educational research about how people change misconceptions suggests this is possible. Its no surprise that simply informing a person they are wrong while simultaneously pointing out what is right is not an effective strategy. This research suggests that a more effective strategy is to engage people in analyzing the veracity of all claims—those that support the prevailing consensus, and those that support dissenting perspectives (see Bedford for a more detailed description of the agnotological approach).[3] By replacing a '"teach the controversy" approach with an, "explain the controversy" approach, a teacher can bridge the divide between science and the social controversies that surround it, and provide opportunities for expansive thinking for all parties. It moves beyond the simple, "I'm right, and you're wrong" tactic by validating the critical thinking capabilities of all parties and allowing conceptual space to open up between one's carefully held beliefs and a more objective analysis of the data. In other words, it appeals to reason without threatening a person's judgment of self-worth. This, I think is precisely what teachers trained within a Lutheran liberal arts college are prepared to do: love one's neighbor, tell the truth, think critically, and act in the best interest of those for whom one is called to serve.

ENDNOTES

1 E. Plutzer, et. al, "Climate Confusion Among U.S. Teachers," in *Science* 351, no. 6274 (February 12, 2016).

2 John Cook, J. (2016). "How Should We Teach Students About Climate Change?," *Bulletin of the Atomic Scientists* (March 3, 2016), accessed at http://thebulletin.org/how-should-we-teach-students-about-climate-change9202.

3 D. Bedford, "Agnotology as a Teaching Tool: Learning Climate Science by Studying Misinformation," *Journal of Geography*, 109, no.4 (2010): 159-165.

THE ELEPHANT IN THE ROOM

Helping First-Year College Students Rethink the Value of Food

DR. JOAN KOPPERUD
Professor of English

"Every month at Anderson Commons dining hall at Concordia College, an elephant quietly walks out of the room, but no one seems to notice." The student is right. Every month, on average, Concordia students who eat in the campus dining center leave approximately 9,870 pounds of uneaten, edible food on their plates, equaling more than the average weight of an elephant. She's also correct that few students seem to notice the staggering food waste they generate each day. When asked to estimate the weight of uneaten food left on their plates on a typical day in Anderson Commons, my students guessed far less than the 329 pound *daily* average. Most students acknowledged that, on occasion, they leave small amounts of uneaten food on their plates, but they did not realize the shocking weight of accumulated wasted food—on average, almost 10,000 pounds of plate waste for *one* month at *one* small Midwestern liberal arts college.

Most students also did not realize the effect their plate waste has on the environment. When I asked students what they thought happened to the food left on their plates in Anderson, students weren't exactly sure, other than saying they thought the uneaten food was "thrown away" or "maybe composted." Most students didn't give the wasted food another thought—out of sight, out of mind, as the adage suggests. In reality, Concordia does not compost plate waste at this time because Moorhead does not have city-wide composting, so plate waste and other prepared, unserved food from Anderson that cannot be reused or donated ends up in the water treatment plant or local landfill, eventually turning into methane gas that directly contributes to climate change.

I doubt the plate waste lack of awareness and its effect on the environment is unique to Concordia students. In fact, according to Recycling Works, the average college student generates close to 142 pounds of food waste per year, contributing their share of the approximately 133 billion pounds of food waste in America, according to the USDA's Economic Research Service.[1] In short, America, including college campuses like Concordia College, is in the midst of a food waste crisis, with an estimated 30 to 40 percent of the food supply in this country never eaten, according to the USDA.[2]

The elephant metaphor for food waste in Anderson Commons was the opening sentence of a student essay based on a field research assignment in my first-year composition class, Food as Identity, Culture, and Conflict. With this course theme in mind, I wanted my students to wrestle firsthand with a food sustainability issue. *Sustainability* is murky to define, let alone teach students, so recognizing the benefits of place-based education, I designed students' field research to connect to a place close at hand. We first posed the question—just how much food is wasted by Concordia students every day? Concordia's Anderson Commons, which provides daily meals for many of our students, seemed like a good hands-on opportunity to narrow our focus and find out.

Since 2009, Concordia Dining Services has tracked front-of-the-house food waste. Specifically, once per semester two to three dietetic interns collect and weigh the edible food left on students' plates, referred to as *plate waste*, and then analyze the results in various ways, such as waste per student, the dollar cost of wasted food, and comparisons to previous years. I arranged with the Director of Dining Services for my students to participate in a plate food waste study during breakfast, lunch, and dinner meal periods for two consecutive days at the end of October 2016. To prepare for and maximize the field research experience, I designed a number of assignments to introduce the topic of food waste and to help students observe keenly and think critically about the place, people, and habits, including their own, for eating in Anderson Commons. Lively class discussions based on their food observation journals followed, and after considering their personal food waste habits, many said, "I just hadn't thought much about food waste until now."

To further prepare students and to pique interest in their upcoming field research experience, dietetic interns created a non-graded multiple choice questionnaire based on facts, statistics, and patterns related to food waste data previously collected and analyzed at Concordia. Students also toured the dining services to learn about the vast system in place and number of people involved in the back-of-the-house efforts of food planning and preparation to bring students their daily food in Anderson Commons and to find out what happens to recoverable food and to wasted food.

For the plate waste study itself, supervised by the dietetic interns, my students worked in the dish room to collect the edible food waste left on students' plates during the two-day study period; the accumulated food waste was then weighed, with the resulting data analyzed by the interns to ensure accuracy for Concordia's official documentation purposes. The data analysis from the study shocked the students: The October 2016 plate waste during the two-day study generated approximately 658 pounds of food waste. When the interns analyzed this staggering statistic from a financial point of view, the plate waste for three meals per day during a typical five-day week costs Concordia and, ultimately our students, approximately $4,966 *per week*. Multiply that amount for an entire academic year of two 15-week semesters, on average, totaling more than $148,980. Students now realized the financial cost of leaving food on their plates, a personal connection that impacts them more directly than simply knowing their wasted food is trucked to a landfill they likely will never see.

The pre- and post-field research experience and data results helped bring into focus not only a clearer picture of food waste in America, but also a picture of food waste closer to home—*their* home at Concordia. The United States has a food waste crisis, and we—the Concordia community—are contributing to the problem every day. How can a nation simply throw edible food into landfills when in 2014, 48.1 million Americans lived in food insecure households, including 32.8 million adults and 15.3 million children, according to the Feeding America website?[3] But as serious as the food crisis is, however, I didn't want to leave students with a sense of despair. Instead, I wanted them to harness creative ideas and to propose solutions to support and practice food sustainability efforts on the Concordia campus. What actions can we take right now at Concordia to reduce *our* food waste?

Students used their observations and field research, including additional interviews with appropriate sources, to write research-based problem/solution essays, keeping a specific audience in mind that they identified, preferably someone in a position to seriously consider their proposed solution to plate food waste. For example, one student shared his problem/solution essay with his coach, encouraging the coach to help change the campus culture from one that lacks awareness of food waste to one that is more food conscious by talking to his athletes about food waste and asking that they help hold each other accountable for mindful food practices. Another student directed her problem/solution essay to the director of the first-year orientation program, asking her to encourage peer mentors to talk about food waste and to model sustainable food practices during orientation meals in Anderson Commons. Other students focused solutions on better signage and publicity to raise awareness of the problem as well as other ideas about how a social media campaign could help Concordia students reduce food waste. By the end of the field research project, students said they believed they could be part of the solution to the food wasted at Concordia and beyond.

I hoped the field research experience would impact not only their daily campus lives, but also give students new knowledge, understanding, and experience that would impact their future decisions and practices. It is one thing to *imagine* that we can reduce food waste, the single largest component of municipal landfills, according to the USDA website, but it is another to *practice* food sustainability—one day, one meal, one plate at a time. While we cannot completely eliminate food waste at Concordia or anywhere else, what we *can* do is practice more sustainable daily food habits to help change the composition of American landfills. In his book *Sustainability*, Leslie Paul Thiele points out that sustainability is

> much more than imagining a better world. It is a practice. To speak of *practicing* sustainability underlines two important points. First, sustainability is an activity. Second, sustainability is something we pursue but never perfect. We *practice* sustainability in the same way we *practice* a musical instrument. There is always room for improvement. That is the point of practicing.[4]

Theile's emphasis on *practicing* sustainability challenged me to design a field research project for my first-year writing class that would provide them with an opportunity to directly study the food waste problem in a place familiar to them, imagine creative solutions, and practice sustainability.

Concordia students are ready to change their food waste habits. They have an opportunity to join all American citizens by becoming part of an unprecedented national effort to reduce food waste. In fall 2015, Agriculture Secretary Tom Vilsack and Environmental Protection Agency Deputy Administrator Stan Meiburg announced the United States' national goal to reduce food waste by 50 percent by 2030. Titled the U.S. "Food Waste Challenge,"[5] the USDA and EPA already are working in partnership with private and public sectors of local, state and tribal governments to reduce food loss and improve overall food security and conserve America's natural resources. On November 1, 2016, President Bill Craft announced Concordia's commitment "to beat the [U.S. Food Waste] Challenge and reach the 50 percent reduction by 2020, a full decade ahead of the national goal. Concordia's core curriculum (Becoming Responsibly Engaged in the World), current sustainability plans, and the strong desire of students to make a positive difference in the world position us to succeed in this effort." The commitment to reduce food waste in Anderson Commons meaningfully and directly connects our students' lives to the community in which they live and learn, better preparing them today as citizens for tomorrow.

Addendum, May 2017

Since Concordia set a 50 percent plate waste reduction goal in Anderson Commons by 2020, the campus has embraced a number of initiatives to raise awareness and change food waste habits. For example, Concordia hosted a community-wide event with Jonathan Bloom (*American Wasteland*),[6] a national expert, author, and food waste reduction activist, for four days in February 2017, sponsored, in part, by a Margaret A. Cargill grant. With Bloom's help, and that of many committed campus partners, Concordia also started the Taste Not Waste campaign; this effort intends to further raise awareness of the food waste problem, not only in Anderson Commons, but also to help students become engaged citizens who understand the impact of food waste, especially in the face of increasing food insecurity and global famines.

There is evidence that Concordia's commitment to change in plate waste is paying off. According to the most recent data collected during a two-day study period in March 2017 in Anderson Commons, **plate waste was down 26 percent from the previous October**. This rapid, sizable decrease in plate waste is worth noting. To help ensure this trend continues, a food waste study group with representatives from diverse perspectives across campus—both Academic and Student Affairs, athletics, dining services, and various environmental and student groups—will continue to find ways to call for action toward meeting the 2020 goal.

Leslie Paul Thiele was right—sustainability is "much more than imagining a better world. It is a practice," and that's what the Concordia community is doing with reducing plate at Concordia College. Little did my first-year writing students and I know that their field research would inspire this kind of positive change at Concordia. Coincidentally, during the semester that initiated the plate waste reduction effort campus-wide, my students had read *A Path Appears: Transforming Lives, Creating Opportunity*,[7] a collection of narratives about people who had effected change, often drawn to causes in surprising, unanticipated ways—but, just as it did for my students, a path for change appeared, and they embraced the challenge.

ENDNOTES

1 Food Waste Estimation Guide, Recycling Works Massachusetts, accessed August 4, 2016, http://recyclingworksma.com/food-waste-estimation-guide/#Jump01.

2 "Frequently Asked Questions" prepared for United States Department of Agriculture, accessed August 4, 2016, http://www.usda.gov/oce/foodwaste/faqs.htm.

3 "Hunger and Poverty Facts and Statistics" prepared for Feeding America, accessed August 4, 2016, http://www.feedingamerica.org/hunger-in-america/impact-of-hunger/hunger-and-poverty/hunger-and-poverty-fact-sheet.html.

4 Leslie Paul Thiele, *Sustainability* (Malden, MA: Polity, 2013), 8.

5 "USDA and EPA Join with Private Sector, Charitable Organizations to Set Nation's First Food Waste Reduction Goals," news release from the United States Department of Agriculture, September 16, 2015, accessed at www.usda.gov/media/press-releases/2015/09/16/usda-and-epa-join-private-sector-charitable-organizations-set.

6 Jonathan Bloom, *American Wasteland: How America Throws Away Nearly Half of Its Food (and What We Can Do About It)* (Cambridge, MA: Da Capo Press, 2010).

7 Nicholas D. Kristof and Sheryl WuDunn, *A Path Appears: Transforming Lives, Creating Opportunity* (New York: Alfred A. Knopf, 2014).

EMBRACING LIMITS IN CREATING A RESPONSIBLE SCIENTIST/CITIZEN

DR. GRAEME WYLLIE
Assistant Professor of Chemistry

"Anthropo-what?—We already live in the Anthropocene so let us get used to this ugly word and the reality it names."[1] This opening statement by Bonneuil and Fressoz proves appropriate since the intent of this piece is not to debate the validity of the Anthropocene and mankind's impact upon the planet. And as we consider the nature and magnitude of changes we have wrought on the world, there is no denying that science has played a significant role in much of this. My intention, though, is not to look backwards but rather discuss briefly how a traditional venue such as the general chemistry teaching laboratory can serve in the initial steps of better preparing our students as responsible citizens, a critical goal which has been discussed at length elsewhere in this volume. This vision is also shared within the scientific community. The American Chemical Society (ACS), the professional body for all chemists in the United States, recently prepared and released a vision statement "to advance the broader chemistry enterprise and its practitioners for the benefit of Earth and its people."[2] This statement makes clear the responsibility of the chemist to the world at large and, for myself, creates the challenge of imbuing that responsibility within the students in my teaching laboratory, something that I have found over the past decade is more than synchronous with the concepts of sustainability.

So how do we define sustainability? Many definitions abound and there is much focus placed on serving current needs without compromising the needs of future generations. A key practical aspect of implementing sustainable practices may therefore lie in the placing of limitations on the resources used for a project, something that is not actually far removed from the development of the optimal conditions for a chemical reaction. Indeed, in the laboratory, the concept of limiting reagent is often utilized to yield the maximum product based on the scarcest or most expensive reagent.

But in a teaching laboratory, what should these limiting conditions be? As part of a direction to better prepare our students spanning the last decade, the general chemistry teaching laboratory has undergone many reforms whether it be behind the scenes or in the materials presented to students. These changes were initially driven by both the desire to decrease the environmental footprint of the class and to increase participant awareness of environmental issues that have grown to incorporate more and more sustainability. The general chemistry teaching laboratory provides an ideal venue to introduce such reforms for a number of reasons. In terms of participant numbers, it is the largest enrollment class in chemistry and previously required larger amounts of resources and generated significant volumes of chemical waste. In both course hierarchy and chronology, it serves as a formative laboratory experience for many students who commonly take the two semester program in their freshman year. So the opportunity is there to plant an early seed in creating not only a more responsible scientist, but a better, more aware global citizen. As we move further into the Anthropocene accompanied by the breathtaking advances in technology, perhaps it is the focus on educating on connections, on our impacts and responsibilities, and our place in the world that is as important as the range of technical abilities.

The main objective of the general chemistry teaching laboratory is traditionally to serve students in providing hands-on examples of concepts discussed in the accompanying lecture course along with teaching both practical laboratory skills and critical thinking. While this may have seemed like a restricting framework to operate within, in reforming the class to better prepare participants for their life and responsibility within the Anthropocene, it soon became clear this was simply another limit and one that could be worked under. In all of the changes of the last decade, there has always been the goal of continuing to teach the material and skills with the required rigor and this was achieved with the re-theming to focus on environment and sustainability. While the changes made over the years are numerous, it is not the intention of the remainder of this case study to go through each one but rather focus on a few major points and describe how an outside limitation inspired perhaps the greatest change.

The initial efforts at reform in the general chemistry teaching laboratory, in fact, took place away from the average participant's viewpoint. Perhaps more than any other class on campus, the environmental footprint of a large enrollment chemistry teaching laboratory can be significant. The volumes of waste generated that required specialized disposal in the early years was easily measured in multiple five-gallon buckets per semester. We redesigned the experiments to use less environmentally concerning materials that resulted in a final non-disposable waste total per semester that fills a medium size jelly-jar. These changes were initially made with little announcement to students. Yet, over the past few years, pedagogical materials emphasize not only the small amount of waste generated each week, but why this is important. It can be said that the greatest impact here is not just in making the changes but in the education and increased awareness for the reasons and philosophy that have informed so much of the latter course design.

To reflect this increasing awareness of environmental issues, the theme of the experiments used in the class have also undergone a significant shift. The original model of the general chemistry teaching laboratory consisted of an "Experiment of the Week" format with little connection between experiments, other than perhaps a shared technique. Incorporation of environmental themes, especially in the second semester, has created not only a more coherent and linked course, but also one that educates on real-world issues outside the laboratory. The limitation in this case proved to be able to teach all of the required skills but the growing interest in incorporating an environmental theme in chemistry pedagogy has resulted in a wealth of experiments being available. Using materials in experiments that participants utilize in their lives outside the laboratory, such as anti-bacterial soaps, teaches the broader impacts of their use. This serves to increase interest and engagement and, anecdotally, several students have mentioned making changes in products they use. The choice of materials also allows students to draw both from the scientific literature and the popular press when preparing background materials, which further increases engagement and awareness of real-world issues and the science behind them.

If this were simply the extent of the reforms made in the class, the efforts made would not be insignificant but the most recent and impactful changes are perhaps those inspired by an enforced outside set of limitations, specifically the reduction in resources arising from the transition period surrounding the science building renovation. In the transition, physical laboratory spaces—in terms of both volume and time—are much reduced, as is the range of equipment available. One could simply have tried to maintain the barest minimum of a program during this time but instead, the challenge was to create something different that went beyond the now demolished walls of Ivers Science Room 359. Serving as the prime example of these new non-laboratory projects is the collaboration with the Concordia organic garden facility which resulted in over 100 students visiting the site and developing, at least for the initial year, theoretical proposals that encompass both science and sustainability. Student and colleague responses were overwhelmingly positive and, even as we move back to the science building, the seeds planted here in this particular project will hopefully continue to grow.

For all the efforts described previously, it is worth mentioning while the goal of creating a better and more responsible and engaged scientist seems to prove successful, there remains some significant deficiencies. True sustainability incorporates not only the environmental but also aspects of community (social) and economic. These have not yet been fully incorporated in this course. This was made apparent in a simple class project that required students to define sustainability using the most common words in the English language. Student responses skewed overwhelmingly to the environmental with little acknowledgement of the other aspects. As Fisher suggests in his chapter, "Hearing the Cries of the World,"[3] it is our responsibility as chemistry educators to better incorporate all three aspects. As we move forward at Concordia though, I choose to acknowledge but not to dwell too long on the deficiencies in balance illustrated in these student responses. I want to celebrate the successes that have been achieved and look with hope for the future in what can still be achieved.

ENDNOTES

1 Christophe Bonneuil and John-Baptiste Fressoz, *The Shock of the Anthropocene* (Brooklyn, NY: Verso Press, 2016).

2 See the American Chemical Society website at https://www.acs.org/content/acs/en/about/aboutacs.html

3 Matthew A. Fisher "Hearing the Cries of the World" in *Teaching and Learning About Sustainability*, eds. Irvin J. Levy and Catherine H. Middlecamp for the ACS Symposium Series (Oxford, England: Oxford University Press, 2015).

CONCLUSION

CONCLUSION

DR. WILLIAM CRAFT
President

Knowing that we will die, how shall we live?

That question haunted Martin Luther. His response fired a Reformation whose past, present, and future inspires the book you have now read. Luther's great epiphany was that the love of God sets us free: free from dread of sin and death to live embracing the goodness of creation and the sacred worth of our neighbor. To use the language of the book my colleagues have written, the liberating force of reformation generates the resilience needed to sustain both self and world. And it defines the work of liberal education at Concordia College, founded 125 years ago by a faith that enkindled a love of learning.

If we look both back at the Reformation's consequences and around at its manifestation in our present life, we see two forces of tremendous power: the energy of liberation, and the lifting up of everyday human life and work. As all great forces do, these have the strength both to bless and to break us. In other words, they require continual reflection and courageous initiative if they are to work in our lives for good. That reflection and courage are exactly the project of this book. The subtext of every essay here is that reformation is a live wire, charged with energy that can build resilience—or, I would add, confuse and distract.

Luther writes in *The Freedom of a Christian* that because God's love sets us free, we can

> be guided in all our works by this one thought alone—
> that we may serve and benefit others in everything that

> is done, having nothing else before our eyes except the need and advantage of the neighbor . . . . This [action] demonstrates that we are children of God, caring and working for the well-being of others and fulfilling the law of Christ by bearing one another's burdens. Here you have the true Christian life.[1]

As many have noted from Luther's day through our own, this is freedom *from* paralyzing fear and freedom *for* good work in the world. What I would suggest now is that the interpretation and practice of that freedom have had a mixed legacy in those who have lived in the Reformation's wake, a legacy that now requires of us both thought and action.

Freedom unbinds: in Luther's case, it unbound him from peril for his own soul and turned his life outward to the world and its creatures; at the same time, it unbound him from the church he had served, however his original intention may have been otherwise. Those of us who stand in the Protestant tradition have, for good and ill, followed suit. We inherit both the outward turn and the division of this liberation. And here, now, in this American life, we stand at a moment in which divisiveness has reached a fierce potency, even a kind of inner contradiction where individual "freedom" of conscience and association can all too easily turn us away from neighbor and more broadly, from the virtue of common work.

Not a single candidate in America's 2016 presidential election told us that citizenship requires shared labor and sacrifice. I find this deeply disturbing but no longer surprising. In matters of faith, centuries of ongoing division and subdivision, much of it based on the questionable assumption that faith is chiefly a matter of "accepting" a fixed set of creedal assertions, have created a fragmented church in which people keep on leaving one another because they cannot agree on—you name it: the meaning of the Eucharist, ordination, the nature of human sexuality, even the value of communal worship. It is not that these things don't matter—they do, a great deal—but that the end of such division is the Church of Me, or at best, of Me and My Friends, present or virtual. The neighbor, or in the nation, the fellow citizen, the child of God who is at once beautiful and broken, gifted and in need, disappears.

The Reformation's powerful legacy of freedom is matched by its legacy of what the philosopher Charles Taylor has called "the sanctification of ordinary life."[2] If my life is good because of the incarnation, death, and resurrection of Christ, I can direct that life to the world in which I live: to my life as child, spouse, parent, student, teacher, artist, business leader, or elected official. To farm and to eat, to compose and to perform, to design and to build, to learn and to teach: these are the fruits of God's gracious gift. The full drama of the incarnation affirms the God-established goodness of the world and its creatures, human and other. The hierarchy in which those of a strictly religious vocation stand apart from and above the carpenter, the sculptor, or the nurse is now gone, and every good calling becomes holy.

A gift of the Reformation every bit as precious as its legacy of freedom, this heritage too has the power to diminish human and earthly community. The sanctification of everyday life retains its meaning and virtue only if its holiness—its sacred worth—is everywhere affirmed. If that life is severed from its root, from the blessing and call of the divine to live in gratitude and love, then a whole world "charged with the grandeur of God"[3] becomes a mere collection of things: soil, water, sky, plants and animals, human beings. Things we can use and abuse, things we can discard, things we can forget, as we will be forgotten.

What I admire most about this book is that it calls us to practice a freedom that binds us to neighbor and to sustain a sanctified and radically interdependent world in which the holiness of creation demands our very best respect and care. Organized in accord with the wholeness that Concordia College seeks for self, life, and world, *Reformation and Resilience* recognizes that we cannot—not now or ever—afford to treat our neighbors as alien or the earth and all its creatures as disposable things. I commend each of these thoughtful essays not only to your private study but also to your conversation with those around you, especially with those with whom you may disagree.

Knowing that we will die, how shall we live?

In the Book of Revelation, John sees "a great multitude that no one could count, from every nation, from all tribes and peoples and languages, standing before the throne and before the Lamb" (NRSV

7:9). Robed in white, palm branches in hand, in the company of angels, they sing of "blessing and glory and wisdom and thanksgiving and honor and power and might" that belong not to empire but to the maker and redeemer of the world.[4] Asked who this multi-national, multi-lingual, multi-ethnic communion may be, an elder tells John that they are those "who are coming out of the great ordeal."[5] They are neither past nor future but present. And the heart-lifting declaration that they "will hunger no more and thirst no more," that "God will wipe away every tear from their eyes," is not only or primarily a picture of what may someday come but of God's eternal, loving embrace of creation in its beauty and its frailty. Not in the sweet by and by alone, but even now.

Good readers pay close attention to beginnings and endings. The scriptural tradition whose vitality the Reformation championed begins with an affirmation that the created world is good, loved by its creator, and in need of care from those made in that creator's image. It ends with the vision cited above, and the story of Christ as redeemer ends not with some ghostly image of a savior withdrawing from the world, glad to be done with it. It ends with Mary Magdalene mistaking Jesus for a gardener, with Jesus cooking breakfast on the lake shore even as he gives fishing instructions to his bewildered disciples, with Jesus walking and talking on the Emmaus road, with Christ revealed in the communion of an evening meal, bread broken and shared. In John's Gospel, it is the resurrected Jesus who turns to Peter and tells him, if you love me, "feed my sheep" (NRSV 21:17).

Emmanuel, God with us still so that we are set free to love and care for the whole world God has made. "We live with all other people on earth," Luther said,[6] and as this book reminds us, with all creation. C. S. Lewis once wrote that there are no *ordinary* human beings.[7] To that we can say amen, and we add in this our moment of reformation, there are no ordinary creatures at all.

ENDNOTES

1 Martin Luther, *The Freedom of a Christian*, trans. Mark D. Tranvik (Minneapolis: Fortress Press, 2008), 79-80.

2 Charles Taylor, *Sources of the Self* (Cambridge: Harvard University Press, 1989), 221.

3 Gerard Manley Hopkins, "God's Grandeur" in *Gerard Manley Hopkins: Poems and Prose* (Penguin Classics, 1985) found at https://www.poetryfoundation.org/poems-and-poets/poems/detail/44395.

4 See Barbara Rossing's reminder that "Revelation's audience was not state-sponsored persecution but rather the social, economic, and religious marginalization of those who refused to participate in Roman imperial system." Her commentary may be found at https://www.workingpreacher.org/preaching.aspx?commentary_id = 1694.

5 For this translation of Revelation 7:14, I am indebted to Walter Taylor. See his commentary at https://www.workingpreacher.org/preaching.aspx?commentary_id=568.

6 Luther, *The Freedom of a Christian*, 79.

7 C.S. Lewis, *The Weight of Glory*: "There are no *ordinary* people." See online at http://www.verber.com/mark/xian/weight-of-glory.pdf, 9.

FURTHER READING

Luther and Reformation: Tradition and Change

Bayer, Oswald. *Martin Luther's Theology: A Contemporary Interpretation*. Grand Rapids, Michigan: Wm. B. Eerdmans Pub. Co., 2008.

Chung, Paul S. *Liberating Lutheran Theology: Freedom for Justice and Solidarity with Others in a Global Context*. Edited by Ulrich Duchrow, Craig L. Nessan. Minneapolis: Fortress Press, 2011.

Crompton, Samuel Willard. *Martin Luther*. Philadelphia: Chelsea House, 2004.

Drescher, Elizabeth. *Tweet if You [Love] Jesus: Practicing Church in the Digital Reformation*. Harrisburg, Pennsylvania: Morehouse Pub., 2011.

Harvesting Martin Luther's Reflections on Theology, Ethics, and the Church. Edited by Timothy J. Wengert. Grand Rapids, Michigan: Wm. B. Eerdmans Pub. Co., 2004.

Hendrix, Scott H. *Martin Luther: Visionary Reformer*. New Haven: Yale University Press, 2015.

Kasper, Walter. *Martin Luther: An Ecumenical Perspective*. New York: Paulist Press, 2016.

Kittelson, James M. *Luther the Reformer: The Story of the Man and His Career*. Minneapolis: Fortress Press, 2003.

Lange, Dirk G. *Trauma Recalled: Liturgy, Disruption, and Theology*. Minneapolis: Fortress Press, 2010.

Lazareth, William. *Christians in Society: Luther, the Bible and Social Ethics*. Minneapolis: Fortress Press, 2001.

Levi, Anthony. *Renaissance and Reformation: The Intellectual Genesis*. New Haven: Yale University Press, 2002.

Ozment, Steven E. *The Serpent & the Lamb: Cranach, Luther, and the Making of the Reformation*. Edited by Lucas Cranach. New Haven: Yale University Press, 2011.

Pettegree, Andrew. *Brand Luther: 1517, Printing, and the Making of the Reformation*. New York: Penguin Press, 2015.

Reformation Luther and the Protestant Revolt. Directed by Claude Theret. Princeton, New Jersey: Films for the Humanities & Sciences, 2004. DVD.

A Reformation Reader: Primary Texts with Introductions. Edited by Denis Janz. 2nd ed. Minneapolis: Fortress Press, 2008.

The Reformation to the Modern Church: A Reader in Christian Theology. Edited by Keith D. Stanglin. Minneapolis: Fortress Press, 2014.

The Reformation World. Edited by Andrew Pettegree. New York: Routledge, 2000.

Reston, James,Jr. *Luther's Fortress: Martin Luther and His Reformation under Siege*. New York: Basic Books, 2015.

Russell, William R. *Praying for Reform: Martin Luther, Prayer, and the Christian Life*. Minneapolis: Augsburg Fortress, 2005.

Watson, Philip. *Let God Be God: An Interpretation of the Theology of Martin Luther.* Eugene, Oregon: Wipf & Stock, 2000.

Waibel, Paul R. *Martin Luther: A Brief Introduction to His Life and Works*. Wheeling, Illinois: Harlan Davidson, 2005.

Wengert, Timothy J. *Martin Luther's Ninety-Five Theses: With Introduction, Commentary, and Study Guide*. Edited by Martin Luther. Minneapolis: Fortress Press, 2015.

Reform and Higher Education

Barbezat, Daniel. *Contemplative Practices in Higher Education: Powerful Methods to Transform Teaching and Learning*. Edited by Mirabai Bush. San Francisco, California: Jossey-Bass, 2014.

Bennett, Douglas C., Grant H. Cornell, Haifa Jamal Al-Lail, and Celeste Schenck. "An Education for the Twenty-First Century: Stewardship of the Global Commons." *Liberal Education* 98, no. 4 (Fall 2012): 34-41.

Brub, Michael. *The Humanities, Higher Education, and Academic Freedom: Three Necessary Arguments*. Edited by Jennifer Ruth. New York: Palgrave Macmillan, 2015.

Burke, Joseph C. *Achieving Accountability in Higher Education: Balancing Public, Academic, and Market Demands*. 1st ed. San Francisco: Jossey-Bass, 2005.

Carnes, Mark C. *Minds on Fire: How Role-Immersion Games Transform College*. Cambridge, Massachusetts: Harvard University Press, 2014.

Christenson, Tom. *The Gift and Task of Lutheran Higher Education*. Minneapolis: Augsburg Fortress, 2004.

College Learning for the New Global Century. Washington: American Association of Colleges and Universities, 2007.

Craig, Ryan. *College Disrupted: The Great Unbundling of Higher Education*. 1st ed. New York: Palgrave Macmillan Trade, 2015.

A Crucible Moment: College Learning and Democracy's Future. Washington: Association of American Colleges and Universities, 2012.

Dovre, Paul J. *The Cross and the Academy*. Minneapolis: Lutheran University Press, 2011.

Governance and the Public Good. Edited by William G. Tierney. Albany, NY: State University of New York Press, 2006.

Hora, Matthew T. *Beyond the Skills Gap: Preparing College Students for Life and Work*. Edited by Ross J. Benbow and Amanda K. Oleson. Cambridge, Massachusetts: Harvard Education Press, 2016.

Integrating Information & Communications Technologies into the Classroom. Edited by Lawrence A. Tomei. Hershey PA: InfoSci., 2007.

Jodock, Darrell. "Vocation of the Lutheran College and Religious Diversity." *Intersections* 33 (Spring 2011): 5-12.

Jonas, Hans. *The Imperative of Responsibility: In Search of an Ethics for the Technological Age*. Translated by Hans Jonas with David Herr. Chicago: University of Chicago, 1984.

Keeling, Richard P. *We're Losing our Minds: Rethinking American Higher Education*. Edited by Richard H. Hersh. 1st ed. New York: Palgrave Macmillan, 2011.

Kennedy, James C. *Can Hope Endure? : A Historical Case Study in Christian Higher Education*. Edited by Caroline Joyce Simon. Grand Rapids, Michigan: Wm. B. Eerdmans Pub. Co., 2005.

The LEAP Vision for Learning: Outcomes, Practices, Impact, and Em-

ployers' Views. Washington: American Association of Colleges and Universities, 2011.

Mahn, Jason A., ed. *The Vocation of Lutheran Higher Education*. Minneapolis: Lutheran University Press, 2016.

Making Space for Active Learning: The Art and Practice of Teaching. Edited by Anne C. Martin. New York: Teachers College Press, 2014.

Greater Expectations: A New Vision for Learning as a Nation Goes to College. Washington, D.C.: American Association of Colleges and Universities, 2002.

Nussbaum, Martha. *Cultivating Humanity: A Classical Defense of Reform in Liberal Education*. Cambridge: Harvard University Press, 1997.

Orr, David W. "What is Education For." In *Hope is an Imperative*, edited by David W. Orr, 237-245. Washington, D.C.: Island Press, 2011.

Rosen, Andrew S. *Change.Edu: Rebooting for the New Talent Economy*. New York: Kaplan Pub., 2011.

Simmons, Ernest. *Lutheran Higher Education: An Introduction*. Minneapolis: Augsburg Fortress, 1998.

Solberg, Richard. *Lutheran Higher Education in North America*. Minneapolis: Augsburg Publishing House, 1985.

Taylor, Mark C. *Crisis on Campus: A Bold Plan for Reforming our Colleges and Universities*. 1st ed. New York: Alfred A. Knopf, 2010.

Wolterstorff, Nicholas. *Educating for Shalom: Essays on Christian Higher Education*. Edited by Clarence W. Joldersma and Gloria Goris Stronks. Grand Rapids, Michigan: Wm. B. Eerdmans Pub. Co., 2004.

The Anthropocene: Spirituality, Education, and Reform

Aber, John, Tom Kelly, and Bruce Malloy, eds. *The Sustainable Learning Community: One University's Journey to the Future*. Durham, New Hampshire: University of New Hampshire Press, 2009.

Ackerman, Diane. *The Human Age: The World Shaped by Us*. 1st ed. New York: W. W. Norton & Company, 2014.

After Modernity?: Secularity, Globalization, and the Re-Enchantment of the World. Edited by James K. A. Smith. Waco, Texas: Baylor University Press, 2008.

Barbezat, Daniel. *Contemplative Practices in Higher Education: Powerful Methods to Transform Teaching and Learning*. Edited by Mirabai Bush. San Francisco, California: Jossey-Bass, 2014.

Brown, Lester R. *Building a Sustainable Society.* New York: W.W. Norton, 1981.

Costanza, Robert and Ida Kubiszewski, eds. *Creating a Sustainable and Desirable Future: Insights from 45 Global Thought Leaders.* Hackensack, New Jersey: World Scientific, 2014.

Creating a Sustainable and Desirable Future: Insights from 45 Global Thought Leaders. Edited by Robert Costanza and Ida Kubiszewski. New Jersey: World Scientific, 2014.

Creation in Crisis: Christian Perspectives on Sustainability. Edited by White, R. S. London: SPCK, 2009.

Disasters and Politics Materials, Experiments, Preparedness. Edited by Chris Shilling, Manuel Tironi Rod, Michael Guggenheim, Israel Rodriguez-Giralt, Nigel Clark, Francisco Tirado, Ignacio Farias, et al. Chichester, West Sussex: Wiley Blackwell, 2014.

Eck, Dianna. *Encountering God: A Spiritual Journey from Bozeman to Banaras*. Boston: Beacon Press, 2003.

Hannesson, Rgnvaldur. *Ecofundamentalism: A Critique of Extreme Environmentalism*. Lanham, Maryland: Lexington Books, 2014.

Jamieson, Dale. *Reason in a Dark Time: Why the Struggle against Climate Change Failed—and What it Means for our Future*. Oxford: Oxford University Press, 2014.

Jenkins, Willis. *The Future of Ethics: Sustainability, Social Justice, and Religious Creativity*. Washington, D.C.: Georgetown University Press, 2013.

Johnston, Lucas F. *Religion and Sustainability: Social Movements and the Politics of the Environment*. New York: Routledge, 2014.

Kolbert, Elizabeth. *Field Notes from a Catastrophe: Man, Nature, and Climate Change*. 1st U.S. ed. New York: Bloomsbury Pub., 2006.

Lange, Dirk G. *Trauma Recalled: Liturgy, Disruption, and Theology*. Minneapolis: Fortress Press, 2010.

Martin-Schramm, Jim and Lisa Dahill, eds. *Eco-Reformation: Grace and Hope for a Planet in Peril*. Eugene, Oregon: Wipf and Stock, 2016.

McCabe, Viki. *Coming to Our Senses: Perceiving Complexity to Avoid*

Catastrophes. New York: Oxford University Press, 2014.

Northcott, Michael S. *A Political Theology of Climate Change*. Grand Rapids, Michigan: Wm. B. Eerdmans Pub. Co., 2013.

On Secular Governance: Lutheran Perspectives on Contemporary Legal Issues. Edited by Ronald W. Duty and Marie A. Failinger. Grand Rapids, Michigan: Wm. B. Eerdmans Pub. Co., 2016.

The Oxford Handbook of Environmental Ethics. Edited by Stephen Mark Gardiner. New York: Oxford University Press, 2017.

Peppard, Christiana Z. *Just Water: Theology, Ethics, and the Global Water Crisis*. Maryknoll, New York: Orbis Books, 2014.

Purdy, Jedediah. *After Nature: A Politics for the Anthropocene*. Cambridge, Massachusetts: Harvard University Press, 2015.

Rolston, Holmes. *A New Environmental Ethics: The Next Millennium for Life on Earth*. New York: Routledge, 2012.

Ryan, Mark. *Human Value, Environmental Ethics and Sustainability.* London: Rowman & Littlefield, 2016.

Sachs, Jeffrey. *The Age of Sustainable Development*. New York: Columbia University Press, 2015.

Schwgerl, Christian. *The Anthropocene: The Human Era and How it Shapes Our Planet*. Santa Fe, New Mexico: Synergetic Press, 2014.

Thiele, Leslie Paul. *Sustainability.* Cambridge: Polity Press, 2013.

Thomashow, Mitchell. *The Nine Elements of a Sustainable Campus.* Cambridge: MIT Press, 2015.

Young, Alistair. *Environment, Economy, and Christian Ethics: Alternative Views on Christians and Markets*. Minneapolis: Fortress Press, 2015.

Zapf, Hubert. *Literature as Cultural Ecology: Sustainable Texts*. London: Bloomsbury Academic, 2016.